W9-CAA-720

Study Guide

for Wayne Weiten's

PSYCHOLOGY
Themes and Variations
BRIEFER VERSION
FIFTH EDITION

Study Guide

for Wayne Weiten's

PSYCHOLOGY
Themes and Variations
BRIEFER VERSION
FIFTH EDITION

Richard B. Stalling
Bradley University

Ronald E. Wasden
Bradley University

WADSWORTH

THOMSON LEARNING

Australia • Canada • Mexico • Singapore • Spain • United Kingdom • United States

Philosophy Editor: *Edith Beard Brady*
Assistant Editor: *Julie Dillemuth*
Editorial Assistant: *Maritess Tse*
Ancillary Coordinator: *Rita Jaramillo*
Print Buyer: *Chris Burnham*
Permissions Editor: *Robert Kauser*

Printer: *Globus Printing*
Cover artist/title: *Victor de Vasarely, Untitled*
Cover Image: *©2001 Artists Rights Society (ARS), New York/ADAGP, Paris*
Cover art from: *Private collection/Bridgeman Art Library*

COPYRIGHT © 2002 Wadsworth Group. Wadsworth, is an imprint of the Wadsworth Group, a division of Thomson Learning, Inc. Thomson Learning™ is a trademark used herein under license.

ALL RIGHTS RESERVED. No part of this work covered by the copyright hereon may be reproduced or used in any form or by any means—graphic, electronic, or mechanical, including photocopying, recording, taping, Web distribution, or information storage and retrieval systems—without the prior written permission of the publisher.

Printed in the United States of America.
1 2 3 4 5 6 7 05 04 03 02 01

For permission to use material from this text, contact us by **Web**: http://www.thomsonrights.com
Fax: 1-800-730-2215 **Phone:** 1-800-730-2214

For more information, contact
Wadsworth/Thomson Learning
10 Davis Drive
Belmont, CA 94002-3098
USA

For more information about our products, contact us:
Thomson Learning Academic Resource Center
1-800-423-0563
http://www.wadsworth.com

International Headquarters
Thomson Learning
International Division
290 Harbor Drive, 2nd Floor
Stamford, CT 06902-7477
USA

UK/Europe/Middle East/South Africa
Thomson Learning
Berkshire House
168-173 High Holborn
London WC1V 7AA
United Kingdom

Asia
Thomson Learning
60 Albert Complex, #15-01
Singapore 189969

Canada
Nelson Thomson Learning
1120 Birchmount Road
Toronto, Ontario M1K 5G4
Canada

ISBN 0-534-59312-7

Contents

To the Student

The two of us have written about eight study guides in our careers and we've used a number of them written by others as well. Our goal in writing this study guide was to make it as useful to students as possible. We've tried to present clear examples that provide practice with the conceptually complex material which makes up an introductory course.

The first and major section of each chapter in the study guide is the Review of Key Ideas, consisting of 20 or so objectives and several questions or exercises relating to each objective. The learning objectives tell you what you are expected to know; the exercises quiz you, sometimes tutor you, and occasionally provide additional information. Answers are presented at the end of each set of exercises.

The second section is the Review of Key Terms, which asks you to match 20 to 50 terms from the chapter with their definitions. The third section is the Review of Key People, a matching exercise confined to the major researchers and theorists presented in each chapter. Finally, the Self-Quiz for each chapter gives you some idea of whether or not your studying has been on target.

What's the best way to work with this book? We suggest that you try this: (1) read each learning objective; (2) read the part of the textbook that relates to that learning objective; (3) complete the exercises for that learning objective; (4) check your answers. After you finish the objectives, do the matching exercises and take the self-quiz. Of course, you may find a different procedure that works better for you. Whatever method you use, the learning objectives will serve as an excellent review. At the end of your study of a particular chapter you can quiz yourself by reading over the learning objectives, reciting answers aloud, and checking your answers. This procedure roughly parallels the SQ3R study technique introduced in the Personal Application section of Chapter 1.

To the extent that the goal of this study guide is achieved we acknowledge the help of the author of your textbook, Wayne Weiten. Wayne received his undergraduate degree from Bradley University, where we are professors. Wayne was one of our students. Across five editions of this study guide Wayne, recognized by the American Psychological Association as one of America's outstanding teachers, has been our teacher. Wayne's writing ability and enthusiasm have made our task much easier, and we owe the success of this project to him.

Rick Stalling and Ron Wasden

Study Guide

for Wayne Weiten's

PSYCHOLOGY
Themes and Variations
BRIEFER VERSION
FIFTH EDITION

1 THE EVOLUTION OF PSYCHOLOGY

REVIEW OF KEY IDEAS

FROM SPECULATION TO SCIENCE • HOW PSYCHOLOGY DEVELOPED

1. Summarize Wundt's accomplishments and contributions to the evolution of psychology.

1-1.   If you ask most college graduates to name the founder of psychology they might well mention the name of a famous psychologist (for example, maybe Sigmund Freud), but they almost certainly would not say Wilhelm Wundt. Yet among psychologists Wundt is generally acknowledged to be the "____founder____" of our field.

1-2.   Wundt established the first experimental psychology ____lab____, in Leipzig, Germany, in 1879. He also established the first ____journal____ devoted to publishing psychological research.

1-3.   The subject matter of Wundt's psychology was (consciousness/behavior).

1-4.   Wundt's major contributions to the evolution of psychology may be summarized as follows: He is the ____founder____ of psychology as an independent academic field; and he insisted that psychology can and must use the ____scientific____ method.

Answers: 1-1. founder 1-2. laboratory, journal 1-3. consciousness 1-4. founder, scientific (experimental). (Personal note from RS: I visited Leipzig in the former East Germany during summer 1996 and looked for the famous founding laboratory. It wasn't there! I found Wundt Street, but no lab. Had I read World War II history more carefully I would have known that an English-U. S. bombing raid destroyed the laboratory in 1943.)

2. Compare structuralism and functionalism and discuss their impact on the subsequent development of psychology.

2-1.   Which "school" is characterized by each of the following descriptions? Place an "S" for structuralism or "F" for functionalism in the appropriate blanks.

   __F__   Concerned with the purpose (or function) of consciousness.

   __S__   Trained human beings to introspect about consciousness.

self observation

_S_ Assumed that consciousness could be broken down into basic elements (in the same way that physical matter is comprised of atoms).

_F_ Interested in the flow of consciousness.

✳ → _F_ Focused on the adaptive (evolutionary) value of consciousness.

_S_ Emphasized sensation and perception in vision, hearing, and touch.

_F_ Founded by William James.

2-2. While neither structuralism nor functionalism survived as viable theories of psychology, functionalism had a more lasting impact. What was that impact?

✳ *led to behaviorism and applied psych*

Answers: 2-1. F, S, S, F, F, S, F 2-2. The emphasis of functionalism on the practical (or the adaptive or purposeful) led to the development of two areas of modern psychology: behaviorism and applied psychology.

③ **Summarize Watson's view on the appropriate subject matter of psychology, nature versus nurture, and animal research.**

3-1. A literal translation of the root words of psychology (psyche and logos) suggests that psychology is the study of the ___*soul or mind*___ For both Wundt and James, this was the case: they studied human ___*consciousness*___. For Watson, however, the subject matter of psychology was ___*behavior*___.

3-2. Watson believed that psychology could not be a science unless it, like the other sciences, concentrated on ___*observable*___ rather than unobservable events.

3-3. Which of the following are observable behaviors? Place an 'O' in the blank if the event is observable and an 'N' if it is not.

_O_ writing a letter

_N_ feeling angry

_O_ saying "Please pass the salt"

_O_ passing the salt

_N_ perceiving a round object

_N_ experiencing hunger

_O_ walking rapidly

3-4. Watson largely discounted the importance of genetic inheritance. For Watson, behavior was governed by the ___*environment*___.

3-5. Watson also made a shift away from human introspection by using ___*animals*___ as the subjects for research. Why the change in orientation? First, animal behavior is observable; human consciousness is not. Second, the environment of laboratory animals, in contrast to that of humans, is subject to much more ___*control*___.

4. Summarize Freud's principal ideas and why they inspired controversy.

4-1. Recall that for Wundt, the subject matter of psychology was human consciousness. For Freud, a major subject of study was what he termed the _unconscious_. With this concept, Freud asserted that human beings are (aware/**unaware**) of most of the factors that influence their thoughts and behavior.

4-2. There is a word beginning with s that means the same thing as feces. This word, however, may be more likely to cause laughter, embarrassment, or anger than the word feces. Why do two words that mean the same thing produce such differing reactions? Freud would assert that our more emotional response to one of the words would be caused by the _unconscious_.

4-3. Although generally not accessible to us, the unconscious is revealed in several ways, according to Freud. Freud thought, for example, that the unconscious is revealed in mistakes, such as " _slips_ of the tongue," or the symbolism in nighttime _dreams_.

4-4. Freud's ideas were (and still are) quite controversial. The general public tended to find Freud's ideas unacceptable because of his emphasis on _sex_. And scientific psychologists, with their increasing emphasis on observable behavior, rejected Freud's notion that we are controlled by _unconscious_ forces. Nonetheless, Freud's theory gradually gained prominence and survives today as an influential theoretical perspective.

Answers: **4-1.** unconscious, unaware **4-2.** unconscious **4-3.** slips, dreams **4-4.** sex (sexuality, sexual instincts), unconscious.

5. Summarize Skinner's work, views, and influence.

5-1. While he did not deny their existence, Skinner said that (**mental**/environmental) events are not observable and cannot be studied scientifically.

5-2. The fundamental principle of behavior, according to Skinner, is that organisms will tend to _repeat_ behaviors that lead to positive outcome (and tend not to repeat responses that lead to neutral or negative outcomes).

not choose

5-3. Skinner asserted that because behavior is under the lawful control of the environment, our feeling of _free will_ is an illusion.

5-4. According to Skinner, to adequately account for and predict behavior psychologists must understand:

a. the relationship between thinking and behavior

b. the physiological basis of action

c. the way environmental factors affect behavior

d. all of the above

Answers: **5-1.** mental **5-2.** repeat **5-3.** free will **5-4.** c (Not d. Although Skinner acknowledged that thinking exists and that physiology is the basis of behavior, he thought that explanations in terms of these factors did not contribute to a science of behavior.)

(6.) **Summarize Rogers's and Maslow's ideas and the contributions of humanistic psychology.**

⋆

6-1. Both Rogers and Maslow, like other ___*humanistic*___ psychologists, emphasized the (similarities/ (differences)) between human beings and the other animals.

6-2. While Freud and Skinner stressed the way in which behavior is controlled (by unconscious forces or by the environment), Rogers and Maslow emphasized human beings' ___*choice*___ to determine their own actions. *freedom*

6-3. Rogers and Maslow also asserted that human beings have a drive to express their inner potential, a drive toward personal ___*growth*___.

6-4. Perhaps the greatest contribution of the humanistic movement has been in producing (scientific findings/ (new approaches)) in psychotherapy.

Answers: 6-1. humanistic, differences 6-2. freedom 6-3. growth (expression) 6-4. new approaches.

(7.) **Explain how historical events since World War I have contributed to the emergence of psychology as a profession.**

⋆ *even better word*
(psychological intelligence)

7-1. World War I ushered in the field of applied psychology, primarily the extensive use of ___*intelligence*___ testing. World War II created demand for yet another applied area, the field of ___*clinical*___ psychology.

7-2. World War II brought an increased need for screening recruits and treating emotional casualties. With the increased demand, the Veterans Administration began funding many new training programs in ___*clinical*___ psychology.

⋆

7-3. In contrast to its founding in the 19th century as a research or academic endeavor, psychology in the 20th century developed a prominent ___*professional*___ *(applied)* branch devoted to solving practical problems. These applied fields, which emerged in large part as a result of two world wars, included psychological ___*testing*___ and ___*clinical*___ psychology.

Answers: 7-1. intelligence (psychological, mental), clinical 7-2. clinical 7-3. applied (or professional), testing, clinical.

(8.) **Describe two recent trends in research in psychology that reflect a return to psychology's intellectual roots.**

8-1. Two recent trends in research in psychology involve the reemergence of areas largely discarded or ignored by the behaviorists. What are these two areas?
cognitive
physiological

8-2. Think about sucking on a lemon. When you do, the amount of saliva in your mouth will actually increase a measurable amount. While it would be enough to describe your observable response as a function of my observable instruction, it is also obvious that thinking, or cognition, is involved: My instruction changed your ___*mental*___ image, which was accompanied by a change in salivation.

8-3. The study of mental imagery, problem solving, and decision making involves _cognitive_ processes. The second more recent trend also concerns "internal" processes. Research on electrical stimulation of the brain, brain specialization, and biofeedback involves _physiological_ processes.

Answers: **8-1.** cognition (consciousness or thinking) and physiological (or biological) processes **8-2.** mental (cognitive) **8-3.** cognitive, physiological (biological).

9. Explain why Western psychology has shown increased interest in cultural factors in recent years.

9-1. In part because they assumed that they were discovering general principles, psychologists saw little need to test their theories in other cultures. The situation has begun to change in recent years primarily due to (a) increased communication and trade between countries, the so-called worldwide or _global_ economy or interdependence between nations; and to (b) increased diversity of ethnic groups within countries of the Western World, such as the _cultural_ mosaic characteristic of the United States.

9-2. This new orientation of psychological research is directed toward testing the generality of earlier findings; exploring both the differences and _similarities_ among cultural groups; looking for ways to reduce intergroup _conflict_; and, in general, understanding the role that culture plays in human behavior.

Answers: **9-1.** global; multicultural (cultural) **9-2.** similarities, misunderstandings (conflict, hostility).

10. Summarize the basic tenets of evolutionary psychology.

10-1. According to evolutionary psychologists, all aspects of human behavior–including not only aggression and mate selection but perception, language, personality, and cognition–are strongly influenced by the _survival or adaptive_ value that these factors have had for the human species.

10-2. While Darwin's influence is clear in other psychological theories (e.g., James, Freud, and Skinner), the new emphasis on natural selection is (less/_more_) comprehensive and widely researched than the earlier versions.

10-3. The viewpoint has its critics. Some charge that the theory is not subject to scientific _proof_ and that evolutionary conceptions are simply post hoc accounts rather than explanations. Nonetheless, _evolutionary_ psychology has gained a high degree of acceptance as the first major new perspective in psychology since the 1960s.

Answers: **10-1.** survival (adaptive) **10-2.** more **10-3.** test (evaluation, disconfirmation, proof), evolutionary.

PSYCHOLOGY TODAY • VIGOROUS AND DIVERSIFIED

11. List and describe seven major research areas in psychology.

11-1. Read over the descriptions of the research areas in Figure 1.6. Then match the names of the areas with the correct research topics by placing the appropriate letters in the blanks. (Note that the separation between these areas is not always perfect. For example, a personality theorist might also be a psychometrician with an interest in genetics or child development. Nonetheless, the following topics have been chosen so that one answer is correct for each.)

A. Experimental   _G_ attitude change, group behavior

B. Physiological   _E_ personality and intelligence assessment, test design, new statistical procedures

C. Cognitive   _F_ personality assessment, personality description

D. Developmental   _A_ "core" topics (e.g., perception, conditioning, motivation)

E. Psychometrics   _B_ influence of the brain, bodily chemicals, genetics

F. Personality   _D_ child, adolescent, and adult development

G. Social   _C_ memory, decision making, thinking

11-2. In case you want to remember the list of seven research areas, here's a mnemonic device: Peter Piper Picked Some Exquisite California Dills. List the seven research areas by matching them with the first letter of each word.

Answers: 11-1. G, E, F, A, B, D, C **11-2.** physiological, psychometrics, personality, social, experimental, cognitive, developmental.

12. **List and describe the four professional specialties in psychology.**

12-1. Review Figure 1.7. Then match the following specialties with the descriptions by placing the appropriate letter in the blanks.

A. Clinical   _B_ Treatment of less severe problems and problems involving family, marital, and career difficulties.

B. Counseling   _A_ Treatment of psychological disorders, behavioral and emotional problems.

C. Educational and school   _C_ Involves work on curriculum design and achievement testing in school settings.

D. Industrial and organizational   _D_ Psychology applied to business settings; deals with personnel, job satisfaction, etc.

Answers: 12-1. B, A, C, D.

PUTTING IN PERSPECTIVE • SEVEN KEY THEMES

13. **Discuss the text's three organizing themes relating to psychology as a field of study.**

13-1. When my (R. S.'s) older daughter Samantha was about three years old, she pulled a sugar bowl off a shelf and broke it while I was not present. Later, when I surveyed the damage, I said, "I see you've broken something." She said, "How do yer know, did yer see me do it?" I was amused, because while it was obvious who had broken it, her comment reflected psychology's foundation in direct observation. Theme 1 is that psychology is ___*empirical*___. Empiricism is the point of view that knowledge should be acquired through ___*observation*___

13-2. My daughter's comment caused me to think about one other aspect of empiricism: she expressed doubt (albeit somewhat self-serving with regard to the sugar bowl). One can describe belief systems along a continuum from credulity, which means ready to believe, to skepticism, which means disposed toward doubt. Psychology, and the empirical approach, is more disposed toward the ___*skepticism*___ end of the continuum.

13-3. We would ordinarily think that if one theory is correct, any other used to explain the same data must be wrong. While scientists do pit theories against each other, it is also the case that apparently contradictory theories may both be correct—as with the explanation of light in terms of both wave and particle theories. Thus, Theme 2 indicates that psychology is ___*multiple causes*___ *theoretically diverse*.

✗ I got wrong answer

13-4. Psychology tolerates (and in fact encourages) different theoretical explanations because: *complex - need more than 1 to explain diff. aspects or diff way of looking at B*

13-5. As is the case with science in general, psychology does not evolve in a vacuum. It is influenced by and influences our society. For example, the current interest in cultural diversity has prompted increased interest in cross-cultural research, which in turn affects the viewpoints in our society. As stated in Theme 3, psychology evolves in a ___*sociohistorical*___ context.

Answers: **13-1.** empirical, observation **13-2.** skepticism **13-3.** theoretically diverse **13-4.** more than one theory may be correct; or, one theory may not adequately explain all of the observations **13-5.** sociohistorical.

14. **Discuss the text's four organizing themes relating to psychology's subject matter.**

14-1. When looking for an explanation of a particular behavior, someone might ask: "Well, why did he do it? Was it greed or ignorance?" The question implies that if one cause is present another cannot be, and it illustrates the very human tendency to reason in terms of (one cause/multiple causes).

14-2. What influences the course of a ball rolled down an inclined plane? Gravity. And also friction. And the presence of other objects, and a number of other factors. That is the point of Theme 4: even more than is the case for physical events, behavior is determined by ___*multiple*___ *causes*.

14-3. Among the multiple causes of human behavior is the category of causes referred to as culture. Cultural factors include the customs, beliefs, and values that we transmit across generations—what we eat, how we walk, what we wear, what we say, what we think, and so on. Theme 5 indicates that our behavior is shaped by our ___*cultural*___ heritage.

14-4. For example, I have observed that many American students traveling abroad initially think that their European lecturers talk down to them; the lecturers, in turn, may regard our students as spoiled and insolent. Perhaps closer to the truth is that there is a clash of customs invisible to both cultures. While we are shaped by our ___*cultural heritage*___ we are often ___*unaware*___ (aware/unaware) of the precise rules and customs that affect us.

yes is → typo

Ans key says aware?? → typo

14-5. Theme 6 relates to the influence of heredity and environment. What is the current consensus about the effect of heredity and environment on behavior?

both. just argue over relative importance now.

14-6. The scientific method relies on observation, but observation by itself isn't sufficient. Why isn't it?

peoples experience of world highly subjective

14-7. Theme 7 indicates that our experience is subjective. What does this mean?

we observe what we want to + what we expect to selectively focus or ignore

Answers: **14-1.** one cause **14-2.** multiple causes **14-3.** cultural **14-4.** cultural heritage, aware **14-5.** Theme 6 states that behavior is affected by both heredity and environment operating jointly. While the relative influence of each is still debated, theorists no longer assert that behavior is entirely a function of one or the other. **14-6.** Because (Theme 7) people's experience of the world is highly subjective **14-7.** Different people experience different things; even if we observe the same event at the same time, we do not "see" the same things; we selectively focus on some events and ignore others.

PERSONAL APPLICATION • IMPROVING ACADEMIC PERFORMANCE

15. Discuss three important considerations in designing a program to promote adequate studying.

15-1. Three features of successful studying are listed below. Elaborate them by providing some of the details asked for.

(a) A schedule: When should you plan your study schedule? Should you write it down? Do the routine or simpler tasks first, or begin with the major assignments?

yes

beginning of quarter or semester - get specific at start each week

do small tasks and small parts of big tasks first, then small tasks

(b) A place: What are the major characteristics of a good study place?

minimal distractions + interruptions can concentrate

maybe even place only used for study

(c) A reward: When should you reward yourself? What kinds of rewards are suggested?

immed after meet goals   *snack, tv, call to friend*

Answers: **15-1.** (a) It's probably useful to set up a general schedule for a particular quarter or semester and then, at the beginning of each week, plan the specific assignments you intend to work on during each study session. Put your plans in writing. It's probably best to tackle the major assignments first, breaking them into smaller components as needed. (b) Find a place to study with minimal distractions: little noise, few interruptions. (c) Reward yourself shortly after you finish a particular amount of studying; snacking, watching TV, or calling a friend are suggested. Suggestion: You are studying now. Is this a good time for you? If it is, why not write out your weekly schedule now. Include schedule preparation as part of your study time.

16. **Describe the SQ3R method and explain what makes it effective.**

16-1. Below are descriptions of an individual applying the five steps of the SQ3R method to Chapter 1 of your text. The steps are not in the correct order. Label each of the steps and place a number in the parentheses to indicate the correct order.

(2) _Question_ Vanessa is taking introductory psychology using this book. She looks at the title of the first subsection of the chapter. After wondering briefly what it means for psychology to have "parents," she formulates this question: How was the field of psychology influenced by philosophy and physiology?

(1) _Survey_ She turns to the back of Chapter 1 and notes that there is a chapter review. She turns back to the first page of the chapter, sees that the outline on that page matches the review at the end, and browses through some of the other parts of the chapter. She has a rough idea that the chapter is going to define the field and discuss its history.

(3) _Read_ Keeping in mind the question she has posed, she reads the section about the meeting of psychology's "parents" and formulates a tentative answer to her question. She also asks some additional questions: "Who was Descartes?" and "What method did philosophers use?"

(4) _Recite_ She answers her first question as follows: "Philosophy (one of the parents) posed questions about the mind that made the study of human thinking and actions acceptable; physiology (the other parent) contributed the scientific method." She decides to note down her answer for later review.

(5) _Review_ When she has finished steps 2 through 4 for all sections, Vanessa looks over the entire chapter, section by section. She repeats the questions for each section and attempts to answer each one.

16-2. What makes the SQ3R technique so effective?

breaks reading into parts
can't go on until understand

Answers: 16-1. (2) Question (1) Survey (3) Read (4) Recite (5) Review 16-2. It breaks the reading assignment into manageable segments; it requires understanding before you move on.

17. **Summarize advice provided on how to get more out of lectures.**

17-1. Using a few words for each point, summarize the four points on getting more out of lectures.
1) active listening (full attention) 3) write notes in own words of key points
2) read before class 4) ask questions

Answers: 17-1. Listen actively; focus full attention on the speaker and try to anticipate what's coming. For complex material, read ahead. Take notes in your own words and attend to clues about what is most important. Consider asking questions during lectures (to keep involved and to clarify points presented).

18. **Summarize advice provided on improving test-taking strategies.**

18-1. Is it better to change answers on multiple-choice tests or to go with one's first hunch?
(wrong to right more than 2x more likely than right → wrong)

18-2. Following are situations you might encounter while taking a test. Reread the section on general test-taking tips and then indicate what you would do in each situation.

(a) You run into a particularly difficult item: *guess or skip + mark it to come back later*

(b) The answer seems to be simple, but you think you may be missing something: *Reread. It may be just simple.*

(c) The test is a timed test: *Check at a midpoint ($\frac{1}{3}$) that you're $\frac{1}{3}$ done.*

(d) You have some time left at the end of the test: *Review answers.*

18-3. Following are samples of the situations mentioned under the discussion of tips for multiple-choice and essay exam questions. Based on the suggestions, what would you do?

(a) In a multiple-choice test, item *c* seems to be correct, but you have not yet read items *d* and *e*: *read all*

(b) You know that items *a* and *b* are correct, are unsure of items *c* and *d*, and item *e* is an "all of the above" option. *choose e*

(c) You have no idea which multiple-choice alternative is correct. You note that option *a* has the word "always" in it, items *b* and *c* use the word "never," and item *d* says "frequently." *item d more likely than a, b, c*

(d) You have read the stem of a multiple-choice item but you have not yet looked at the options. *try to anticipate answer before reading them*

Answers: 18-1. In general, changing answers seems to be better. Available research indicates that people are more than twice as likely to go from a wrong answer to a right one as from a right answer to a wrong one. **18-2.** (a) Skip it and come back to it if time permits. (b) Maybe the answer is simple! Don't make the question more complex than it was intended to be. (c) Budget your time, checking the proportion of the test completed against the time available. (d) Review, reconsider, check over your answers. **18-3.** (a) Read all options. (b) Answer e. (c) Answer d. (Still good advice and generally the best procedure to follow. But note that some professors, aware of the strategy, may throw in an item in which "always" is part of a correct answer! It's sort of like radar detectors: someone builds a better detector and someone else builds radar that can't be detected.) (d) Try to anticipate the correct answer before reading the options.

19. Explain the nature of critical thinking skills and why they need to be taught.

19-1.   The previous section on test-taking strategies asked whether or not it is better to change answers or go with one's first hunch. Actually, that is a critical thinking question. While our hunches are often pretty good, sometimes they don't lead to the desired outcome. When we use critical thinking we use the same principles that we would use in a ___*scientific*___ investigation, apply the formal and informal rules of ___*logic*___, and analyze events in terms of likelihood or ___*probability*___.

19-2.   Critical thinking is not something that we come by naturally, and it (is/*is not*) a normal part of instruction in most subject areas. So, for people to develop the skill of critical thinking, it has to be deliberately and consciously ___*taught*___.

Answers: **19-1.** scientific, logic, probability **19-2.** is not, taught.

20. Identify two "standard" critical thinking questions that were illustrated in the Critical Thinking Application.

20-1.   Some evidence suggests that males tend to have better visual-spatial perception than females and that females have better memories for locations. The reason for these gender differences, according to evolutionary psychologists, is that in our evolutionary past natural selection favored a division of labor in which men were ___*hunters*___ and women were ___*gatherers*___. Hunting (aiming a spear, traveling long distances) required ___*visual-spatial*___ perception, while gathering required ___*memory*___ for locations of food.

20-2.   As previously discussed, evolutionary psychology is a major new theoretical perspective in psychology. While the interpretation of the evolutionary psychologists is certainly plausible, critical thinking urges us to consider the following two questions when assessing a truth claim: (1) Are there ___*alternative/other*___ explanations for these results? And, (2) are data available that ___*contradicts*___ the evidence provided?

20-3.   It turns out that the answer to both of these questions is a qualified "yes." For example, it may be that most cultures encourage male children to engage in visual-spatial activities, such as playing with blocks, a difference in experience that would provide an ___*alternative*___ interpretation to one based on evolutionary principles. In addition, some scholars have suggested that women in early hunter-gatherer societies often did, in fact, travel long distances to obtain food and were also involved in hunting. While far from established, this type of evidence would ___*contradict*___ data collected by evolutionary psychologists.

Answers: **20-1.** hunters, gatherers, visual-spatial, memory **20-2.** alternative, contradicts **20-3.** alternative, contradict (challenge, dispute).

REVIEW OF KEY TERMS

Applied psychology
Behavior
Behaviorism
Clinical psychology
Cognition
Critical thinking
Culture

Empiricism
Evolutionary psychology
Functionalism
Humanism
Introspection
Natural selection
Psychoanalytic theory

Psychology
SQ3R
Structuralism
Testwiseness
Theory
Unconscious

theory **1.** A system of ideas used to link together or explain a set of observations.

applied psychology **2.** The branch of psychology concerned with practical problems.

structuralism **3.** School of thought based on notion that the task of psychology is to analyze consciousness into its basic elements.

introspection **4.** Observation of one's own conscious experience.

functionalism **5.** School of thought asserting that psychology's major purpose was to investigate the function or purpose of consciousness.

behaviorism **6.** The theoretical orientation asserting that scientific psychology should study only observable behavior.

behavior **7.** An observable activity or response by an organism.

evolutionary psych **8.** Examines behavioral processes in terms of their adaptive or survival value for a species.

critical thinking **9.** The use of cognitive skills and strategies to increase the probability of a desirable outcome.

natural selection **10.** The Darwinian principle that characteristics that have a survival advantage for a species are more likely to be passed on to subsequent generations.

psychoanalytic theory **11.** Freudian theory that explains personality and abnormal behavior in terms of unconscious processes.

unconscious **12.** According to psychoanalytic theory, that portion of the mind containing thoughts, memories, and wishes not in awareness but nonetheless exerting a strong effect on human behavior.

humanism **13.** The psychological theory asserting that human beings are unique and fundamentally different from other animals.

empiricism **14.** The point of view that knowledge should be based on observation.

culture **15.** Widely shared customs, beliefs, values, norms, and institutions that are transmitted socially across generations.

clinical psychology **16.** The branch of psychology concerned with the diagnosis and treatment of psychological disorders.

cognition **17.** Mental processes or thinking.

psychology **18.** The science that studies behavior and the physiological and cognitive processes that underlie it, and it is the profession that applies this knowledge to solving various practical problems.

_SQ3R_ **19.** A five-step procedure designed to improve study skills.

testwiseness **20.** Ability to use the characteristics and formats of a test to maximize one's score.

Answers: 1. theory 2. applied psychology 3. structuralism 4. introspection 5. functionalism 6. behaviorism 7. behavior 8. evolutionary psychology 9. critical thinking 10. natural selection 11. psychoanalytic theory 12. unconscious 13. humanism 14. empiricism 15. culture 16. clinical psychology 17. cognition 18. psychology 19. SQ3R 20. Testwiseness.

REVIEW OF KEY PEOPLE

Sigmund Freud✓
William James✓

Carl Rogers
B. F. Skinner

John B. Watson
Wilhelm Wundt✓

Wundt

1. Founded experimental psychology and the first experimental psychology laboratory.

James

2. Chief architect of functionalism; described a "stream of consciousness."

Watson

3. Founded behaviorism.

Freud

4. Devised the theory and technique known as psychoanalysis.

Skinner

5. Identified operant conditioning.

Rogers

6. A major proponent of "humanistic" psychology.

Answers: 1. Wundt 2. James 3. Watson 4. Freud 5. Skinner 6. Rogers.

SELF-QUIZ

1. Structuralism is the historical school of psychology that asserted that the purpose of psychology was to:
   a. study behavior
   b. discover the smaller elements that comprise consciousness
   c. explore the unconscious
   d. examine the purposes of conscious processes

2. Of the two parents of psychology, physiology and philosophy, which provided the method? What is the method?
   a. philosophy; logic, reasoning
   b. philosophy; intuition, introspection
   c. physiology; observation, science
   d. physiology; anatomy, surgery

3. Who is Wilhelm Wundt?
   a. He founded the first experimental laboratory.
   b. He founded the American Psychological Association.
   c. He discovered the classically conditioned salivary reflex.
   d. He founded behaviorism.

4. For John B. Watson, the appropriate subject matter of psychology was:
   a. animal behavior
   b. the unconscious
   c. consciousness
   d. human physiology

5. Which of the following represents a major milestone in the development of applied psychology?
   a. use of the method of introspection by Wundt at Leipzig
   b. development of mental testing during World War I
   c. founding of an animal laboratory at Johns Hopkins
   d. use of Gestalt psychology in the field of perception

6. Within the field of psychology, Freud's ideas encountered resistance because he emphasized:
   a. human consciousness
   b. human behavior
   c. introspection
   d. the unconscious

7. Which of the following would be considered the major principle of operant conditioning?
   a. Human behavior derives in part from free will; animal behavior is determined by the environment.
   b. Humans and other animals tend to repeat responses followed by positive outcomes.
   c. The majority of human behavior is based on thoughts, feelings, and wishes of which we are unaware.
   d. Human beings are fundamentally different from other animals.

8. Which of the following theorists would tend to emphasize explanations in terms of freedom and potential for personal growth?
   a. Carl Rogers
   b. Sigmund Freud
   c. B. F. Skinner
   d. All of the above

9. Recent research trends in psychology involve two areas largely ignored by early behaviorists. These two areas are:
   a. observable and measurable responses
   b. cognition (thinking) and physiological processes
   c. classical and operant conditioning
   d. the effect of environmental events and the behavior of lower animals

10. Which core psychological research area is primarily devoted to the study of such topics as memory, problem solving, and thinking?
    a. physiological
    b. social
    c. cognitive
    d. personality

11. Critical thinking refers to:
    a. analysis of problems in terms of scientific principles
    b. making decisions based on formal and informal logic
    c. thinking that includes consideration of probabilities
    d. All of the above

12. The assertion that "psychology is empirical" means that psychology is based on:
    a. introspection
    b. logic
    c. observation
    d. mathematics

13. In looking for the causes of a particular behavior, psychologists assume:
    a. one cause or factor
    b. multifactorial causation
    c. free will
    d. infinite causation

14. Contemporary psychologists generally assume that human behavior is determined by:
    a. heredity
    b. environment
    c. heredity and environment acting jointly
    d. heredity, environment, and free will

CHAPTER ONE

15. What does SQ3R stand for?
    a. search, question, research, recommend, reconstitute
    b. silence, quietude, reading, writing, arithmetic
    c. summarize, quickly, read, research, reread
    (d) survey, question, read, recite, review

Answers: 1. b **2.** c **3.** a **4.** a **5.** b **6.** d **7.** b **8.** a **9.** b **10.** c **11.** d **12.** c **13.** b **14.** c **15.** d.

INFOTRAC

Applied Psychology	Humanism	Psychoanalytic Theory
Clinical Psychology	Natural Selection	

2 THE RESEARCH ENTERPRISE IN PSYCHOLOGY

REVIEW OF KEY IDEAS

LOOKING FOR LAWS • THE SCIENTIFIC APPROACH TO BEHAVIOR

1. **Explain science's main assumption, and describe the goals of the scientific enterprise in psychology.**

   Study ✗ **1-1.** A major assumption of science is that events occur in a (an) ___*lawful*___ (*predictable, constant, regular, orderly*) manner.

   1-2. The three interrelated goals of psychology and the other sciences are: (a) measurement and description, (b) understanding and prediction, and (c) application and control. Match each of the following descriptions with the goal it represents by placing the appropriate letters in the blanks. (There is considerable overlap among these goals; pick the closest match.)

   _c_ Muscle relaxation techniques are found to be useful in reducing anxiety and improving concentration and memory.

   _a_ A psychologist develops a test or procedure that measures anxiety.

   _b_ Researchers find that when individuals are exposed to an object they happen to fear (e.g., a cliff, rats, roaches, snakes, spiders, etc.), their concentration and memory deteriorate.

   Answers: 1-1. lawful (predictable, consistent, regular, orderly) **1-2.** c, a, b.

2. **Explain the relations between theory, hypotheses, and research.**

   2-1. A theory is a system of ideas used to explain a set of observations. One could devise an exhaustive description of human behavior, but the description wouldn't be a theory unless it also included concepts that would ___*explain*___ why the behavior occurs.

   2-2. Researchers can't test a theory all at once, but they can test one or two hypotheses derived from a theory. For example, evolutionary theory asserts that humans form groups because this behavioral tendency has had survival value. To reflect on this idea, one could test the ___*hypothesis*___ that certain specific aspects of group-oriented behavior occur in all cultures.

2-3. The relationship between theory, hypothesis, and research is this: theories suggest _hypotheses_ (questions or predictions), which are then tested in _research_. If the hypotheses are supported, confidence in the _theory_ is strengthened. If the findings fail to support the hypothesis, confidence in the theory decreases and the theory may be revised or discarded. In this way theory building is a gradual process with the result that over time theories (remain fixed/are subject to revision).

Answers: **2-1.** explain **2-2.** hypothesis **2-3.** hypotheses, experiments (research), theory, are subject to revision.

3. Outline the steps in a scientific investigation.

3-1. The process of doing a scientific study may be broken down into five steps, as follows. Fill in the missing key words.

1. Formulate a testable _hypothesis_.

2. Select the research _method_ and design the study.

3. _Collect/gather_ the data.

4. _Analyze_ the data and draw conclusions.

5. _Report_ the findings.

3-2. Following are descriptions of various phases in the study by Cole and his co-workers (Cole et al., 1996). Indicate which step of this study is being described by placing a number from the previous question (1, 2, 3, 4, or 5) in the appropriate blank.

_5_ The authors prepared a report of their findings that was accepted for publication in a technical journal.

_4_ The patients' responses were expressed as numbers and analyzed with statistics. The data indicated that higher scores on closetedness were associated with higher incidences of physical illness.

_1_ Cole and his co-workers thought that concealment of homosexual identify might be associated with increased illness. Before they began they made precise operational definitions of both concealment (closetedness) and illness.

_2_ The researchers decided to use a survey procedure involving administering questionnaires to a large number of people.

_3_ The researchers gathered questionnaire and medical data from gay men over a period of several years.

Answers: **3-1.** (a) hypothesis (b) method (c) collect (d) analyze, conclusions (e) report (publish, write up) **3-2.** 5, 4, 1, 2, 3.

4. Discuss the advantages of the scientific approach.

4-1. We all tend to agree with the idea that "haste makes waste." We are also likely to agree with a commonsense saying that has the opposite implication: "a stitch in time saves nine." What are the two major advantages of the scientific approach over the commonsense approach?

precise - (is measurable, specific when/what/how)

intolerance for contradiction/error

Answers: 4-1. First, scientific descriptions generally have a clarity and precision lacking in commonsense proverbs. While we have a general idea about the meaning of haste, for example, we don't know precisely when or in what way or how much haste we should avoid. Second, science has an intolerance for error or for contradictory conclusions; commonsense sayings are likely to be contradictory. (Note that the proverbs in our example have contradictory messages: one says to slow down, the other says to hurry up.)

LOOKING FOR CAUSES • EXPERIMENTAL RESEARCH

5. Describe the experimental method of research, explaining independent and dependent variables, experimental and control groups, and extraneous variables.

5-1. Schachter proposed that affiliation is caused (in part) by level of anxiety. What was his independent variable? ___*anxiety*___ The dependent variable? ___*affiliation*___

5-2. The variable that is manipulated or varied by the experimenter is termed the ___*independent*___ variable. The variable that is affected by, or is dependent on, the manipulation is termed the ___*dependent*___ variable.

5-3. What is the name of the variable that results from the manipulation? ___*dependent*___ What is the name of the variable that produces the effect? ___*independent*___

5-4. The group of subjects that receives the experimental treatment is known as the ___*experimental*___ group; the group that does not is known as the ___*control*___ group.

5-5. Control and experimental groups are quite similar in most respects. They differ in that the experimental group receives the experimental ___*treatment*___ and the control group does not. Thus, any differences found in the measure of the ___*dependent*___ variable are assumed to be due to differences in manipulation of the ___*independent*___ variable.

5-6. In Schachter's study, the experimental group was subjected to instructions that produced a high level of ___*anxiety*___. Results were that the experimental group was higher than the control group on the dependent measure, the tendency toward ___*affiliation*___ with others.

5-7. An extraneous variable is any variable other than the ___*independent*___ variable that seems likely to cause a difference between groups as measured by the ___*dependent*___ variable.

5-8. To review the parts of an experiment: Suppose a researcher is interested in the effect of a drug on the running speed of rats. The ___*experimental*___ group is injected with the drug and the ___*control*___ group is not. Whether or not the rats received the drug would be the ___*independent*___ variable, and running speed would be the ___*dependent*___ variable.

5-9. Suppose also that the average age of the experimental rats is two years while the average age of the control rats is 3 months. What is the extraneous variable in this experiment? _____*age*_____
Why does this variable present a problem?

may affect data (dependent variable)

5-10. Researchers generally control for extraneous variables through random _____*selection*_____ of
subjects to groups. Write a definition of this procedure:

each one has = chance to go to any group

Answers: **5-1.** anxiety, affiliation **5-2.** independent, dependent **5-3.** dependent, independent **5-4.** experimental, control **5-5.** treatment, dependent, independent **5-6.** anxiety, affiliation **5-7.** independent, dependent **5-8.** experimental, control, independent, dependent **5-9.** age, any difference between groups could be due to age rather than the independent variable **5-10.** assignment, all subjects have an equal chance of being assigned to any group or condition.

6. Explain the major advantages and disadvantages of the experimental method.

6-1. What is the major advantage of the experimental method?

cause/effect conclusions

6-2. What are the two major disadvantages of the experimental method?

— is contrived, may not apply to real world outside lab
— can't manipulate all variables due to ethics or practicality

6-3. Suppose a researcher is interested in the effect of drinking large amounts of alcohol on health (e.g., 15 glasses of wine per day over an extended period of time). What would be a major disadvantage of using the experimental method to examine this particular question? *(unethical)*

could be harmful to people, but if use animals, may not apply to people. People may not be able to drink that much (impractical)

Answers: **6-1.** The major advantage is that it permits researchers to make cause-effect conclusions. **6-2.** The major disadvantages are that (a) precise experimental control may make the situation so artificial that it does not apply to the real world, and (b) ethical or practical considerations may prevent one from manipulating independent variables of interest. **6-3.** To the extent that excessive coffee drinking is a suspected factor in health problems, it would be unethical and perhaps impossible to require an experimental group to drink that much per day.

LOOKING FOR LINKS • DESCRIPTIVE RESEARCH

7. Explain how experimental and descriptive/correlational research methods are different.

7-1. The major difference between the experimental method and descriptive research is that with descriptive research the experimenter cannot _____*manipulate/control*_____ variables. For this reason, the descriptive methods do not permit one to demonstrate _____*cause/effect*_____ relationships between variables.

7-2. For example, suppose you have data indicating that people who drink a lot of coffee _{or alcohol} tend to have cardiovascular problems. Is this experimental or descriptive research? Why?

descriptive or correlational. Can't make test subjects drink lg amts of something which could be harmful. ∴ no control (or manipulation) of variables

Answers: 7-1. manipulate, cause-effect (causal) **7-2.** descriptive, because the variables are not manipulated by the experimenter.

8. Distinguish between positive and negative correlations and explain how the size of a correlation coefficient relates to the strength of an association.

8-1. Some examples will help illustrate the difference between positive and negative correlations. Which of the following relationships are positive (direct) and which are negative (inverse)? (Indicate with a + or - sign.)

_+_ The better that students' grades are in high school, the better their grades tend to be in college.

_−_ The more alcohol one has drunk, the slower his or her reaction time.

_−_ The higher the anxiety, the poorer the test performance.

_+_ The greater the fear, the greater the need for affiliation.

8-2. Which of the following indicates the strongest *correlational relationship*?

(a) 1.12 (b) -.92 (c) .58 (d) .87   *Can't be > ±1.00!*

Answers: 8-1. +, -, -, + **8-2.** b (not a, because correlations cannot exceed +1.00 or -1.00).

9. Explain how correlations relate to prediction and causation.

9-1. Suppose you have data indicating that the more money people make (e.g., the higher their annual incomes), the less depressed they report being on a mood survey. Thus, if you know the incomes of people in that group you should be able to ___predict___, with some degree of accuracy, their self-reported depressed mood.

9-2. The accuracy of your prediction will depend on the size of the correlation coefficient. Which of the following correlation coefficients would allow you to predict with the greatest accuracy?

(a) +.41 (b) +.54 (c) -.65 (d) +.20

9-3. From the (hypothetical) correlational data on mood and income, what kind of conclusion is justified, a conclusion involving prediction or one involving a statement about causation? ___prediction___

9-4. Consider the correlational relationship discussed in the earlier question: You discover that the more money people make, the greater their happiness. Which of the following conclusions is justified? Explain.

(a) Money makes people happy.

(b) Happiness causes people to earn more money.

(c) Both happiness and money result from some unknown third factor.

(d) None of the above.

[handwritten: Could be ⓐ, ⓑ or ⓒ but can't know for sure.]

9-5. Again consider the relationship between money and happiness. Assume that money does not cause happiness and happiness does not cause money. What possible third factor can you think of that could cause both? (I'm asking you to make a wild speculation here just to get the idea of how third variables may operate.)

[handwritten left margin: $ ↛ H / H ↛ $]

[handwritten: sex, age, job satisfaction, marital status, etc. book gives poor health, aggressiveness, stubbornness]

9-6. We aren't justified in making causal conclusions from a correlation, but we can predict. Let's examine what prediction means in the case of our hypothetical example. If the relationship really exists, what prediction would you make about people who are rich? What prediction would you make concerning people who are unhappy?

[handwritten: rich people tend to be happier / poor " " " " less happy / no causal effect]

Answers: 9-1. predict 9-2. c. 9-3. prediction (Generally one can't make causal conclusions from a correlation.) 9-4. d, while any of the statements is a possible causal explanation of the relationship, we don't know which one(s) may be correct because the data are correlational. Therefore, no causal conclusions are justified! 9-5. For example, poor health might cause one to be both unhappy and poverty stricken (while good health would cause one to be both happy and wealthy). Intelligence or aggressiveness or stubbornness or a number of other physiological or behavioral factors could be causally related both to income and to happiness without those two factors being causes of one another. 9-6. You would predict that a group that was rich would also be happy and that a group that was unhappy would be poor. No causation is implied in these statements.

10. **Discuss three descriptive/correlational research methods.**

10-1. Naturalistic observation involves study of human beings or animals in their natural environments conducted (with/without) direct intervention from the observer.

10-2. A case study is an in-depth and generally highly subjective or impressionistic report on (a group of people/a single individual) that may be based on interviews, psychological testing, and so on.

[handwritten left margin: study]

10-3. The third descriptive procedure is the survey technique. Surveys use _questionnaires_ to find out *[handwritten: (or interviews)]* about specific aspects of human attitudes or opinions.

10-4. List the three descriptive/correlational methods in the space below.

[handwritten: natural observation, case study, survey]

Answers: 10-1. without 10-2. a single individual 10-3. questionnaires (or interviews) 10-4. naturalistic observation, case studies, surveys.

11. **Explain the major advantages and disadvantages of descriptive/correlational research.**

11-1.   The major difference between the experimental method and descriptive research is that with descriptive/correlational research the experimenter cannot _control/manipulate_ variables. For this reason, the descriptive methods generally do not permit one to demonstrate _causal_ relationships between variables.

11-2.   For example, suppose you have data indicating that people who happen to drink a lot of coffee tend to have cardiovascular problems. Is this experimental or (descriptive/correlational research?) _descriptive/corr_, Would it be correct to conclude (from these data) that coffee drinking causes cardiovascular problems? _no_

11-3.   An advantage of the descriptive/correlational methods is that they allow researchers to study phenomena that they could not study with experimental methods. Thus, the descriptive/correlational methods (narrow/broaden) the scope of phenomena studied. A major disadvantage of these techniques is that one generally cannot make _causal_ conclusions from the resulting data.

Answers: 11-1. manipulate (control), cause-effect (causal) **11-2.** descriptive/correlational, because the variables are not manipulated by the experimenter; no **11-3.** broaden, cause-effect (causal).

LOOKING FOR FLAWS • EVALUATING RESEARCH

12. **Describe the four common flaws in research (sampling bias, placebo effects, distortions in self-report, and experimenter bias).**

12-1.   Dr. Brutalbaum distributes a questionnaire in an attempt to find out how the students in a particular course react to his teaching. Unfortunately, the day he selects for the evaluation is the day before a scheduled vacation, and about half the students are absent. He knows, however, that he does not have to test the entire class, and the sample that remains is large enough. Is the sample representative? Define the concept representative sample. Which of the four common flaws is illustrated? _NO._
Rep sample = similar composition of whole popn being studied
∴ Sampling bias

12-2.   Brutalbaum is now concerned about class attendance and decides to find out what proportion of students miss class regularly. He distributes a questionnaire that asks students to indicate how many classes they have missed during the course of the semester. Which of the four common flaws is he likely to encounter? _distortions in self report_

12-3.   A student in Brutalbaum's class orders some audio tapes that promise sleep learning for psychology students. (Brutalbaum is dubious, because from his observations students sleep a lot in his classes but still don't seem to learn much.) The student obtains an appropriate sample of psychology students, distributes the tapes to a random half, tells the experimental subjects about the anticipated sleep-learning benefits, and instructs them to use the tapes each night for one month. She has no contact with the remaining random half, his "control" group. After the next test the student analyzes the results. The mean test score of the experimental group is statistically significantly higher than that of the control group. She concludes that the higher grades are due to the taped messages.

(a) For review: What is the independent variable?

sleep learning audio tapes

(b) What are the names of two flaws (of the four discussed in the text) illustrated in this study? (Note that these two flaws overlap somewhat in meaning.)

placebo effect + experimenter bias

(c) What two procedures could have been used to correct the student's experiment?

don't contact them about the tapes

double blind ~~~~ procedure (neither experimenter nor test subjects know which group is which)

Answers: 12-1. Probably not representative. A representative sample is one that is similar in composition to the population from which it is drawn. In this case, it seems likely that students who attend are different from those who do not (e.g., perhaps more enthusiastic, harder working, etc.). Thus, the flaw illustrated is sampling bias. **12-2.** He is likely to encounter distortions in self-report, which may include the social desirability bias, misunderstanding of the question-naire, memory errors, and response set (e.g., tendencies to agree or disagree regardless of content). **12-3.** (a) the tapes (versus no tapes) (b) Through contact with the experimental group the experimenter may have produced a placebo effect and unintentionally influenced subjects through experimenter bias. (c) A fake or placebo condition (in which subjects receive a fake experimental treatment) and a double-blind procedure (in which neither the experimenter nor subjects would know who is in the experimental group and who is in the control group).

LOOKING AT ETHICS • DO THE ENDS JUSTIFY THE MEANS?

13. **Discuss the pros and cons of deception in research with human subjects.**

   13-1.   In the space below present one or two of the arguments in favor of using deception and one or two arguments against.

   pro

   allows research that couldn't do otherwise

   usually harmless "white lies"

   con

   lying – undermines trust
   – causes stress

Answers: 13-1. On the con side, deception is, after all, lying; it may undermine people's trust in others; it may cause distress. On the pro side, many research issues could not be investigated without deception; the "white lies" involved are generally harmless; research indicates that deception studies are not actually harmful to subjects; the advances in knowledge obtained may improve human well-being.

14. **Discuss the controversy about the use of animals as research subjects.**

   14-1.   What is the major reason that some people object to using animal subjects in research? In view of this objection, what moral considerations are raised by those who favor using animals in research?

Answers: 14-1. Many people believe that it is morally wrong to use animals in research, especially in painful or harmful treatments that would be unacceptable for human subjects. In defense of the practice, others cite the significant advances in treatment of a variety of mental and physical disorders that have resulted from animal research. The question to some degree involves the issue of whether or not saving human lives or finding remedies for human illnesses justifies the sacrifice of, or pain or discomfort inflicted on, research animals.

PUTTING IN PERSPECTIVE

15. **Explain how this chapter highlighted two of the text's unifying themes.**

   15-1.   One of the text's unifying themes is that psychology is _____ , which means that its conclusions are based on systematic _____ and that it tends to be (<u>skeptical/credulous</u>).

   15-2.   In what way did the discussion of methodology suggest that psychology tends to be skeptical of its results?

   15-3.   People's experience of the world is also highly subjective. Which of the methodological problems discussed point up psychology's awareness of the subjective nature of our experience?

   Answers: 15-1. empirical, observation (experience), skeptical **15-2.** Researchers constantly look for methodological flaws and subject their results to critical scrutiny by other scientists. **15-3.** Behavioral scientists try to guard against subjective reactions by building in appropriate experimental controls for placebo effects and experimenter bias.

PERSONAL APPLICATION • FINDING AND READING JOURNAL ARTICLES

16. **Describe PsychINFO and explain how it can be used to locate information.**

   16-1.   PsychINFO is a computerized database that contains abstracts or a concise _____ of articles published in psychological journals.

   16-2.   To find information about a particular journal article referred to in the popular press, for example, you could begin your search by entering the name of the author. You could further narrow your search by entering the approximate _____ in which the article might have been published

   16-3.   You can also search under topic. To further reduce your search, enter _____ topics (e.g., insomnia and mood). By pairing two topics you are more likely to find articles relevant to your particular question.

   Answers: 16-1. summaries **16-2.** years (dates, time period) **16-3.** two.

17. **Describe the standard organization of journal articles reporting on psychological research.**

   17-1.   In the blanks below list the six parts of the standard journal article in the order in which they occur. (As a hint, the initial letters of each section are listed on the left.)

   A   _____

   I   _____

M   _____

R   _____

D   _____

R   _____

17-2. In the blanks below match the names of the sections of the standard journal article with the descriptions.

_____ States the hypothesis and reviews the literature relevant to the hypothesis.

_____ A list of all the sources referred to in the paper.

_____ A summary.

_____ Presents the data; may include statistical analyses, graphs, and tables.

_____ Describes what the researchers did in the study; includes subjects, procedures, and data collection techniques.

_____ Interprets or evaluates the data and presents conclusions.

Answers: 17-1. abstract, introduction, method, results, discussion, references **17-2.** introduction, references, abstract, results, method, discussion, critical thinking application – The perils of anecdotal evidence: "I have a friend who . . . "

18. Explain why anecdotal evidence is flawed and unreliable.

18-1. Anecdotal evidence consists of personal stories that support a particular point of view. Anecdotes are frequently persuasive because they are concrete and vivid and, therefore, easy to _____.

18-2. What's wrong with anecdotal evidence? First, one cannot generalize from a single case. Although a political candidate's story about a coal minor named Bob (or a physician named Alice, etc.) may be memorable, Bob's experiences cannot be _____ to other people or situations.

18-3. Second, people tend to represent themselves in the most favorable light. To the extent that Bob is the source of the anecdote, Bob's self-report data may reflect the social _____ bias.

18-4. In addition, stories change with the telling, so that later versions may bear little resemblance to the original event. Stories one has heard second- or third-hand, so-called _____ evidence, are likely to be particularly unreliable.

18-5. Nor is it likely that Bob, or the story about Bob, was picked randomly. The candidate selects an anecdote to make a particular point, a process similar to _____ bias in a research setting. The clear alternative to anecdotal evidence is to solve problems based on solid evidence, the so-called _____-based decision-making process.

Answers: 18-1. remember **18-2.** generalized **18-3.** desirability **18-4.** hearsay **18-5.** sampling, evidence.

REVIEW OF KEY TERMS

Case study
Confounding of variables
Control group
Correlation
Correlation coefficient
Data collection techniques
Dependent variable
Double-blind procedure
Experiment
Experimental group
Experimenter bias

Extraneous variables
Hypothesis
Independent variable
Journal
Naturalistic observation
Participants
Operational definition
Placebo effects
Population
Random assignment

Replication
Research methods
Sample
Sampling bias
Social desirability bias
Statistics
Subjects
Survey
Variables
Theory

_____ 1. Any of the factors in an experiment that are controlled or observed by an experimenter or that in some other way affect the outcome.

_____ 2. A tentative statement about the expected relationship between two or more variables.

_____ 3. Precisely defines each variable in a study in terms of the operations needed to produce or measure that variable.

_____ 4. Term used to refer to nonhuman animals whose behavior is being systematically observed in a study.

_____ 5. Differing ways of conducting research, which include experiments, case studies, surveys, and naturalistic observation.

_____ 6. A research method in which independent variables are manipulated and which permits causal interpretations.

_____ 7. A condition or event that an experimenter varies in order to observe its impact.

_____ 8. The variable that results from the manipulation in an experiment.

_____ 9. The group in an experiment that receives a treatment as part of the independent variable manipulation.

_____ 10. The group in an experiment that does not receive the treatment.

_____ 11. Any variables other than the independent variables that seem likely to influence the dependent measure in an experiment.

_____ 12. Distribution of subjects in an experiment in which each subject has an equal chance of being assigned to any group or condition.

_____ 13. A link or association between variables such that one can be predicted from the other.

_____ 14. The statistic that indicates the degree of relationship between variables.

_____ 15. A research method in which the researcher observes behavior in the natural environment without directly intervening.

_____ 16. An in-depth, generally subjective, investigation of an individual subject.

_____ 17. A questionnaire or interview used to gather information about specific aspects of subjects' behavior.

_____ 18. Procedures for making empirical observations, including questionnaires, interviews, psychological tests, and physiological recordings.

_____ 19. Mathematical techniques that help in organizing, summarizing, and interpreting numerical data.

_____	20.	A repetition of a study to determine whether the previously obtained results can be duplicated.
_____	21.	A group of subjects taken from a larger population.
_____	22.	A larger group from which a sample is drawn and to which the researcher wishes to generalize.
_____	23.	Exists when a sample is not representative of the population from which it was drawn.
_____	24.	Occurs when a researcher's expectations influence the results of the study.
_____	25.	Effects that occur when subjects experience a change due to their expectations (or to a "fake" treatment).
_____	26.	Occurs when an extraneous variable makes it difficult to sort out the effects of the independent variable.
_____	27.	The tendency to answer questions about oneself in a socially approved manner.
_____	28.	A research strategy in which neither the subjects nor experimenters know which condition or treatment the subjects are in.
_____	29.	A periodical that publishes technical and scholarly material within a discipline.
_____	30.	A system of interrelated ideas used to explain a set of observations.
_____	31.	Term generally used to refer to the people whose behavior is being systematically observed in a study.
_____	32.	Support for a particular point of view through the use of personal and vivid (but frequently misleading) stories.

Answers: 1. variables 2. hypothesis 3. operational definition 4. subjects (or participants) 5. research methods 6. experiment 7. independent variable 8. dependent variable 9. experimental group 10. control group 11. extraneous variables 12. random assignment 13. correlation 14. correlation coefficient 15. naturalistic observation 16. case study 17. survey 18. data collection techniques 19. statistics 20. replication 21. sample 22. population 23. sampling bias 24. experimenter bias 25. placebo effects 26. confounding of variables 27. social desirability bias 28. double-blind procedure 29. journal 30. theory 31. participants 32. anecdotal evidence.

REVIEW OF KEY PEOPLE

Neal Miller   Robert Rosenthal   Stanley Schachter

_____		
_____	1.	Studied the effect of anxiety on affiliation.
_____	2.	Studied experimenter bias, a researcher's unintended influence on the behavior of subjects.
_____	3.	Asserted that the benefits of animal research (e.g., the resulting treatments for mental and physical disorders) far outweigh the harm done.

Answers: 1. Schachter 2. Rosenthal 3. Miller.

1. Which of the following is a major assumption of science?
   a. Events occur in a relatively orderly or predictable manner.
   b. Cause and effect is indicated by correlational relationships.
   c. In contrast to the behavior of lower animals, human behavior is in part a function of free will.
   d. Events are largely randomly determined.

2. An experimenter tests the hypothesis that physical exercise helps people's mood (makes them happier). Subjects in the experimental group participate on Monday and Tuesday and those in the control group on Wednesday and Thursday. What is the independent variable?
   a. the hypothesis
   b. day of the week
   c. the exercise
   d. the mood (degree of happiness)

3. Regarding the experiment described in the previous question: What is the dependent variable?
   a. the hypothesis
   b. day of the week
   c. the exercise
   d. the mood (degree of happiness)

4. Regarding the experiment described above: What is an extraneous (confounding) variable?
   a. the hypothesis
   b. day of the week
   c. the exercise
   d. the mood (degree of happiness)

5. The major advantage of the experimental method over the correlational approach is that the experimental method:
   a. permits one to make causal conclusions
   b. allows for prediction
   c. is generally less artificial than correlational procedures
   d. permits the study of people in groups

6. In looking through some medical records you find that there is a strong relationship between depression and chronic pain: the stronger the physical pain that people report, the higher their scores on an inventory that measures depression. Which of the following is the best statement of conclusions?
   a. Depression tends to produce chronic pain.
   b. Chronic pain tends to produce depression.
   c. Both chronic pain and depression result from some unknown third factor.
   d. Depression could have caused the pain, pain could have caused the depression, or both pain and depression could have been caused by an unknown third factor.

7. In an experiment, neither the experimenter nor the subjects know what treatment condition they are in (e.g., whether they are in the experimental or control group). What has occurred?
   a. a confounding or extraneous variable
   b. the double-blind has been used
   c. experimenter bias
   d. a correlation coefficient

8. In his experiment on the effect of anxiety on affiliation, Schachter defined anxiety in terms of the specific instructions given by "Dr. Zilstein." In Schachter's experiment anxiety was the:
   a. independent variable
   b. dependent variable
   c. extraneous variable
   d. intervening variable

9. Suppose that researchers find an inverse relationship between alcohol consumption and speed of response: the more alcohol consumed, the slower the response. Which of the following fictitious statistics could possibly represent that correlation?
   a. -4.57
   b. -.87
   c. .91
   d. .05

10. The specific prediction that an experimenter wishes to test in an experiment is referred to as the:
    a. hypothesis
    b. theory
    c. dependent variable
    d. intervening variable

11. An instructor wishes to find out whether a new teaching method is superior to his usual procedures, so he conducts an experiment. Everyone in his classes is quite excited about the prospect of learning under the new procedure, but of course he cannot administer the new teaching method to everyone. A random half of the students receive the new method and the remaining half receive the old. What is the most obvious flaw in this experiment?
    a. Subjects should have been systematically assigned to groups.
    b. The sample is not representative of the population.
    c. Placebo effects or experimenter bias are likely to affect results.
    d. Distortions in self-report will affect results.

12. What procedure helps correct for experimenter bias?
    a. extraneous or confounding variables
    b. sleep learning or hypnosis
    c. a higher standard for statistical significance
    d. use of the double-blind procedure

13. With regard to the topic of deception in research with human subjects, which of the following is true?
    a. Researchers are careful to avoid deceiving subjects.
    b. Some topics could not be investigated unless deception was used.
    c. It has been empirically demonstrated that deception causes severe distress.
    d. All psychological research must involve some deception.

14. Which of the following is not one of the six standard parts of a psychological journal article?
    a. Abstract
    b. Method
    c. Statistics
    d. Discussion

15. PsychINFO is a computerized database containing:
    a. standard diagnostic information for classifying behavior disorders
    b. abstracts of and bibliographical information about journal articles
    c. psychological profiles of known felons
    d. names of authors who specialize in abstractions

Answers: 1. a **2.** c **3.** d **4.** b **5.** a **6.** d **7.** b **8.** a **9.** b **10.** a **11.** c **12.** d **13.** b **14.** c **15.** b.

Anecdotal Evidence   Correlation   Placebo Effects

3 THE BIOLOGICAL BASES OF BEHAVIOR

REVIEW OF KEY IDEAS

COMMUNICATION IN THE NERVOUS SYSTEM

1. **Describe the main functions of the two types of nervous tissue.**

   1-1. One of the major types of nervous tissue provides very important services to the other type: such as removing waste, supplying nutrients, insulating, and providing structural support. Individual members of this kind of nervous tissue are called _____ cells.

   1-2. The other type of nervous tissue receives, integrates, and transmits information. Individual members of this type of tissue are called _____.

   1-3. While most neurons just receive and transmit information from one neuron to another, one kind is specialized to carry information from the _____ organs to the brain and another kind is specialized to carry information from the brain to the _____ that move the body.

   Answers: 1-1. glia **1-2.** neurons **1-3.** sensory, muscles.

2. **Describe the various parts of the neuron.**

   2-1. The neuron has basic parts: the dendrites, the cell body or soma, and the axon. The major mission of the average neuron is to receive information from one neuron and pass it on to the next neuron. The receiving part is the job of the branch-like parts called _____. They then pass the message along to the nucleus of the cell, called the cell body, or_____. From there the message is sent down the _____to be passed along to other neurons.

   2-2. Many axons are wrapped in a fatty jacket called the _____ sheath, which permits three for faster transmission of information and prevents messages from getting on to the wrong track. Like the covering on an electrical cord, myelin acts as an _____ material.

2-3. When the neural message reaches the end of the axon it excites projections called terminal _____, which then release a chemical substance into the junction that separates them from other neurons. This junction between neurons is called the _____.

2-4. Identify the major parts of a neuron in the figure below. Note that the arrow indicates the direction of the flow of information.

(a) _____   (b) _____   (c) _____   (d) _____

Answers: **2-1.** dendrites, soma, axon **2-2.** myelin, insulating **2-3.** buttons, synapse **2-4.** (a) dendrites, (b) cell body or soma, (c) axon, (d) terminal buttons.

3. Describe the neural impulse.

3-1. When at rest, the neuron is like a tiny battery in that it contains a weak (<u>negative/positive</u>) charge. When the neuron is stimulated, the cell membrane becomes more permeable. This allows positively charged _____ ions to flow into the cell, thus lessening the cell's negative charge.

3-2. The change in the electrical charge of the cell caused by the inflow of positively charged sodium ions is called an _____ potential, which travels down the _____ of the neuron. After the firing of an action potential, there is a brief period in which no further action potentials can be generated. This brief period is called the absolute _____ period.

3-3. The text likens the neuron to a gun in that it either fires or it does not fire. This property of the neuron is called the _____ law. Neurons transmit information about the strength of a stimulus by variations in the number of action potentials generated. For example, in comparison to a weak stimulus, a strong stimulus will generate a (<u>higher/lower</u>) rate of action potentials.

Answers: **3-1.** negative, sodium **3-2.** action, axon, refractory **3-3.** all-or-none, higher.

4. Describe how neurons communicate at chemical synapses.

4-1. A neuron passes its message on to another neuron by releasing a chemical messenger into the gap or _____ cleft that separates it from other neurons. The sending neuron, called the _____ neuron, releases a chemical messenger into the synaptic cleft, which then excites the _____ neuron.

4-2. The chemical messenger that provides this transmitting service is called a _____. The chemical binds with specifically tuned receptor sites on the postsynaptic neurons. In other words, the receptor sites accept some neurotransmitters and reject _____, much like a lock and key.

4-3. When the neurotransmitter combines with a molecule at the receptor site it causes a voltage change at the receptor site called an _____ potential (PSP). One type of PSP is excitatory and (increases/decreases) the probability of producing an action potential in the receiving neuron. The other type is inhibitory and _____ the probability of producing an action potential.

4-4. Whether or not a neuron fires depends on the number of excitatory PSPs it is receiving and the number of _____ PSPs it is receiving. PSPs (do/do not) follow the all-or-none law.

4-5. Put the following four steps of communication at the synapse in their correct order (by using the numbers 1 through 4):

_____ (a) The reuptake of transmitters by the presynaptic neuron.

_____ (b) The enzyme inactivation or drifting away of transmitters in the synapse.

_____ (c) A voltage change occurs (PSP) at the receptor site on the postsynaptic neuron.

_____ (d) The release of transmitters into the synaptic cleft by the presynaptic neuron.

Answers: **4-1.** synaptic, presynaptic, postsynaptic **4-2.** neurotransmitter, others **4-3.** postsynaptic, increases, decreases **4-4.** inhibitory, do not **4-5.** (a) 4 (b) 3 (c) 2 (d) 1.

5. Discuss how acetylcholine, the monoamines, and endorphins are related to behavior.

5-1. Our moods, thoughts, and actions all depend on the action of neurotransmitters. For example, the movement of all muscles depends on _____ (ACh).

5-2. Three neurotransmitters, dopamine, norepinephrine, and serotonin, are collectively known as _____. Both Parkinsonism and schizophrenia have been linked with alterations in _____ activity, while regulation of sleep and wakefulness appear to be regulated in part by _____. The mood changes found in depression have been linked to receptor sites for both serotonin and _____.

5-3. Endorphins are a family of internally produced chemicals that have effects similar to those produced by the drug _____ and its derivatives. That is, they are able to reduce pain and also induce _____.

Answers: **5-1.** acetylcholine, Alzheimer's **5-2.** monoamines , dopamine, serotonin, norepinephrine **5-3.** opium, pleasure (euphoria).

ORGANIZATION OF THE NERVOUS SYSTEM

6. Provide an overview of the organization of the nervous system.

With approximately 85 to 180 billion individual neurons to control, it is important that the central nervous system have some kind of organizational structure. This organizational structure is depicted in Figure 3.5 of the text, and it will prove helpful if you have this figure in front of you while answering the following questions.

6-1. Answer the following questions regarding the organization of the nervous system.

(a) What are the two major divisions of the nervous system?

(b) What two subdivisions make up the peripheral nervous system?

(c) What two subdivisions make up the autonomic nervous system?

(d) What are the two major divisions of the central nervous system?

6-2. What are the roles of the afferent and efferent fibers in the somatic nervous system?

6-3. With respect to the opposing roles of the sympathetic and parasympathetic nervous systems, which system:

(a) prepares the body for fight or flight?

(b) conserves the body's resources?

6-4. Besides nourishing the brain and spinal chord, what other role does the cerebrospinal fluid play?

Answers: 6-1. (a) The central nervous system and the peripheral nervous system. (b) The somatic nervous system and the autonomic nervous system. (c) The sympathetic nervous system and the parasympathetic nervous system. (d) The brain and the spinal cord. **6-2.** Afferent fibers carry information inward (to the central nervous system) and efferent fibers carry information outward (to the periphery of the body). **6-3.** (a) The sympathetic system. (b) The parasympathetic system. **6-4.** It provides a protective cushion for the brain and spinal cord.

7. **Describe the brain-imaging methods that are used to study brain structure and function.**

   7-1. Three kinds of brain-imaging procedures are currently being used. One of these procedures consists of a computer-enhanced X-ray machine that compiles multiple X-rays of the brain into a single vivid picture. The resulting images are called _____ scans. An even newer device that produces clearer three-dimensional images of the brain goes by the name of magnetic resonance imaging scanner, and the images it produces are known as _____ scans.

   7-2. Unlike CT and MRI scans, which can only show the structure of the brain, the positron emission tomography scanner can portray the brain's actual _____ across time. The images produced by this procedure are called _____ scans.

   Answers: **7-1.** CT, MRI **7-2.** activity, PET.

8. **Summarize the key structures and functions of the hindbrain and midbrain.**

   8-1. The brain can be subdivided into three major structures. Moving up from the top of the spinal cord, one first encounters the hindmost part of the brain, or _____. Next comes the middle part or _____. At the top we encounter the _____.

   8-2. Three separate structures make up the hindbrain: the cerebellum, the pons, and the medulla. The structure that attaches to the top of the spinal cord and controls many essential functions such as breathing and circulation is called the _____. The section that forms a bridge of fibers between the brainstem and the cerebellum is called the _____. The structure that is essential for executing and coordinating physical movement is called the _____.

   8-3. Helping to control sensory processes and voluntary movements is one of the major roles of the _____. It also shares a structure with the hindbrain that is essential for the regulation of sleep and wakefulness as well as modulation of muscular reflexes, breathing, and pain perception. This structure is called the _____ formation.

   Answers: **8-1.** hindbrain, midbrain, forebrain **8-2.** medulla, pons, cerebellum **8-3.** midbrain, reticular.

9. **Summarize the key functions of the thalamus, hypothalamus, and limbic system.**

   9-1. The structure that serves as a way station for all sensory information (except for smell) headed for the brain is called the _____. The thalamus also appears to play an active role in _____ sensory information.

   9-2. In addition to its role in controlling the autonomic nervous system, the hypothalamus also plays a major role in regulating basic biological drives such as fighting, _____, feeding, and _____.

   9-3. An interconnected network of structures involved in the control of emotion, motivation, and memory are collectively known as the _____ system. One of these structures, the hippocampus, is known to play a key role in the formation of _____. However, the limbic system is best known for its role as the seat of _____. Electrical stimulation of particular areas of the limbic system in rats and monkeys appears to produce intense _____. The key neurotransmitter in these pleasure centers appears to be _____.

Answers: **9-1.** thalamus, integrating **9-2.** fleeing, mating **9-3.** limbic, memories, emotion, pleasure, dopamine.

10. Describe the structure of the cerebrum and the key function of the four lobes in the cerebral cortex.

10-1. The cerebrum is the brain structure that is responsible for our most complex _____ activities. Its folded outer surface is called the _____ cortex. The cerebrum is divided into two halves, known as the _____ and _____ cerebral hemispheres. The two hemispheres communicate with each other by means of a wide band of fibers called the _____ _____.

10-2. Each cerebral hemisphere is divided into four parts called lobes. Match these four lobes (occipital, parietal, temporal, and frontal) with their key function:

(a) Contains the primary motor cortex, which controls the movement of muscles _____

(b) Contains the primary visual cortex, which initiates the processing of visual information _____

(c) Contains the primary auditory cortex, which initiates the processing of auditory information _____

(d) Contains the somatosensory cortex, which registers the sense of touch _____

10-3. What appears to be the possible role of the prefrontal cortex in monitoring, organizing, and directing thought?

Answers: **10-1.** mental, cerebral, right, left, corpus callosum **10-2.** (a) frontal (b) occipital (c) temporal (d) parietal **10-3.** It functions as an executive control system.

RIGHT BRAIN/LEFT BRAIN • CEREBRAL SPECIALIZATION

11. Summarize evidence that led scientists to view the left hemisphere as the dominant hemisphere and describe how research on cerebral specialization changed this view.

11-1. Until recent years, it was believed that the left hemisphere dominated a submissive right hemisphere. Evidence for this belief came from several sources, which all seemed to indicate that the left hemisphere played the dominant role with respect to the use of _____. For example, damage to an area in the frontal lobe known as _____ area was associated with speech deficits. Also, damage to another area located in the temporal lobe was found to be associated with difficulty in speech comprehension. This area is called _____ area. Both of these areas are located in the _____ cerebral hemisphere.

11-2.   Answer the following questions regarding split-brain research.

   (a) What was the result of severing the corpus callosum in these patients?

   (b) Which hemisphere was found to be primarily responsible for verbal and language tasks in general?

   (c) Which hemisphere was found to be primarily responsible for visual and spatial tasks?

11-3.   What can be concluded with respect to hemispheric domination from both split-brain and intact-brain studies?

Answers: 11-1. language, Broca's, Wernicke's, left **11-2.** (a) The two cerebral hemispheres could no longer communicate with each other. (b) The left cerebral hemisphere. (c) The right cerebral hemisphere. **11-3.** Neither hemisphere dominates, rather each has its own specialized tasks.

THE ENDOCRINE SYSTEM • ANOTHER WAY TO COMMUNICATE

12. Describe the workings of the endocrine system.

   12-1.   Answer the following questions regarding the workings of the endocrine system.

   (a) What is the role played by the hormones in the endocrine system?

   (b) While many glands comprise the endocrine system, which one functions as a master gland to control the others?

   (c) What structure is the real power behind the throne here?

   12-2.   Fill in the boxes in the diagram below showing the role of the pituitary gland and adrenal gland in the "fight or flight" response to stress.

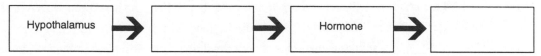

12-3. What is the role of sexual hormones:

(a) Prior to birth?

(b) At puberty?

Answers: 12-1. (a) They serve as chemical messengers. (b) The pituitary gland. (c) The hypothalamus. **12-2.** Pituitary, Adrenal **12-3.** (a) They direct the formation of the external sexual organs. (b) They are responsible for the emergence of the secondary sexual characteristics.

HEREDITY AND BEHAVIOR • IS IT ALL IN THE GENES?

13. Describe the structures and processes involved in genetic transmission.

13-1. Except for the sex cells each cell in humans contains 46 chromosomes that operate in 23 pairs, half of which are contributed by each _____. Each member of a pair operates in conjunction with its _____ member.

13-2. Each chromosome is actually a threadlike strand of a _____ molecule, and along this threadlike structure are found the individual units of information, called _____, that determine our biological makeup. Like chromosomes, genes operate in _____. Most human traits are influenced by (one pair/several pairs) of genes and are thus said to be _____ with respect to hereditary influence.

Answers: 13-1. parent, opposite **13-2.** DNA, genes, pairs, several pairs, polygenic.

14. Explain the special methods used to investigate the influence of heredity on behavior.

14-1. If a trait is due to heredity, then more closely related members of a family should show (lesser/greater) resemblance on this trait than less closely related family members. Studies using this method are called _____studies. Data gathered from family studies (can/cannot) furnish conclusive proof as to the heritability of a specific trait. Even when it is demonstrated that a particular trait is highly related to the degree of family relationship, the cause for this relationship could be either heredity or

_____.

14-2. A second method in this line of investigation is to compare specific traits across identical twins and fraternal twins. This method, called _____studies, assumes that inherited traits are much more likely to be found among _____ twins than among fraternal twins. These studies do in fact show that for many characteristics, such as intelligence and extraversion, the resemblance is closest for _____ twins. However, since identical twins are far from identical on these characteristics, _____ factors must also play a role here.

14-3. A third method in this line of investigation is to study children who have been separated from their biological parents at a very early age and raised by adoptive parents. The idea behind these _____ studies is that if the adoptive children more closely resemble their biological parents with respect to a specific trait, then it can be assumed that _____ plays a major role. On the other hand, if the adoptive children more closely resemble their adoptive parents with respect to a specific trait it would indicate that _____ plays a major role. Studies using this method to study the inheritabilty of intelligence have found that children appear to be equally influenced by both their biological and adoptive parents. This would indicate that a trait such as intelligence is influenced by both heredity and _____.

Answers: **14-1.** greater, family, cannot, environment **14-2.** twin, identical, identical, environmental **14-3.** adoption, heredity, environment, environment.

THE EVOLUTIONARY BASES OF BEHAVIOR

15. Explain the four key insights that represent the essence of Darwin's theory.

15-1.   Darwin's four key insights are listed below. Match each one with the statement that best reflects the essence of the insight.

1.   Organisms vary in endless ways.

2.   Some of these characteristics are heritable.

3.   Organisms tend to reproduce faster than the available resources necessary for their survival.

4.   If a specific heritable trait contributes to survival or reproductive fitness its prevalence will increase over generations.

_____ (a) The gazelle that runs the fastest is most likely to leave offspring behind.

_____ (b) The members of most species die from starvation or other side effects of overcrowding.

_____ (c) Birds fly, fish swim, and lions roar.

_____ (d) We all have some traits that are very similar to our grandparents.

Answers: **15-1.** (a) 4 (b) 3 (c) 1 (d) 2.

16. Describe some subsequent refinements to evolutionary theory.

16-1.   While contemporary theorists accept Darwin's basic theory of natural selection, they have found that natural selection operates on a gene pool that is also influenced by adaptations and inclusive fitness. Match these terms with the definitions given below.

(a)   The sum of an individual's own reproductive success plus the effects the organism has on the reproductive success of related others.

(b)   An inherited characteristic that increased in a population because it helped solve a problem of survival or reproduction during the time it emerged.

16-2. (a) Which of these processes explain why our ancient ancestors developed a taste for fatty foods?

(b) Which of these processes explain why black birds risk death from a hawk to alert other members of the flock?

Answers: **16-1.** (a) inclusive fitness (b) adaptations **16-2.** (a) adaptations (b) inclusive fitness.

17. Provide some examples of animal behavior that represent adaptations.

17-1. Answer the following questions about behavioral adaptations.

(a) What advantage do females gain by trading sex for material goods?

(b) What advantage do rats gain by only eating only a small amount when they first encounter a new food?

Answers: **17-1.** (a) The females and their offspring are more likely to survive. (b) It decreases their chances of being poisoned.

PUTING IT IN PERSPECTIVE

18. Explain how this chapter highlighted three of the text's unifying themes.

18-1. Indicate which of the three unifying themes–heredity and environment jointly influence behavior, behavior is determined by multiple causes, and psychology is empirical–is particularly illustrated in each of the following situations.

(a) The development of schizophrenic disorders.

(b) The new discoveries of cerebral specialization and the impact of heredity on behavior.

(c) The development of personal characteristics such as sarcasm and artistic interest.

Answers: **18-1.** (a) Behavior is determined by multiple causes. (b) Psychology is empirical. (c) Heredity and environment jointly influence behavior.

19. **Outline four popular ideas linking cerebral specialization to cognitive processes and evaluate each of these in light of currently available evidence.**

   19-1.   Your text lists four popular ideas that have found support among some neuroscientists and psychologists. These ideas are:

   (a) The two hemispheres are _____ to process different cognitive tasks.

   (b) The two hemispheres have _____ modes of thinking.

   (c) People vary in their _____ on one hemisphere as opposed to the other.

   (d) Schools should place more emphasis on teaching the _____ side of the brain.

   19-2.   We will now proceed through each of these four assumptions to show how each has to be qualified in light of currently available evidence.

   (a) The idea that the left and right brains are specialized to handle different kinds of information (is/is not) supported by research. However, there is evidence that this specialization hardly occurs in some persons, while in other persons the specialization is reversed, particularly among _____ - handed persons. Moreover, most tasks require the ongoing cooperation of _____ hemispheres.

   (b) The assertion that each hemisphere has its own mode of thinking is (plausible/confirmed). A big problem here, however, is that mode of thinking, or cognitive style, has proven difficult to both define and _____.

   (c) The assertion that some people are left-brained while other are right-brained (is/is not) conclusive at this time. Abilities and personality characteristics (do/do not) appear to be influenced by brainedness.

   (d) The notion that most schooling overlooks the education of the right brain (does/does not) really make sense. Since both hemispheres are almost always sharing in accomplishing an ongoing task, it would be _____ to teach only one hemisphere at time.

   Answers: 19-1. (a) specialized (b) different (c) reliance (dependence) (d) right 19-2. (a) is, left, both (b) plausible, measure (c) is not, do not (d) does not, impossible.

CRITICAL THINKING APPLICATION • BUILDING BETTER BRAINS: THE PERILS OF EXTRAPOLATION

20. **Explain how neuroscience research has been overextrapolated by some education and child care advocates who have campaigned for infant schooling.**

   20-1.   Answer the following questions regarding neuroscience research.

   (a) What happened to kittens deprived of light to one eye for the first 4-6 weeks of life?

(b) What happened to kittens deprived of light to one eye for the same amount of time after 4 months of age?

(c) What is the name given to that early period in the kitten's life when light is essential for the normal development of vision?

(d) What difference was found in synapses in rats that were raised in "enriched" environments when compared to rats raised in "impoverished" environments?

20-2. Answer the following questions regarding the overextrapolation of neuroscience findings.

(a) What findings argue against the notion that brain development is more malleable during the first three years of life?

(b) There are findings that argue against the notion that greater synaptic density is associated with greater intelligence. Which of the following is correct?

1. Infant animals and human beings begin life with an overabundance of synaptic connections.

2. Infant animals and human beings begin life with an insufficient number of synaptic connections.

3. Learning involves the pruning of inactive synapses and reinforcing heavily used neural pathways.

Answers: 20-1. (a) They became blind in the light-deprived eye. (b) They did not suffer blindness in that eye. (c) critical period (d) They had more synapses. **20-2.** (a) It has been found that the brain remains malleable throughout life. (b) 1 and 3 are correct.

REVIEW OF KEY TERMS

Absolute refractory period	Cerebral cortex	Fitness
Action potential	Cerebral hemispheres	Forebrain
Adaptation	Chromosomes	Genes
Adoption studies	Corpus callosum	Hindbrain
Afferent nerve fibers	Critical period	Hormones
Agonist	Dendrites	Hypothalamus
Antagonist	Efferent nerve fibers	Inclusiveness fitness
Autonomic nervous system (ANS)	Endocrine System	Limbic system
Axon	Endorphins	Midbrain
Central nervous system (CNS)	Family studies	Natural selection

Neurons
Neurotransmitters
Parental investment
Peripheral nervous system
Pituitary gland
Polygenic traits

Polygyny
Postsynaptic potential (PSP)
Resting potential
Reuptake
Soma
Somatic nervous system

Split-brain surgery
Synapse
Synaptic cleft
Terminal buttons
Thalamus
Twin studies

_____ 1. Individual cells in the nervous system that receive, integrate, and transmit information.

_____ 2. Neuron part that contains the cell nucleus and much of the chemical machinery common to most cells.

_____ 3. Branchlike parts of a neuron that are specialized to receive information.

_____ 4. A long, thin fiber that transmits signals away from the soma to other neurons, or to muscles or glands.

_____ 5. A process in which neurotransmitters are sponged up from the synaptic cleft by the presynaptic membrane.

_____ 6. Small knobs at the end of the axon that secrete chemicals called neurotransmitters.

_____ 7. A junction where information is transmitted between neurons.

_____ 8. The stable, negative charge of an inactive neuron.

_____ 9. A brief change in a neuron's electrical charge.

_____ 10. The minimum length of time after an action potential during which another action potential cannot begin.

_____ 11. A microscopic gap between the terminal buttons of the sending neuron and the cell membrane of another neuron.

_____ 12. Holds that heritable characteristics that provide a survival or reproductive advantage are more likely than alternative characteristics to be passed on to subsequent generations and thus they come to be "selected" over time.

_____ 13. A voltage change at the receptor site of a neuron.

_____ 14. A technique for assessing hereditary influence by examining blood relatives to see how much they resemble each other on a specific trait.

_____ 15. A chemical that mimics the action of a neurotransmitter.

_____ 16. A chemical that opposes the action of a neurotransmitter.

_____ 17. An entire family of internally produced chemicals that resemble opiates in structure and effects.

_____ 18. Chemicals that increase or decrease (modulate) the activity of specific neurotransmitters.

_____ 19. System that includes all those nerves that lie outside the brain and spinal cord.

_____ 20. An inherited characteristic that increased in a population because it helped solve a problem of survival or reproduction during the time it emerged.

_____ 21. System made up of the nerves that connect to voluntary skeletal muscles and sensory receptors.

_____ 22. Axons that carry information inward to the central nervous system from the periphery of the body.

_____ 23. Axons that carry information outward from the central nervous system to the periphery of the body.

_____ 24. System made up of the nerves that connect to the heart, blood vessels, smooth muscles and glands.

_____ 25. Refers to the reproductive success of an individual organism relative to the average reproductive success in the population.

_____ 26. The sum of an individual's own reproductive success plus the effects the organism has on the reproductive success of related others.

_____ 27. System that consists of the brain and spinal cord.

_____ 28. A limited time span in the development of an organism when it is optimal for certain capacities to emerge because the organism is especially responsive to certain experiences.

_____ 29. Assessing hereditary influence by comparing the resemblance of identical twins and fraternal twins on a trait.

_____ 30. Part of the brain that includes the cerebellum and two structures found in the lower part of the brainstem – the medulla and the pons.

_____ 31. The segment of the brainstem that lies between the hindbrain and the forebrain.

_____ 32. Part of the brain encompassing the thalamus, hypothalamus, limbic system, and cerebrum.

_____ 33. A structure in the forebrain through which all sensory information (except smell) must pass to get to the cerebral cortex.

_____ 34. A structure found near the base of the forebrain that is involved in the regulation of basic biological needs.

_____ 35. A densely connected network of structures located beneath the cerebral cortex, involved in the control of emotion, motivation, and memory.

_____ 36. The convulated outer layer of the cerebrum.

_____ 37. The right and left halves of the cerebrum.

_____ 38. The structure that connects the two cerebral hemispheres.

_____ 39. Assessing hereditary influence by examining the resemblance between adopted children and both their adoptive and biological parents.

_____ 40. Surgery in which the corpus callosum is severed to reduce the severity of epileptic seizures.

_____ 41. System of glands that secrete chemicals into the bloodstream that help control bodily functioning.

_____ 42. The chemical substances released by the endocrine glands.

_____ 43. The "master gland" of the endocrine system.

_____ 44. Threadlike strands of DNA molecules that carry genetic information.

_____ 45. DNA segments that serve as the key functional units in hereditary transmission.

_____ 46. Characteristics that are influenced by more than one pair of genes.

_____ 47. Refers to what each sex has to invest – in terms of energy, survival, and forgone opportunities – to produce and nurture offspring.

_____ 48. A mating system in which each male seeks to mate with multiple females, whereas each female mates with only one male.

Answers: 1. neurons **2.** soma **3.** dendrites **4.** axon **5.** reuptake **6.** terminal buttons **7.** synapse **8.** resting potential **9.** action potential **10.** absolute refractory period **11.** synaptic cleft **12.** natural selection **13.** postsynaptic potential (PSP) **14.** family studies **15.** agonist **16.** antagonist **17.** endorphins **18.** neuromodulators **19.** peripheral nervous system **20.** adaptation **21.** somatic nervous system **22.** afferent nerve fibers **23.** efferent fibers **24.** autonomic nervous system (ANS) **25.** fitness **26.** inclusive fitness **27.** central nervous system (CNS) **28.** critical period **29.** twin studies **30.** hindbrain **31.** midbrain **32.** forebrain **33.** thalamus **34.** hypothalamus **35.** limbic system **36.** cerebral cortex **37.** cerebral hemispheres **38.** corpus callosum **39.** adoption studies **40.** split-brain surgery **41.** endocrine system **42.** hormones **43.** pituitary gland **44.** chromosomes **45.** genes **46.** polygenic traits **47.** parental investment **48.** polygyny.

REVIEW OF KEY PEOPLE

Alan Hodgkin & Andrew Huxley   Candice Pert & Solomon Snyder   Roger Sperry & Michael Garzzaniga
James Olds & Peter Milner   Robert Plomin

_____   **1.** Unlocked the mystery of the neural impulse.

_____   **2.** Known for their work with the split brain.

_____   **3.** Showed that morphine works by binding to specific receptors.

_____   **4.** Discovered "pleasure centers" in the limbic system.

_____   **5.** One of the leading behavior genetics researchers in the last decade.

Answers : 1. Hodgkin & Huxley **2.** Sperry & Garzzaniga **3.** Pert & Snyder **4.** Olds & Milner **5.** Plomin.

SELF-QUIZ

1. Most neurons are involved in transmitting information:
   a. from one neuron to another
   b. from the outside world to the brain
   c. from the brain to the muscles
   d. from the brain to the glands

2. Which part of the neuron has the responsibility for receiving information from other neurons?
   a. the cell body
   b. the dendrites
   c. the axon
   d. the soma

3. The myelin sheath serves to:
   a. permit faster transmission of the neural impulse
   b. keep neural impulses on the right track
   c. add structural strength
   d. permit faster transmission and keep neural impulses on the right track

4. The change in the polarity of a neuron that results from the inflow of positively charged ions and the outflow of negatively charged ions is called the:
   a. presynaptic potential
   b. postsynaptic potential
   c. action potential
   d. synaptic potential

5. The task of passing a message from one neuron to another is actually carried out by:
   a. the myelin sheath
   b. the glia cells
   c. the action potential
   d. neurotransmitters

6. What is the key neurotransmitter found in the "pleasure centers" of the limbic system?
   a. acetycholine
   b. dopamine
   c. norepinephrine
   d. serotonin

7. Which of the following brain-imaging techniques portray the brain's actual activity across time?
   a. CT scans
   b. PET scans
   c. MRI Scans
   d. ESB scans

8. The seat of emotion is to be found in the:
   a. reticular formation
   b. hindbrain
   c. limbic system
   d. forebrain

9. Persons having difficulty with language and speech following an accident that resulted in injury to the brain are most likely to have sustained damage in the:
   a. right cerebral hemisphere
   b. left cerebral hemisphere
   c. cerebellum
   d. thalamus

10. In carrying out the "fight or flight" response, the role of master supervisor is assigned to the:
    a. adrenal gland
    b. pituitary gland
    c. hypothalamus
    d. parasympathetic nervous system

11. Adoption studies show that the intelligence of adopted children is:
    a. most influenced by the biological parents
    b. most influenced by the adoptive parents
    c. equally influenced by the biological and adoptive parents
    d. most influenced by the other children of the adoptive parents

12. Current evidence indicates that schizophrenia results from:
    a. genetic factors
    b. environmental factors
    c. completely unknown factors
    d. multiple factors that involve both genetic and environmental factors

13. Which evolutionary principle is used to explain why a woman may risk her life to save another person?
    a. inclusive fitness
    b. adaptations
    c. polygyny
    d. parental investment

14. Which of the following statements is/are correct?
    a. the left side of the brain is the dominant side
    b. the right and left brains are specialized to handle different kinds of information
    c. personality characteristics appear to be influenced by brainedness
    d. most schooling overlooks the education of the right brain

15. Which of the following statements is correct?
    a. Human beings begin life with an insufficient number of synapses.
    b. Human beings begin life with an overabundance of synapses.
    c. Intelligence is associated with synaptic density.
    d. The brain is only malleable during the first 3 years of life.

Answers: 1. a 2. b 3. d 4. c 5. d 6. b 7. b 8. c 9. b 10. c 11. c 12. d 13. a 14. b 15. b.

INFOTRAC

Critical Period   Family Studies   Twin Studies
Endorphins

4 SENSATION AND PERCEPTION

REVIEW OF KEY IDEAS

OUR SENSE OF SIGHT • THE VISUAL SYSTEM

1. **List the three properties of light and the aspects of visual perception that they influence.**

   Before we can see anything, _____ must be present. There are three characteristics of light waves that directly affect how we perceive visual objects; match each of these characteristics with its psychological effect.

   (a) _____ wavelength   1. color

   (b) _____ amplitude   2. saturation (or richness)

   (c) _____ purity   3. brightness

   Answers: 1-1. light waves or light, (a) 1 (b) 3 (c) 2.

2. **Describe the role of the lens and pupil in the functioning of the eye.**

   2-1. Getting light rays entering the eye to properly focus on the retina is the job of the _____. It accomplishes this task by either thickening or flattening its curvature, a process called _____. The amount of light entering the eye is controlled by the opening in the center of the iris called the _____.

   Answers: 2-1. lens, accommodation, pupil.

3. **Describe the role of the retina in light sensitivity and in visual information processing.**

   3-1. The structure that transforms the information contained in light rays into neural impulses that are then sent to the brain is called the _____. All of the axons carrying these neural impulses exit the eye at a single opening in the retina called the optic _____. Since the optic disk is actually a hole in the retina, this part of the retina cannot sense incoming visual information and for this reason it is called the _____ _____.

3-2. The specialized receptor cells that are primarily responsible for visual acuity and color vision are called the _____. The cones are mainly located in the center of the retina in a tiny spot called the _____. The specialized receptor cells that lie outside of the fovea and toward the periphery of the retina are called the _____. The rods are primarily responsible for peripheral vision and for _____ vision.

3-3. Answer the following questions regarding light and dark adaptation.

(a) What form of adaptation occurs when you walk into a darkened theatre?

(b) What form of adaptation occurs when you leave the darkened theatre?

3-4. Light rays striking the rods and cones initiate neural impulses that are then transmitted to _____ cells and then to _____ cells. From here the visual information is transmitted to the brain via the axons running from the retina to the brain, collectively known as the _____ nerve.

3-5. The processing of visual information begins within the receiving area of a retinal cell called the _____ field. Stimulation of the receptive field of a cell causes signals to be sent inward toward the brain and sideways, or laterally to nearby cells, thus allowing them to _____ with one another.

Answers: 3-1. retina, disk, blind spot **3-2.** cones, fovea, rods, night (low light) **3-3.** (a) dark adaptation (b) light adaptation **3-4.** bipolar, ganglion, optic **3-5.** receptive, interact.

4. Describe the routing of signals from the eye to the brain and the brain's role in visual information processing.

4-1. Visual information from the right side of the visual field (see Figure 4-8 in the text) exits from the retinas of both eyes via the optic nerves and meet at the _____ _____ , where it is combined and sent to the _____ side of the brain. Visual information from the left side of the visual field follow a similar pattern, meeting at the optic chiasm, and then on to the _____ side of the brain.

4-2. After leaving the optic chiasm on their way to the visual cortex, the optic nerve fibers diverge along two pathways before reaching (the same/different) areas in the occipital cortex.

4-3. The main visual pathway is subdivided into two more specialized pathways called the magnocellular and parvocellular channels.

(a) What kind of information is extracted by the parvocelluar channel?

(b) What kind of information is extracted by the magnocellular channel?

(c) What is the benefit of this kind of parallel processing?

4-4.   Because the cells in the visual cortex respond very selectively to specific features of complex stimuli, they have been described as _____ detectors. There are three major types of cells in the visual cortex: simple cells, complex cells, and hypercomplex cells. Identify them from their descriptions given below.

(a) These cells are particular about the width and orientation of a line but respond to any position in their receptive field.

(b) These cells are very particular about the width, orientation, and position of a line.

(c) These cells are very particular about the length of the lines that will cause them to fire.

4-5.   After information is processed in the primary visual cortex it is sent on to other areas in the cortex and as the information moves along the neurons become (much less/even more) fussy about what turns them on.

Answers: 4-1. optic chiasm, left, right 4-2. (a) different 4-3. (a) What objects are out there (perception of color form and texture) (b) Where the objects are (perception of motion and depth) pathway (c) It allows for simultaneously extracting different information from the same input). 4-4. feature, (a) complex cells (b) simple cells (c) hypercomplex cells 4-5. even more.

5. **Discuss the trichromatic and opponent process theories of color vision, and the modern reconciliation of these theories.**

5-1.   The trichromatic theory of color vision, as its name suggests, proposes three different kinds of receptors (channels) for the three primary colors red, _____, and _____. The opponent process theory of color vision also proposes three channels for color vision, but these channels are red versus _____, yellow versus _____, and black versus _____.

5-2.   These two theories of color vision can be used to explain different phenomena. Use T (trichromatic) or O (opponent process) to indicate which theory best explains the following phenomena.

_____ (a) The color of an afterimage is the complement of the original color.

_____ (b) The different kinds of color blindness suggest three different kinds of receptors.

_____ (c) Any three appropriately spaced colors can produce all other colors.

_____ (d) People describing colors often require at least four different names.

5-3. The evidence is now clear that both theories are (incorrect/<u>correct</u>). Each is needed to explain all of the phenomena associated with color vision. Three different kinds of cones have been found in the retina that are sensitive to one of the three primary colors; this supports the _____ theory. It has also been found that once information leaves the cones and is processed in the retina and brain the cells respond in opposite (antagonistic) ways to colors, thus supporting the _____ _____ theory.

Answers: **5-1.** green, blue, green, blue, white **5-2.** (a) O (b) T (c) T (d) O **5-3.** correct, trichromatic, opponent process.

6. **Explain the basic premise of Gestalt psychology and describe Gestalt principles of visual perception.**

6-1. The Gestalt view of form perception assumes that form perception is not constructed out of individual elements; rather the form, or whole, is said to be _____ than the sum of its individual elements. The illusion of movement, called the _____ phenomenon, is used to support the Gestalt view of form perception because the illusion of movement (<u>is/is not</u>) completely contained in the individual chunks of stimuli that give rise to it.

6-2. Five Gestalt principles of visual perception are illustrated below. Match each illustration with its correct name.

Proximity

Similarity

Continuity

Closure

Simplicity

(a) _____

(b) _____

(c) _____

(d) _____

(e) _____

6-3. What Gestalt principle is illustrated by the fact that the words printed on this page appear to stand out from the white paper they are printed on?

Answers: **6-1.** greater (more), phi, is not, greater (more) **6-2.** (a) proximity (b) closure (c) similarity (d) simplicity (e) continuity **6-3.** figure and ground.

7. **Explain how form perception can be a matter of formulating perceptual hypotheses.**

   7-1.   The objects that surround us in the world outside of our bodies are called _____ stimuli; the images the objects project on our retinas are called _____ stimuli. When perceived from different angles or distances, the same distal stimulus projects (similar/different) proximal images on the retina. This forces us to make perceptual _____ about the distal stimulus.

   Answers: 7-1. distal, proximal, different, hypotheses or guesses.

8. **Describe the monocular and binocular cues employed in depth perception and cultural variations in depth perception.**

   8-1.   There are two general types of cues that allow us to perceive depth and they are easy to remember because one type involve the use of both eyes and are called _____ cues; the other type require the use of only one of the eyes and are called _____ cues. Depth perception (does/does not) require the use of both binocular and monocular cues.

   8-2.   The primary binocular depth arises from the fact that objects within 25 feet project images to slightly different locations on the right and left retinas. This cue is called _____ _____ and the disparity becomes (greater/lesser) as objects move closer to you.

   8-3.   There are two general kinds of monocular cues. One kind involves the active use of the eye, such as the accommodation used for focusing the eye. The other general kind is used to indicate depth in flat pictures and thus is called a _____ cue.

   8-4.   Identify which of the six pictorial cues – light and shadow, interposition, texture gradients, linear perspective, height in plane, relative size – are being described below:

   (a)   Parallel lines grow closer as they recede into the distance.

   (b)   More distant objects are higher in the field than nearer objects.

   (c)   When objects appear to be of the same size, closer ones appear larger than more distant ones.

   (d)   Near objects block or overlap more distant ones.

   (e)   Texture appears to grow finer as viewing distance increases.

   (f)   Patterns of light and dark suggest shadows that can create an impression of three-dimensional space.

8-5. What phenomenon was observed in societies where the people had little exposure to pictures or photos?

(a) What does this tell us about depth cues in pictures?

Answers: **8-1.** binocular, monocular, does not **8-2.** retinal disparity, greater **8-3.** pictorial **8-4.** (a) linear perspective (b) height in plane (c) relative size (d) interposition (e) texture gradients (f) light and shadow **8-5.** They had difficulty perceiving depth in two-dimensional pictures. (a) Perception of depth in pictures is partly an acquired skill that depends on experience.

9. **Describe perceptual constancies and illusions in vision, and discuss cultural variations in susceptibility to certain illusions.**

9-1. The tendency to experience stable perceptions in spite of constantly changing sensory input is called perceptual _____. For instance, the retinal image shrinks as a friend walks away, but she continues to appear her usual height.

9-2. Being fooled by the discrepancy between the appearance of a visual stimulus and its physical reality is what is meant by an optical _____. Both perceptual constancies and optical illusions illustrate the point that we are continually formulating _____ about what we perceive and also that these perceptions can be quite (subjective/objective).

9-3. How do cultures affect susceptibility to certain illusions?

Answers: **9-1.** constancy **9-2.** illusion, hypotheses, subjective **9-3.** They make us more or less susceptible (to certain illusions).

OUR SENSE OF HEARING • THE AUDITORY SYSTEM

10. **List the three properties of sound and the aspects of auditory perception that they influence.**

10-1. Name the perceived qualities that are associated with the following properties of sound waves.

Physical Property	Description	Perceived Quality
(a) purity	kind of mixture	_____
(b) amplitude	wave height	_____
(c) wavelength	wave frequency	_____

Answers: **10-1.** (a) timbre (b) loudness (c) pitch.

11. **Summarize the information on human hearing capacities and describe how sensory processing occurs in the ear.**

11-1. On the following page are questions concerning human hearing capacities. Match the questions with their correct answers.

Answers	Questions
1. 90 to 120 decibels (dB).	_____ (a) What is the frequency range of human hearing?
2. 1,800 to 2,200 Hz.	_____ (b) How loud do sounds have to be to cause damage to human hearing?
3. 20 to 20,000 Hz.	_____ (c) To what frequency range is human hearing the most sensitive?

11-2. Below is a scrambled sequence of events that occurs when a sound wave strikes the ear. Put these events in their correct order using the numbers 1 through 4.

_____ Fluid waves travel down the chochlea causing the hair cells on the basilar membrane to vibrate.

_____ The pinna directs air to the eardrum.

_____ The hair cells convert fluid motion into neural impulses and send them to the brain.

_____ The motion of the vibrating eardrum is converted to fluid motion by the ossicles.

Answers: 11-1. (a) 3 (b) 1 (c) 2 **11-2.** 3, 1, 4, 2.

12. Compare and contrast the place and frequency theories of pitch perception and discuss the resolution of the debate.

12-1. One theory of pitch perception assumes that the hair cells respond differentially to pitch depending on their location along the basilar membrane. This is the main idea of the _____ theory of pitch perception. A second theory assumes a one-to-one correspondence between the actual frequency of the sound wave and the frequency at which the entire basilar membrane vibrates. This is the main idea of the _____ theory of pitch perception.

12-2. Below are two facts uncovered by research. Tell which theory of pitch is supported by each of these facts.

(a) The hair cells along the basilar membrane vibrate in unison and not independently.

(b) A wave pattern caused by the vibrating basilar membrane peaks at a particular place along the membrane.

12-3. The above findings mean that the perception of pitch depends on both _____ and _____ coding.

Answers: 12-1. place, frequency **12-2.** (a) frequency theory (b) place theory **12-3.** place and frequency (in either order).

13. **Describe the stimulus and receptors for taste and discuss factors that may influence perceived flavor.**

    13-1.   The stimuli for taste perception are _____ absorbed in the saliva that stimulate taste cells located in the tongue's _____. It is generally thought that there are four fundamental tastes; these are _____, _____, _____, _____ .

    13-2.   Tell how the following wine-tasting rituals may influence perceived flavor.

        (a) Cleaning the palate with water before tasting wine?

        (b) Swirling the wine in the glass before sipping?

        (c) Rolling a sip of wine around in the mouth before swallowing?

Answers: 13-1. chemicals, taste buds, sweet, sour, salty, bitter (in any order) **13-2.** (a) It lowers the aftereffects associated with sensory adaptation. (b) It helps to release the wine's odor and odor is a major determinant of flavor. (c) It distributes the wine over the full diversity of taste cells.

14. **Describe the stimulus and receptors for smell.**

    14-1.   The stimuli for the sense of smell are volatile _____ molecules floating in the air. The receptors for smell are hairlike structures located in the nasal passages called _____ _____. If there are any primary odors, they must be (<u>large</u>/small) in number. While humans can distinguish between around 10,000 odors, for unknown reasons they find it difficult to attach _____ to these odors.

Answers: 14-1. chemical, olfactory cilia, large, names.

OUR OTHER SENSES

15. **Describe the processes involved in the perception of pressure and pain.**

    15-1.   Answer the following questions concerning the sense of touch.

        (a) What four different perceptions are included in the sense of touch?

        (b) What three body areas are most sensitive to pressure stimulation?

        (c) What is the name of the receiving area in the brain for tactile information?

        (d) What similar mechanism does the tactile and visual system use for processing sensory information?

15-2. Pain signals travel to the brain by two slightly different pathways. One pathway sends signals directly and immediately to the cortex and is called the _____ pathway. The other first sends signals through the limbic system and then on to the cortex and is called the _____ pathway. Lingering, less-localized pain is mediated by the _____ pathway.

15-3. Answer the following questions regarding the perception of pain.

(a) What phenomenon did the gate-control theory of pain perception attempt to explain?

(b) What effect do endorphins have with respect to pain?

(c) A descending pathway originating in the midbrain also appears to inhibit the perception of pain. Where might the controls for this pathway originate?

Answers: **15-1.** (a) pressure, warmth, cold, and pain (b) fingers, lips, and tongue (c) somatosensory cortex (d) receptive fields **15-2.** fast, slow, slow **15-3.** (a) Why the perception of pain is so subjective (b) An analgesic (pain-relieving) effect (c) In higher brain centers.

16. Describe the perceptual experiences mediated by the kinesthetic and vestibular senses.

16-1. The system that monitors the positions of various parts of the body is called the _____ system. This system sends information to the brain about body position and movement obtained from receptors located in the joints and _____.

16-2. The system that monitors the body's location in space is called the _____ system. The receptors for the vestibular system are primarily hair cells contained within the _____ canals in the inner ear.

16-3. What point does the text make about the kinesthetic and vestibular systems, and indeed all sensory systems, in carrying out their tasks?

Answers: **16-1.** kinesthetic, muscles **16-2.** vestibular, semicircular **16-3.** They integrate information from other senses (in carrying out their tasks).

PUTTING IT IN PERSPECTIVE

17. Explain how this chapter highlighted three of the text's unifying themes.

17-1. The fact that competing theories of both color vision and pitch were eventually reconciled attests to the value of theoretical diversity. Why is this?

17-2. Why must our experience of the world always be highly subjective?

17-3. What do cultural variations in depth perception, taste preferences, and pain tolerance tell us about the perceptual processes?

Answers: 17-1. Competing theories drive and guide the resolving research **17-2.** The perceptual processes themselves are inherently subjective **17-3.** They are subject to cultural influences.

PERSONAL APPLICATION • APPRECIATING ART AND ILLUSION

18. **Discuss how the paintings shown in the Application illustrate various principles of visual perception.**

   18-1. After reading the Application section in your text, answer the following questions by only looking at the paintings.

   (a) Which painting uses the Gestalt principles of perceptual organization to build a total picture out of geometric forms?

   (b) Which painting incorporates impossible triangles to achieve its effect?

   (c) Which painting makes particular use of pictorial depth cues (linear perspective, relative size, height in plane and interposition) to enhance the illusion of depth?

   (d) Which painting makes use of color mixing to illustrate how different spots of colors can be blended into a picture that is more than the sum of its parts?

   (e) Which painting makes use of a reversible figure to enhance a feeling of fantasy?

   (f) Which painting uses the pictorial depth cues of texture gradient and linear perspective to convey the look of great depth?

   Answers: 18-1. (a) 4.45 (b) 4.47 (c) 4.43 (d) 4.44 (e) 4.46 (f) 4.49.

CRITICAL THINKING APPLICATION • RECOGNIZING CONTRAST EFFECTS: IT'S ALL RELATIVE

19. **Explain how contrast effects can be manipulated to influence or distort judgments.**

   19-1. Which of the following contrast strategies, the door in the face technique or employing comparitors, is being illustrated in the following situations.

(a) You want to hit the Florida beaches for Spring Break, but you need extra money from home. Realizing this is going to be a hard sell, you first ask for a week in Paris and then try and settle for the beaches.

(b) When your lover catches you in an indiscretion, you quickly point out many more serious infractions by friends and acquaintances.

19-2. Both of these strategies illustrate the point that our perceptions and judgments are both subjective and

_____.

Answers: **19-1.** (a) the foot in the door technique (b) employing comparitors **19-2.** relative.

REVIEW OF KEY TERMS

Additive color mixing
After image
Basilar membrane
Binocular depth cues
Cochlea
Color blindness
Comparitors
Complimentary colors
Cones
Dark adaptation
Depth perception
Distal stimuli
Door-in-the-face technique
Farsightedness
Feature analysis

Feature detectors
Fovea
Gustatory system
Impossible figures
Kinesthetic system
Lens
Light adaptation
Monocular cues
Nearsightedness
Olfactory system
Optical illusion
Parallel processing
Perception
Perceptual constancy
Perceptual hypothesis

Perceptual set
Phi phenomenon
Pictorial depth cues
Proximal stimuli
Pupil
Receptive field of a visual cell
Retina
Retinal disparity
Reversible figure
Rods
Sensation
Sensory adaptation
Subtractive color mixing
Vestibular system

_____ 1. The stimulation of sense organs.

_____ 2. The selection, organization, and interpretation of sensory input.

_____ 3. Involves a gradual decline in sensitivity to prolonged stimulation.

_____ 4. The transparent eye structure that focuses the light rays falling on the retina.

_____ 5. The opening in the center of the iris that helps regulate the amount of light passing into the rear chamber of the eye.

_____ 6. The neural tissue lining the inside back surface of the eye that absorbs light, processes images, and sends visual information to the brain.

_____ 7. Specialized receptors that play a key role in daylight vision and color vision.

_____ 8. Specialized receptors that play a key role in night vision and peripheral vision.

_____ 9. A tiny spot in the center of the retina that contains only cones, where visual acuity is greatest.

_____	10. The process in which the eyes become more sensitive to light in low illumination.
_____	11. The process in which the eyes become less sensitive to light in high illumination.
_____	12. A variety of deficiencies in the ability to distinguish among colors.
_____	13. The retinal area that, when stimulated, affects the firing of a particular cell.
_____	14. Neurons that respond selectively to very specific features of more complex stimuli.
_____	15. Works by removing some wavelengths of light, leaving less light than was originally there.
_____	16. Works by superimposing lights, leaving more light in the mixture than in any one light by itself.
_____	17. Pairs of colors that can be added together to produce gray tones.
_____	18. A visual image that persists after a stimulus is removed.
_____	19. A drawing compatible with two different interpretations that can shift back and forth.
_____	20. A readiness to perceive a stimulus in a particular way.
_____	21. A process in which we detect specific elements in visual input and assemble these elements into a more complex form.
_____	22. An apparently inexplicable discrepancy between the appearance of a visual stimulus and its physical reality.
_____	23. The illusion of movement created by presenting visual stimuli in rapid succession.
_____	24. Stimuli that lie in the distance (in the world outside us).
_____	25. The stimulus energies that impinge directly on our sensory receptors.
_____	26. An inference about what distal stimuli could be responsible for the proximal stimuli sensed.
_____	27. Involves our interpretation of visual cues that tell us how near or far away objects are.
_____	28. Clues about distance that are obtained by comparing the differing views of the two eyes.
_____	29. Clues about distance that are obtained from the image in either eye alone.
_____	30. A tendency to experience a stable perception in the face of constantly changing sensory input.
_____	31. A fluid-filled, coiled tunnel that makes up the largest part of the inner ear.
_____	32. A membrane running the length of the cochlea that holds the actual auditory receptors, called hair cells.
_____	33. Involves simultaneously extracting different information from the same input.
_____	34. Our sense of taste.
_____	35. Our sense of smell.
_____	36. Objects that can be represented in two-dimensional figures but cannot exist in three-dimensional space.
_____	37. The sense that monitors the positions of the various parts of the body.
_____	38. The system that provides the sense of balance.
_____	39. A condition in which close objects are seen clearly but distant objects appear blurry.

_____ 40. A condition in which distant objects are seen clearly but close objects appear blurry.

_____ 41. Refers to the fact that objects within 25 feet project images to slightly different locations on the right and left retinas, so the right and left eyes see slightly different views of the object.

_____ 42. Cues about distance that can be given in a flat picture.

_____ 43. Involves making a large request that is likely to be turned down as a way to increase the chances that people will agree to a smaller request later.

_____ 44. People, objects, events, and other standards that are used as a baseline for comparison in making judgments.

Answers: 1. sensation **2.** perception **3.** sensory adaptation **4.** lens **5.** pupil **6.** retina **7.** cones **8.** rods **9.** fovea **10.** dark adaptation **11.** light adaptation **12.** color blindness **13.** receptive field of a visual cell **14.** feature detectors **15.** subtractive color mixing **16.** additive color mixing **17.** complementary colors **18.** afterimage **19.** reversible figure **20.** perceptual set **21.** feature analysis **22.** optical illusions **23.** phi phenomenon **24.** distal stimuli **25.** proximal stimuli **26.** perceptual hypothesis **27.** depth perception **28.** binocular cues **29.** monocular cues **30.** perceptual constancy **31.** cochlea **32.** basilar membrane **33.** parallel processing **34.** gustatory system **35.** olfactory system **36.** impossible figures **37.** kinesthetic sense **38.** vestibular system **39.** nearsightedness **40.** farsightedness **41.** retinal disparity **42.** pictorial depth cues **43.** door-in-the-face technique **44.** comparitors.

REVIEW OF KEY PEOPLE

Linda Bartoshuk   David Hubel and Torston Weisel   Max Wertheimer
Herman von Helmholtz   Ronald Melzack and Patrick Wall

_____ 1. These two men won the Nobel Prize for their discovery of feature detector cells in the retina.

_____ 2. One of the originators of the trichromatic theory of color vision.

_____ 3. Made use of the phi phenomenon to illustrate some of the basic principles of Gestalt psychology.

_____ 4. A leading authority on taste research.

_____ 5. Proposed a gate-control theory of pain.

Answers: 1. Hubel and Weisel **2.** Helmholtz **3.** Wertheimer **4.** Bartoshuk **5.** Melzack and Wall.

SELF-QUIZ

1. Averting your gaze slightly away from an object you are trying to see under darkened conditions improves your ability to see it. Why is this?
   a. It causes the pupils to open wider.
   b. It allows for stimulation of more cones.
   c. It allows for stimulation of more rods.
   d. It causes the lens to focus more sharply.

2. Information from the right visual field is sent to:
   a. the right side of the visual cortex
   b. the left side of the visual cortex
   c. both the right and left sides of the visual cortex
   d. the right side of the visual cortex and the left side of the auditory cortex

3. The major difference between a green light and a blue light is the:
   a. wave amplitude
   b. wave purity
   c. wavelength
   d. wave saturation

4. If the eye is compared to a camera, the role of the retina would most closely resemble the role of the:
   a. lens
   b. film
   c. shutter
   d. flash cube

5. Which theory of color vision best explains why the color of an afterimage is the complement of the original color?
   a. the trichromatic theory
   b. the opponent process theory
   c. both theories explain this phenomenon equally well
   d. neither theory adequately explains this phenomenon

6. When watching a wild car chase scene in a movie we can be thankful for:
   a. chunking
   b. lateral processing
   c. bottom-up processing
   d. the phi phenomenon

7. Which one of the following is a binocular depth cue?
   a. convergence
   b. linear perspective
   c. relative height
   d. texture gradients

8. Which of the following is an example of what is meant by perceptual constancy?
   a. moths are always attracted to light
   b. a round pie tin always appears to us as round
   c. proximal and distal stimuli are always identical
   d. distal stimuli never change

9. The fact that the words on this page tend to stand out from the paper it is printed on illustrates the Gestalt principle of:
   a. figure and ground
   b. simplicity
   c. proximity
   d. closure

10. Middle C sounded on a piano sounds different than middle C on a violin because of the difference in:
    a. wavelengths
    b. purity
    c. amplitude
    d. frequency

11. Research has shown that the perception of pitch depends on:
    a. the area stimulated on the basilar membrane
    b. the frequency at which the basilar membrane vibrates
    c. both the area stimulated on the basilar membrane and the frequency at which the basilar membrane vibrates
    d. the frequency at which the ossicles vibrate

12. Which of the following is not considered to be one of the four fundamental tastes?
    a. burnt
    b. sweet
    c. sour
    d. bitter

13. Receptive fields and feature detectors are found in:
    a. the visual system
    b. the touch system
    c. the balance system
    d. the visual and touch systems

14. Our sense of balance depends upon:
    a. the semicircular canals
    b. the kinesthetic senses
    c. visual cues
    d. the semicircular canals, the kinesthetic senses, and visual cues

15. The gate-control theory is an attempt to explain:
    a. the subjective nature of pain
    b. the transformation from sensation to perception
    c. the adaptation to strong odors
    d. light and dark adaptation

16. Which of the following terms perhaps best describes human perception?
    a. accurate
    b. objective
    c. subjective
    d. unknowable

Answers: 1. c **2.** b **3.** c **4.** b **5.** b **6.** d **7.** a **8.** b **9.** a **10.** b **11.** c **12.** a **13.** d **14.** d **15.** a **16.** c.

INFOTRAC

Dark Adaptation   Optical Illusions   Reversible Figure
Depth Perception

5 VARIATIONS IN CONSCIOUSNESS

REVIEW OF KEY IDEAS

ON THE NATURE OF CONSCIOUSNESS

1. Discuss the nature of consciousness, including its relation to brain activity.

1-1. The personal awareness of internal and external events is how psychologists define _____. Consciousness is like a moving stream in that it is constantly _____.

1-2. Not only is consciousness constantly changing, but it also may exist at different levels. Freud believed that at its deepest level we would find the _____. For a long time it was believed that the conscious states experienced while under anesthesia or during sleep were very different from the waking state, but recently some theorists have argued that the differences are (less/greater) than originally thought.

1-3. EEG recordings reveal that there (is/is not) some relationship between brain waves and levels of consciousness. There are four principal bands of brain wave activity, based on the frequency of the wave patterns; these are alpha, beta delta, and theta. Identify these wave patterns from their descriptions given below.

_____ (a) alert (13-24 cps)   _____ (c) deep sleep (4-7 cps)

_____ (b) drowsy (8-12 cps)   _____ (d) deepest sleep (1-3 cps)

Answers: **1-1.** consciousness, changing **1-2.** unconscious, less **1-3.** (a) beta (b) alpha (c) theta (d) delta.

2. **Summarize what is known about our biological clocks and the relationship of circadian rhythms to sleep.**

2-1.   Like most living organisms, human beings experience periodic fluctuations in physiological functioning, which are called _____ rhythms. This means that we must have internal "biological _____" that can monitor the passage of time.

2-2.   The daily, or 24-hour, circadian rhythm is responsible for the regulation of sleep and wakefulness. This is accomplished through the regulation of several bodily processes, including body temperature. Describe below what happens to body temperature when we:

(a) begin to fall asleep.

(b) begin to awaken.

2-3.   There is evidence that exposure to _____ is responsible for regulating the 24-hour circadian clock. Sunlight affects the suprachiasmatic nucleus in the hypothalamus, which in turn signals the _____ gland. The pineal gland then secretes the hormone melatonin, which is a key player in adjusting biological clocks.

Answers: **2-1.** biological, clocks **2-2.** (a) temperature decreases (b) temperature begins to increase **2-3.** sunlight, pineal.

3. **Discuss the significance of ignoring circadian rhythms and the value of melatonin for resetting biological clocks.**

3-1.   Getting out of time with the circadian rhythms can greatly affect the quality of _____. This is commonly found among persons suffering from jet lag. Research on jet lag has shown that since there already seems to be a natural tendency to shift to a 25-hour circadian rhythm, most people find it is easier to readjust when they have flown in (an easterly/a westerly) direction.

3-2.   While melatonin has been shown to be helpful in treating sleep problems, other claims of health benefits (have/have not) been proven. Moreover, researchers worry that many people may take too (much/little) of the drug to achieve sleep-related effects. Ill effects (have/have not) been reported from large doses of melatonin.

Answers: **3-1.** sleep, a westerly **3-2.** have not, much, have.

THE SLEEP AND WAKING CYCLE

4. **Compare and contrast REM sleep and NREM sleep.**

4-1.   The four stages of sleep that do not involve rapid eye movement (REM) are collectively called _____ sleep. During NREM sleep one first descends into stage _____ sleep and then continues to descend into stages 2, 3, and 4. Each descent is accompanied by (slower/faster) brain wave activity, along with declines in body temperature, heart rate, respiration rate, and muscle tension.

4-2. What particularly differentiates NREM sleep from rapid eye movement sleep, or _____ sleep, is that during REM sleep the brain wave pattern resembles that of a person who is wide _____. However, REM sleep is actually a deep stage of sleep in which the muscle tone is extremely relaxed and the sleeper is virtually _____. It is also during REM sleep that _____ is most likely to occur.

Answers: **4-1.** NREM, 1, slower **4-2.** REM, awake, paralyzed, dreaming.

5. Describe how sleep cycles evolve through the night and how sleep patterns are related to age and culture.

5-1. The sleep cycle is repeated approximately four times during an average night of sleep. NREM sleep dominates the early part of the sleep period, but light sleep (stages 1 and 2) and _____ sleep dominate the later stages of sleep. As one progresses though the night the depth of NREM sleep tends to progressively (increase/decrease).

5-2. Not only do newborns sleep more frequently and for more total hours during a day than do adults, but they also spend a greater proportion of time in _____ sleep. As they grow older, the children move toward longer but (more/less) frequent sleep periods and the total proportion of REM sleep declines from about 50 percent to the adolescent level of about _____ percent. During adulthood there is a gradual shift toward the (lighter/deeper) stages of sleep.

5-3. Answer the following questions regarding sleeping patterns across cultures.

(a) Which pattern, children sleeping with their parents (co-sleeping) or children sleeping alone, is the most widely practiced in cultures around the world?

(b) Where are the "siesta cultures" generally located?

(c) What is the effect of industrialization on the practice of siestas?

Answers: **5-1.** REM, decrease **5-2.** REM, less, 20, lighter **5-3.** (a) co-sleeping (b) tropical regions (c) The practice declines.

6. Discuss the evolutionary bases of sleep.

6-1. At least three theories have attempted to account for the evolutionary (adaptive) bases of sleep: sleep evolved to conserve energy, sleep evolved to reduce risk to many sources of danger, and sleep evolved to restore energy and other bodily resources. Which theory is best supported by the evidence at this time?

Answers: **6-1.** Sleep evolved to conserve energy (and other bodily resources).

7. **Summarize evidence on the effects of complete, partial, and selective sleep deprivation.**

   7-1.   While research results show rather benign effects from sleep deprivation in laboratory studies, what might be a serious problem when attention lapses due to sleep deprivation as people go about their daily activities?

   7-2.   Studies in which subjects were selectively deprived of REM sleep, leaving NREM sleep undisturbed, found (substantial/little) negative effects from REM deprivation. One curious effect that has been noted from selective REM deprivation is that subjects tend to increase their amount of (NREM/REM) sleep when given the first opportunity to do so. This same rebound effect has also been found with _____-wave sleep.

   Answers: **7-1.** It can lead to serious accidents. **7-2.** little, REM, slow.

8. **Discuss the prevalence, causes, and treatment of insomnia.**

   8-1.   While practically everybody will suffer from occasional bouts of insomnia, it is estimated that chronic problems with insomnia occur in about _____ percent of all adults and another _____ percent complain of occasional insomnia. There are three basic types of insomnia, which are easily remembered because one type occurs at the beginning of sleep, one type during sleep, and the third type at the end of sleep. Thus, one type involves difficulty in _____ asleep; one type involves difficulty in _____ asleep; and one type involves persistent _____ awakening.

   8-2.   There are a number of different causes of insomnia, but perhaps the most common one results from side effects due to_____ problems. Another frequent cause results from pain or from difficulty in breathing due to _____. Certain drugs are also implicated in insomnia.

   8-3.   Researchers agree that the most commonly used form of treatment, using sedatives, or _____ pills, is not the long-term treatment of choice. Evidence shows that while sleeping pills do promote sleep, they also interfere with both the slow-wave and _____ part of the sleep cycle. Moreover, if medication is abruptly stopped, _____ insomnia can result and the insomnia becomes worse than ever.

   Answers: **8-1.** 15, 15, falling, remaining, early **8-2.** emotional, asthma **8-3.** sleeping, REM, rebound.

THE WORLD OF DREAMS

9. **Discuss the nature of dreams and findings on dream content.**

   9-1.   Which of the following statements is/are correct with respect to the changing scientific view with respect to dreams?

   (a) Dreams are not as bizzare as was widely assumed.

(b) Dreams are not the exclusive property of REM sleep.

(c) Non-REM dreams appear to be less vivid and story like than REM dreams.

9-2.   Calvin Hall, who analyzed the contents of more than 10,000 dreams, concluded that the content of most dreams is (<u>exotic/mundane</u>). Moreover, he found that dreams seldom involve events that are not centered around _____. Hall also found that dreams tend to be like soap operas in that they revolve around such common themes as misfortune, _____, and _____.

9-3.   What did Freud mean when he stated that our dreams reflect day residue?

9-4.   What other factor has an inconsistent effect on our dreams?

Answers: 9-1. All are correct. **9-2.** mundane, ourselves, sex, aggression **9-3.** Dream content is influenced by what happens to us in our daily lives **9-4.** External stimuli (dripping water, ringing phones, etc.).

10. Describe some cultural variations in beliefs about the nature and importance of dreams.

10-1.   Say which of the following statements about dreams is more characteristic of Western cultures (W) or non-Western cultures (NW).

_____   (a) Little significance paid as to the meaning of dreams.

_____   (b) Remembering dreams is important.

_____   (c) Believe that dreams may provide information about the future.

_____   (d) Are likely to report frequent dreams involving food.

Answers: (a) W (b) NW (c) NW (d) NW (Or persons from any culture who are chronically hungry).

11. Describe the three theories of dreaming covered in the chapter.

11-1.   The text mentions three theories as to why we need to dream. Tell what emotional or cognitive purpose, if any, each of these theories proposes as to the purpose of dreaming.

(a) Sigmund Freud's theory about the need to dream.

(b) The theory proposed by Rosalind Cartwright is cognizant of the fact that dreams are not restricted by logic or reality.

(c) The activation-synthesis theory of Hobson and McCarley proposes that dreams occur as side effects of neural activation of the cortex by lower brain centers.

Answers: 11-1. (a) Dreams serve the purpose of wish fulfillment. (b) Dreams allow for creative problem solving. (c) Dreams serve no cognitive purpose.

HYPNOSIS • ALTERED CONSCIOUSNESS OR ROLE PLAYING?

12. **Discuss hypnotic susceptibility and list some prominent effects of hypnosis.**

   12-1.   While there are many different hypnotic induction techniques, a common factor among all of them is that they all lead to a heightened state of _____. Research shows that individuals (do/do not) vary in their susceptibility to hypnotic induction. In fact, approximately _____ percent of the population does not respond at all and approximately _____ percent are highly susceptible to hypnotic induction.

   12-2.   The text lists several of the more prominent effects that can be produced by hypnosis. Identify these effects from their descriptions given below.

   (a) Reducing awareness of pain. _____

   (b) Engaging in acts one would not ordinarily do. _____

   (c) Perceiving things that do not exist or failing to perceive things that do exist or claiming sour foods taste sweet. _____

   (d) Carrying out suggestions following the hypnotic induction session. _____.

   Answers: 12-1. suggestibility, do, 10, 10 **12-2.** (a) anesthesia (b) disinhibition (c) hallucinations and sensory distortions (d) posthypnotic suggestions.

13. **Explain the role-playing and altered-state theories of hypnosis.**

   13-1.   A theory of hypnosis proposed by Barber and Orne is that hypnosis is really a form of acting or role playing in which the subjects are simply playing as if they are hypnotized. What two lines of evidence support this theory?

   13-2.   A theory of hypnosis proposed by Hilgard is that hypnosis does in fact result in an altered state of consciousness. This theory holds that hypnosis results in a dissociation or _____ of consciousness into two parts. One half of the divided consciousness communicates with the hypnotist while the other half remains _____, even from the hypnotized subject. In this case, pain perceived by the "hidden" part of the consciousness (is/is not) reported to the "aware" part of consciousness. The divided state of consciousness proposed by Hilgard (is/is not) a common experience in everyday life. One such example of this commonly experienced state is appropriately called "highway _____."

Answers: **13-1.** Nonhypnotized subjects can duplicate the feats of hypnotized subjects and it has been shown that hypnotized subjects are merely carrying out their expectations of how hypnotized subjects should act **13-2.** splitting or dividing, hidden, is not, is, hypnosis.

MEDITATION • PURE CONSCIOUSNESS OR RELAXATION?

14. **Summarize the evidence on the short-term and long-term effect of meditation.**

    14-1. Certain short-term physiological changes may occur during meditation. One of the most prominent of these changes is that EEG brain waves change from the rapid beta waves to the slower _____ and theta waves. This change to slower waves is accompanied by (an increase/a decrease) in metabolic activity, such as heart rate, oxygen consumption, etc. All of these physiological changes are characteristic of a normal state of _____. This state of relaxation (is/is not) unique to meditation.

    14-2. The claims made for the long-term effects of meditation may have some merit in that studies have shown that subjects have shown improved mood and lessened anxiety and fatigue, as well as better physical health and increased longevity. These changes can (also/not) be induced by other commonly used methods for inducing relaxation. The claim that meditation can produce a unique state of pure consciousness (has/has not) been supported by scientific research.

Answers: **14-1.** alpha, a decrease, relaxation, is not **14-2.** also, has not.

ALTERING CONSCIOUSNESS WITH DRUGS

15. **List and describe the major types of abused drugs and their effects.**

    15-1. The text list six different categories of psychoactive drugs (chemical substances that modify mental, emotional, or behavioral functioning): identify these drugs from the descriptions given below.

        (a) This drug is the most widely used, and abused, of all psychoactive drugs and produces a relaxed euphoria that temporarily boosts self-esteem. Wine and beer are both examples of the drug _____.

        (b) While this class of drugs derived from opium is effective at relieving pain, it can also produce a state of euphoria, which is the principal reason that opiates, or _____, are attractive to recreational users.

        (c) The drugs in this class, such as LSD, mescaline, and psilocybin, are known for their ability to distort sensory and perceptual experiences, which is why they are given the collective name of _____.

        (d) The drugs in this class include marijuana, hashish, and THC. Although they vary in potency each of them can produce a mild and an easy-going state of euphoria along with enhanced sensory awareness and a distorted sense of time. This class of drugs gets its name from the hemp plant _____ from which they are all derived.

(e) This class of drugs is known for its sleep-inducing (sedation) and behavioral depression effects, resulting in tension reduction and a relaxed state of intoxication. While there are several different drugs in this class, the barbiturates are the most widely abused. Commonly known as "downers," they are more properly called _____.

(f) This class of drugs produces arousal in the central nervous system and ranges from mildly arousing drugs like caffeine and nicotine, to strongly arousing drugs like cocaine and the amphetamines. Known for their ability to produce an energetic euphoria, the drugs in this class go by the name of _____.

Answers: 15-1. (a) alcohol (b) narcotics (c) hallucinogens (d) cannabis (e) sedatives (f) stimulants.

16. Explain why drug effects vary and how psychoactive drugs exert their effects in the brain.

16-1.   Taking a specific drug (will/will not) always have the same effect on the same person. This is because drug effects have _____ causation; individual, environmental, and drug factors can combine in many ways to produce the final effect. For example, one's expectations can strongly affect reactions to a drug. This is known as the _____ effect. Moreover, as one continues to take a specific drug, it requires a greater amount of the drug to achieve the same effect. This phenomenon is called drug _____.

16-2.   Psychoactive drugs affect the CNS by selectively influencing _____ systems in a variety of ways. The action takes place at the juncture between neurons called the _____. For example, norepinesphrine and dopamine activity is influenced in a variety of ways by the action of _____. Both sedatives and alcohol exert their key effects at GABA synapses. When these two drugs are taken together their combined depressive effect on the CNS may be greater than the sum of their individual effects. Drugs having this effect are said to be _____.

Answers: 16-1. will not, multifactorial, placebo, tolerance 16-2. neurotransmitter, synapse, amphetamines, synergistic.

17. Summarize which drugs carry the greatest risk of tolerance, physical dependence, and psychological dependence.

17-1.   When a person must continue taking a drug to avoid withdrawal illness, addiction, or _____ dependence is said to occur. When a person must continue taking a drug to satisfy intense emotional craving for the drug, then _____ dependence is said to occur. As can be seen in Table 5.4 in the text, the three riskiest drugs in terms of tolerance and physical and psychological dependence are the _____, _____, and _____.

17-2.   How are both physical and psychological dependence established?

Answers: 17-1. physical, psychological, narcotics/opiates, sedatives, stimulants 17-2. Gradually with repeated use of the drug.

CHAPTER FIVE

18. **Summarize evidence on the major physical health risks associated with drug abuse.**

    18-1.   There are three major ways in which drugs may affect physical health. The most dramatic is when a person takes too much of a drug, or drugs, and dies of an _____. Another way is when drug usage directly damages bodily tissue; this is referred to as a _____ effect. The third way is when drug usage results in accidents, improper eating and sleeping habits, infections, etc. These effects are collectively called _____ effects.

    Answers: **18-1.** overdose, direct, indirect.

PUTTING IT IN PERSPECTIVE

19. **Explain how the chapter highlighted four of the unifying themes.**

    19-1.   Identify which of the underlying themes (psychology evolves in a sociohistorical context, experience is subjective, cultures mold some aspects of behavior, and psychology is theoretically diverse) are illustrated by the following statements.

        (a) Psychologists have followed many different approaches and developed many different theories in their attempt to understand consciousness.

        (b) The study of consciousness by psychologists followed rather than preceded renewed public interest in this topic.

        (c) There are striking individual differences in the way people respond to hypnosis, meditation, and drugs.

        (d) The significance given to dreams and sleep patterns can be influenced by this factor.

    Answers: **19-1.** (a) Psychology is theoretically diverse (b) Psychology evolves in a sociohistorical context (c) Experience is subjective (d) Culture molds some aspects of behavior.

PERSONAL APPLICATION • ADDRESSING PRACTICAL QUESTIONS ABOUT SLEEP AND DREAMS

20. **Summarize evidence on common questions about sleep and dreams as discussed in the application.**

    20-1.   Answer the following questions about sleep and napping.

        (a) How much sleep do we require?

(b) While napping can be refreshing for most people, in what way can it prove inefficient?

(c) What does evidence show about the effectiveness of attempting to learn complex material, such as a foreign language, during deep sleep?

20-2. Temporary problems in going to sleep (do/do not) indicate that one is becoming an insomniac. These temporary problems often correct themselves. There are numerous methods for facilitating going to sleep, but a common feature in all of them is that they generate a feeling of _____. Some methods generate a feeling of boredom, which is akin to relaxation. The important point here is that one (does/does not) concentrate on the heavy events in life when attempting to go to sleep.

20-3. While there are some persons who claim they never dream, what is really happening is that they cannot _____ their dreams. Dreams are best recalled when waking occurs during or immediately following the dream. Determination and practice (can/cannot) improve one's ability to recall dreams.

20-4. Freud believed that dreams do require interpretation because their true meaning, which he called the _____ content, is symbolically encoded in the obvious plot of the dream, which he called the _____ content. Freud's theory that dreams carry hidden symbolic meaning would mean that dream interpretation (is/is not) a very complicated affair. Many researchers now believe that dreams are (more/less) complicated than Freud believed. Calvin Hall makes the point that dreams require some interpretation simply because they are mostly (visual/verbal).

Answers: 20-1. (a) It varies across individuals (b) Insufficient time is spent in the deeper stages of sleep (c) It is very ineffective **20-2.** do not, relaxation or calmness, does not **20-3.** remember (or recall), can **20-4.** latent, manifest, is, less, visual.

CRITICAL THINKING APPLICATION • IS ALCOHOLISM A DISEASE? THE POWER OF DEFINITIONS

21. Discuss the influence of definitions and how they are sometimes misused as explanations for the phenomena they describe.

21-1. Whether alcoholism is a disease or a result of personal failure depends on _____ gets to make up the definition. In fact, there is (only one/no) conclusive way to determine if alcoholism is a disease.

21-2. To say that someone drinks too much because she is alcoholic is an example of the _____ fallacy. Definitions can never serve as _____ of the thing they are defining.

Answers: 21-1. who, no **21-2.** nominal, explanations.

REVIEW OF KEY TERMS

Alcohol
Biological rhythms
Cannabis
Circadian rhythms
Consciousness
Dissociation
Electrocardiograph (EKG)
Electroencephalograph (EEG)
Electromyograph (EMG)

Electro-oculograph (EOG)
Hallucinogens
Hypnosis
Insomnia
Latent content
Manifest content
Meditation
Narcotics (opiates)
Non-REM (NREM) sleep

Physical dependence
Psychoactive drugs
Psychological dependence
REM sleep
Sedatives
Slow-wave sleep
Stimulants
Tolerance

_____ 1. Our awareness of internal and external stimuli.

_____ 2. A device that records muscle activity and tension.

_____ 3. A device that monitors the electrical activity of the brain.

_____ 4. A device that records the contractions of the heart.

_____ 5. A device that records eye movements.

_____ 6. Periodic fluctuations in physiological functioning.

_____ 7. The 24-hour biological cycles found in humans and many other species.

_____ 8. Sleep involving rapid eye movements.

_____ 9. Sleep stages 1 through 4, which are marked by an absence of rapid eye movements.

_____ 10. Drugs derived from opium that are capable of relieving pain.

_____ 11. Involves chronic problems in getting adequate sleep.

_____ 12. A condition that exists when a person must continue to take a drug to satisfy mental and emotional craving for the drug.

_____ 13. A systematic procedure that typically produces a heightened state of suggestibility.

_____ 14. Involves a splitting off of mental processes into two separate, simultaneous streams of awareness.

_____ 15. A family of mental exercises in which a conscious attempt is made to focus attention in a nonanalytical way.

_____ 16. Chemical substances that modify mental, emotional, or behavioral functioning.

_____ 17. Sleep stages 3 and 4 in which low-frequency delta waves become prominent in EEG recordings.

_____ 18. Drugs that have sleep-inducing and behavioral depression effects.

_____ 19. Drugs that tend to increase central nervous system activation and behavioral activity.

_____ 20. A diverse group of drugs that have powerful effects on mental and emotional functioning, marked most prominently by distortions in sensory and perceptual experience.

_____ 21. The hemp plant from which marijuana, hashish, and THC are derived.

_____ 22. A variety of beverages containing ethyl alcohol.

_____ 23. A progressive decrease in a person's responsiveness to a drug.

24. A condition that exists when a person must continue to take a drug to avoid withdrawal illness.

25. Freud's term that refers to the plot of a dream at the surface level.

26. Freud's term that refers to the disguised or hidden meaning of events in a dream.

Answers: 1. consciousness **2.** electromyograph (EMG) **3.** electroencephalograph (EEG) **4.** electrocardiograph (EKG) **5.** electro-oculograph (EOG) **6.** biological rhythms **7.** circadian rhythms **8.** REM sleep **9.** non-REM sleep **10.** narcotics or opiates **11.** insomnia **12.** psychological dependence **13.** hypnosis **14.** dissociation **15.** meditation **16.** psychoactive drugs **17.** slow-wave sleep (SWS) **18.** sedatives **19.** stimulants **20.** hallucinogens **21.** cannabis **22.** alcohol **23.** tolerance **24.** physical dependence **25.** manifest content **26.** latent content.

REVIEW OF KEY PEOPLE

William Dement   Calvin Hall   J. Allan Hobson
Sigmund Freud   Ernest Hilgard

1. Argued for the existence of the unconscious and the hidden meaning of dreams.

2. As one of the pioneers in early sleep research, he coined the term REM sleep.

3. After analyzing thousands of dreams, he concluded that their contents are generally quite mundane.

4. A proponent of the altered state (divided consciousness) theory of hypnosis.

5. His activation-synthesis model proposes that dreams are only side effects of neural activation.

Answers: 1. Freud **2.** Dement **3.** Hall **4.** Hilgard **5.** Hobson.

SELF-QUIZ

1. Which brain wave is probably operating while you are taking this quiz?
   a. alpha
   b. beta
   c. theta
   d. delta

2. What did William James mean by his term "the stream of consciousness"?
   a. consciousness always remains at the same level
   b. consciousness never stops
   c. consciousness is constantly changing
   d. consciousness is beyond personal control

3. The circadian rhythm operates around a:
   a. 1-year cycle
   b. 28-day cycle
   c. 24-hour cycle
   d. 90-minute cycle

4. The most vivid dreams generally occur during:
   a. REM sleep
   b. NREM sleep
   c. the early hours of sleep
   d. when alpha brain waves are present

5. What appears to be responsible for regulating the circadian rhythm?
   a. amount of time spent sleeping
   b. amount of time spent awake
   c. cultural practices
   d. exposure to light

6. As adults age they tend to:
   a. spend more time in slow-wave sleep
   b. sleep for a longer period of time at night
   c. shift toward the lighter stages of sleep
   d. shift toward the sleep pattern of newborns

7. What is the purpose of dreams according to the activation-synthesis theory of Hobson and McCarley?
   a. they allow for creative thinking
   b. they serve no useful (cognitive or emotional) purpose
   c. they allow for wish fulfillment
   d. they allow for escape from everyday reality

8. The content of most dreams is usually:
   a. mundane
   b. exotic
   c. exciting
   d. erotic

9. Which theory as to why we need to sleep is best supported by the evidence at this time?
   a. sleep evolved to conserve energy
   b. sleep evolved to reduce risk to many sources of danger
   c. sleep evolved to restore energy
   d. sleep evolved to aid in the consolidation of memory

10. Which of the following physiological changes is unique to meditation?
    a. increased alpha rhythms
    b. decreased heart rate
    c. decreased oxygen consumption
    d. all of these thing are common to many forms of relaxation

11. Psychoactive drugs exert their effect on the brain by:
    a. decreasing blood supply to the brain
    b. altering neurotransmitter activity
    c. breaking down essential brain amino acids
    d. penetrating the nucleus of the neurons

12. The most widely abused drug in the United States is:
    a. alcohol
    b. cocaine
    c. heroin
    d. hallucinogens

13. Which of the following is likely to produce highly subjective events?
    a. hypnosis
    b. meditation
    c. psychoactive drugs
    d. all of the above can produce highly subjective events

14. Which of the following statements is correct?
    a. Most people do not dream in color.
    b. Practice will not improve the ability to recall dreams.
    c. From birth until death everyone dreams.
    d. Dreams generally last only 1 or 2 minutes.

15. Which of the following statements is correct?
    a. alcoholism is a disease
    b. alcoholism is the result of personal failure
    c. alcoholism results from abuse as a child
    d. the cause of alcoholism will depend on who gets to define the term

Answers: 1. b **2.** c **3.** c **4.** a **5.** d **6.** c **7.** b **8.** a **9.** a **10.** d **11.** b **12.** a **13.** d **14.** c **15.** d.

INFOTRAC

Biological Rhythms   Meditation   REM Sleep
Hallucinogens

6 LEARNING THROUGH CONDITIONING

REVIEW OF KEY IDEAS

1. **Describe Pavlov's demonstration of classical conditioning and the key elements in this form of learning.**

   1-1. Classical conditioning is a type of learning that occurs when two stimuli are paired or associated closely in time. In Pavlov's initial demonstration, the two stimuli were a bell and ___meat powder___.

   1-2. The response to one of the two stimuli occurs naturally and does not have to be learned or acquired through conditioning. This "unlearned" stimulus, in this case the food, is technically known as the ___unconditioned___ stimulus.

   1-3. The other stimulus is said to be neutral in the sense that it does not initially produce a response. When a response to this neutral stimulus is *acquired* or *learned*, the technical name for it is the ___conditioned___ stimulus. In Pavlov's initial study the conditioned stimulus was the sound of a ___bell___.

   1-4. The unconditioned stimulus in Pavlov's original study was the ___meat powder___ and the conditioned stimulus was the ___bell___. Salivation to the meat powder is known as the ___unconditioned___ response; salivation to the bell is termed the ___conditioned___ response.

   1-5. Label the parts of the classical conditioning sequence. Place the commonly used abbreviations for these terms in the parentheses.

   (a) meat: ___UCS___ (   )

   (b) salivation to meat: ___UCR___ (   )

   (c) bell: ___CS___ (   )

   (d) salivation to bell: ___CR___ (   )

Answers: 1-1. meat powder (food) **1-2.** unconditioned **1-3.** conditioned, bell **1-4.** meat powder, bell, unconditioned, conditioned **1-5.** (a) unconditioned stimulus (UCS) (b) unconditioned response (UCR) (c) conditioned stimulus (CS) (d) conditioned response (CR).

2. **Discuss how classical conditioning may modulate everyday responses including physiological responses.**

2-1.   The kids in the neighborhood where I (R. S.) grew up used to dig tunnels in a neighbor's backyard. One day a boy got stuck in the tunnel and couldn't get out. Eventually he got out, but after that he didn't want to play in tunnels again. To this day that person still has an intense fear not only of tunnels but of closed-in spaces in general. Label the parts of the classical conditioning process involved in the acquisition of the phobia of closed-in spaces. (Hint: Even though "getting stuck" certainly involves a behavior or response, it also has stimulus components.)

UCS getting stuck

UCR fear produced by getting stuck

_CS_ tunnels and closed-in spaces

_CR_ fear of tunnels and closed-in spaces

2-2.   The individual described above had developed an intense fear or phobia, acquired in part through the process of _classical_ conditioning. Thus, one of the everyday responses that may be modulated by classical conditioning is the emotional response of _fear_ .

2-3.   Other emotions can be conditioned as well. For example, the smell of smoke and Beemans gum described in your text, the playing of "our song," and the sight of one's home after a long absence could all produce a pleasant emotional response (or perhaps a slightly weepy, sentimental feeling). Such smells, sounds, or sights would be considered _conditioned_ stimuli.

2-4.   Similarly, certain physiological responses can be conditioned. Label the parts of the conditioning process in the study on immunosuppression in rats described in the text. (Use the abbreviations CS, CR, UCS, and UCR.)

UCS the immunosuppressive drug

_CS_ unusual taste

UCR decreased antibody production produced by the drug

_CR_ decreased antibody production produced by the taste

2-5.   Apparently sexual arousal can be classically conditioned as well. In quail or in humans, stimuli routinely paired with sex (e.g., red lights in the quail study, lingerie in humans) evidently become _conditioned_ stimuli for sexual arousal.

Answers: 2-1. UCS, UCR, CS, CR **2-2.** classical, fear **2-3.** conditioned **2-4.** UCS, CS, UCR, CR **2-5.** conditioned.

3. **Describe the classical conditioning phenomena of acquisition, extinction, spontaneous recovery, and higher-order conditioning.**

3-1.   *Acquisition* of a conditioned response occurs when the CS and UCS are contiguous, or paired. Not all pairings result in conditioning, however. What characteristics of the CS are more likely to produce acquisition of a CR? _Unique or intense CS_

3-2. Acquisition refers to the formation of a conditioned response. What is the term that refers to the weakening or disappearance of a CR? _extinction_

3-3. Extinction in classical conditioning occurs when the ___CS___ stimulus is presented *alone*, without the ___UCS___ stimulus.

3-4. After CRs are extinguished they may reappear, even without further conditioning.

(a) For example, after being completely extinguished, a dog may again show the conditioned response (e.g., salivation to a bell) when returned to the apparatus in which it was originally conditioned. What is the name of this type of "reappearance" of the CR? _spontaneous recovery_

(b) When, or under what circumstance, is spontaneous recovery likely to occur? _after extinction + after no exposure to CS_

3-5. Suppose a bell and meat powder are paired, as in the original Pavlovian study, until a conditioned salivary response occurs to the bell alone. Suppose that the bell is then paired in a series of new trials with a clicking sound. Assuming that the stimuli are potent enough, that the timing is right, and so on:

(a) Will a CR now occur to the clicking sound? _yes_

(b) What is the name of this conditioning procedure? _higher order conditioning_

(c) Which stimulus acts as the UCS under this new arrangement? _bell acts like a UCS (previous CS)_

Answers: **3-1.** A novel or particularly intense CS is more likely to produce conditioning. **3-2.** extinction **3-3.** CS, UCS **3-4.** (a) spontaneous recovery (b) after extinction, following a period of nonexposure to the CS **3-5.** (a) yes (b) higher-order conditioning (c) The bell, the previous CS, now acts as a UCS.

4. Describe the processes of stimulus generalization and discrimination and summarize the classic study of Little Albert.

4-1. With regard to the case of Little Albert:

(a) What was the CS? _white rat_

(b) The UCS? _loud noise_

4-2. Albert also developed a fear of white dogs and white rabbits, even though he had not been exposed to these stimuli. What is the name of the process that produced these fear responses? _generalization_

4-3. Why would Albert have been more likely to develop a fear of a white rabbit, say, than a white car or a dark horse?

more similar to original CS

4-4. The more similar stimuli are to the CS, the more likely the organism will ___*generalize*___ from the CS to the other stimuli. The less similar stimuli are to the CS, the more likely the organism is to ___*discriminate*___ them from the CS.

4-5. Casey (R. S.'s cat, now deceased) salivates when she hears the sound of food being dumped into her bowl. The process by which this salivary response was learned is ___*Classical Cond.*___ The food is a(an) (CS/(UCS)/CR/UCR). The sound of the food is a(an) ((CS)/UCS/CR/UCR). Salivation to the sound is a(an) (CS/UCS/(CR)/UCR).

4-6. Pets are also likely to salivate when they hear other, similar sounds, like bags rustling in the kitchen or dishes being pulled from the cupboard. Salivation to these other sounds represents stimulus ___*generalization*___

4-7. With continued training, in which food is paired only with the sound of food entering the bowl and not with the other sounds, the animal will learn to salivate only to the rattling bowl. The process of learning to respond only to one particular stimulus and not to a range of similar stimuli is termed ___*discrimination*___

Answers: 4-1. (a) a white rat (b) a loud noise **4-2.** stimulus generalization (or just generalization) **4-3.** Because of similarity. The more similar the other stimuli to the CS, the more likely generalization is to occur. **4-4.** generalize, discriminate **4-5.** classical conditioning, UCS, CS, CR **4-6.** generalization **4-7.** discrimination.

OPERANT CONDITIONING

5. Describe Skinner's principle of reinforcement.

5-1. A reinforcer is a stimulus or event that (1) is presented *after* a response and that (2) increases the tendency for the response to be repeated. Apply that definition to this example: Grundoon, a captive monkey, occasionally swings on a bar in his cage. Suppose that at some point Grundoon's trainers decide to give him a spoonful of applesauce whenever he swings. How would they know whether the applesauce is a reinforcer?

if rate swinging ↑ when given applesauce then is

5-2. The trainers switch to vinegar. Grundoon, an unusual primate, swings quite frequently when this behavior is followed by vinegar. Is vinegar a reinforcer here? How do you know?

yes because vinegar came after response + response rate ↑

5-3. The trainers try another approach. They present Grundoon with fresh fruit *just before* they think he is likely to jump. It so happens that Grundoon's rate of jumping does increase. Is the fruit a reinforcer here? Why or why not? *No because reinforcing stimuli follow response.*

Answers: 5-1. If the animal's rate of swinging increases when followed by applesauce, then applesauce is a reinforcer. **5-2.** Yes. Because the vinegar is presented *after the response*, and because the *response rate increases*. (Note that this is an imaginary example to illustrate the point that reinforcement is defined in terms of *consequences*, not by our subjective judgment. I don't know of any monkeys that will respond for vinegar.) **5-3.** No. Reinforcing stimuli, by definition, follow the response. (Again, this is a contrived example just to illustrate the definition.)

6. Describe the prototype experimental procedures and apparatus used in studies of operant conditioning.

6-1. The prototypic apparatus used in operant conditioning studies is the operant chamber, better known as the *Skinner box*. On one wall of the chamber is mounted some sort of device that makes for an easily recorded response. For rats, the device is usually a small *lever*; for pigeons, the device is a *disk* that the bird learns to peck.

6-2. A press of the lever or peck at the disk may produce a reinforcer, generally a small bit of food dispensed into the food cup mounted to one side or below the manipulandum. Each response is recorded on a *Cumulative recorder*, a device that creates a graphic record of the number of responses per unit time.

6-3. The cumulative recorder records the *rate* of the behavior, that is, the number of *responses* made per unit *time*.

6-4. Below is a highly stylized version of a cumulative record. About how many responses were made during the first 40 seconds? *10* Which section of the graph (a, b, c, d, or e) has the steepest slope? *d* Which section of the graph illustrates the fastest rate of responding? *d* About how many responses were made between the 40th and 70th seconds? *20*

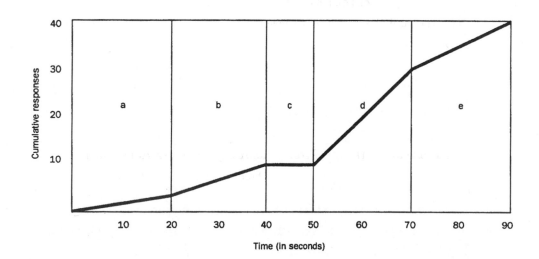

7. **Describe the operant conditioning phenomena of acquisition, shaping, and extinction.**

7-1.   Acquisition refers to the formation of new responses. In classical conditioning, acquisition occurs through a simple pairing of the CS and UCS. In operant conditioning, acquisition involves the procedure known as _shaping_ .

7-2.   What is shaping? When is it used?

reinforce as behavior gets closer to goal to form new long term behavior

7-3.   Extinction in classical conditioning involves removing the UCS while still presenting the CS.

(a) What is the extinction procedure in operant conditioning?

no longer have reinforcers after response

(b) What is the effect of extinction on behavior (response rate)?

response rate ↓ + may stop

(c) What does the term *resistance to extinction* mean?

may continue to respond even though reinforcer no longer

Answers: **7-1.** shaping **7-2.** Shaping involves reinforcing closer and closer approximations to the desired behavior. It is used in the formation of a new response. **7-3.** (a) The extinction procedure involves no longer presenting the reinforcers after the response. (b) Response rate decreases and may eventually stop. (c) Animals may continue to respond, for a period of time, even when reinforcers are no longer presented. The extent to which they will *continue to respond during extinction* is referred to as *resistance* to extinction.

8. **Explain how stimuli govern operant behavior and how generalization and discrimination occur in operant conditioning.**

8-1.   Suppose that a rat has been shaped so that when it presses a lever it receives a food pellet. With further training, the rat may respond only when a light (or sound, etc.) in the chamber is on and not when it is off. The food pellet (which follows the response) is a _reinforcer_ . The light (which precedes the response) is a _discriminative_ stimulus.

8-2.   Reinforcers occur _after_ (after/before) the response occurs. Discriminative stimuli occur _before_ the response occurs.

8-3.   To create a discriminative stimulus, one reinforces a response only in the presence of a particular stimulus and not in its absence. In time that stimulus will gain control of the response: Animals will tend to emit the response only if the discriminative stimulus is (present/absent) and not if it is _absent_ .

8-4. For example, rats can be trained to press a lever when a light comes on and not to press when the light is off. Lever presses that occur when the light is on are followed by a food pellet; those that occur in the dark are not. Label each component of this operant-conditioning process by placing the appropriate letters in the blanks below.

___*a*___ light   a. discriminative stimulus

___*b*___ lever press   b. response

___*c*___ food   c. reinforcer

8-5. "Heel Fido!" says Ralph. Fido runs to Ralph's side. Fido gets a pat on the head. Label the parts of the operant-conditioning sequence by placing the appropriate letters in the blanks. (To avoid confusion, the behavior or response of interest in this example is already labeled.)

___*a*___ "Heel Fido!"   a. discriminative stimulus

___*c*___ Fido gets a pat on the head.   b. response

__b__ Fido runs to Ralph's side.   c. reinforcer

8-6. Phyllis will lend money to Ralph, but only after Ralph promises to pay her back. Ralph is also careful to thank Phyllis for her help. The behavior we are looking at here is Phyllis's lending behavior.

___*c*___ "Thank you very much, Phyllis."   a. discriminative stimulus

__b__ Phyllis lends.   b. response

___*a*___ "I promise I'll pay you back."   c. reinforcer

8-7. Generalization occurs in operant as well as classical conditioning. For example, when I put dishes in the sink, our cat would *run to her bowl* looking for food. In technical terms, our cat *generalized* between the sound of food dropping in her bowl and the *similar* sound of dishes going into the sink. Despite the fact that food does not follow the sound of clattering dishes, our cat did *not* learn to *discriminate* between the sounds in our kitchen.

Answers: 8-1. reinforcer, discriminative **8-2.** after, before **8-3.** present, absent **8-4.** a, b, c **8-5.** a, c, (b) **8-6.** c, (b), a **8-7.** generalized, discriminate.

9. Discuss the distinction between primary and secondary reinforcers.

9-1. Define the following:

(a) Primary reinforcer: *satisfies biological need (food, water, heat, sex)*

(b) Secondary or conditioned reinforcer: *learned through assoc w/ primary reinforcing (ie. praise, $, attention)*

Answers: 9-1. (a) A primary reinforcer satisfies biological needs, such as needs for food, water, warmth, and sex. (b) A secondary, or conditioned, reinforcer is learned or acquired through association with a primary reinforcer. For humans, common secondary reinforcers include praise, attention, and money.

10. **Identify various types of schedules of reinforcement, and discuss their typical effects on responding.**

10-1.   Schedules of reinforcement are either continuous or intermittent. If reinforcers follow each response, the schedule is referred to as a ___Continuous___-reinforcement schedule, abbreviated CRF. If reinforcers only follow some responses and not others (e.g., FR, VR), or occur as a function of the passage of time (e.g., FI, VI), the schedule is referred to as a/(an) ___Intermittent___ schedule .
or partial

10-2.   Identify the following schedules of reinforcement by placing the appropriate abbreviations in the blanks: continuous reinforcement (CRF), fixed ratio (FR), variable ratio (VR), fixed interval (FI), variable interval (VI).

_FR_ A pigeon is reinforced whenever it has pecked a disk exactly 200 times.

_VR_ A pigeon is reinforced for pecking a disk, on the average, 200 times.

_FI_ A rat is always reinforced for the first response that follows a two-minute interval.

_VR_ A slot machine delivers a payoff, on the average, after every 10th pull of the lever.

CRF Every time the pigeon pecks a disk, it receives a pellet of food.

_VI_ A rat is reinforced, on the average, for the first response following a two-minute interval.

_VI_ A pig is reinforced for the first response after 30 seconds, then for the first response after 42 seconds, then for the first response after 5 seconds, and so on.

_FI_ Every two weeks Ralph picks up his payroll check at the office.

_VR_ A rat is reinforced after the 73rd response, then after the 22nd response, then after the 51st response, and so on.

10-3.   Resistance to extinction refers to the extent to which responses occur during a period of extinction. What is the general effect of the intermittent schedules of reinforcement on resistance to extinction?

Intermittent schedules ↑ resistance to extinction

10-4.   In terms of the effect on *rate* of responding, what is the general difference between the *ratio* schedules (FR and VR) and the *interval* schedules (FI and VI)?

ratio schedules tend to produce more rapid responding than interval schedules

10-5.   In terms of the effect on *pattern* of responding, what is the general difference between *fixed* schedules and *variable* schedules?

var. schedules

Answers: 10-1. continuous, intermittent (or partial) **10-2.** FR, VR, FI, VR, CRF, VI, VI, FI, VR **10-3.** The intermittent schedules increase resistance to extinction. **10-4.** Ratio schedules tend to produce more rapid responding than the interval schedules. **10-5.** Variable schedules tend to produce more regular patterns of responding, without pauses or scalloping, than do their fixed counterparts. They also result in more resistance to extinction.

11. Explain how operant psychologists study choice and summarize what they have learned.

11-1. We make choices. Animals make choices also–for example, whether to seek shelter in a tree or on the ground. In operant theory, choice depends on the payoff or _____ available for a particular behavior.

11-2. To study choice behavior psychologists use two or more reinforcement schedules that operate simultaneously, so-called _____ schedules of reinforcement.

11-3. For example, a pigeon might have the choice between pecking Disk A and Disk B. Suppose the two choices were set up on VI schedules, so that Disk A would reinforce the animal once every minute and Disk B once every two minutes. Which disk would the animal tend to choose more frequently, A or B? _____

11-4. How much more frequently would the animal press disk A? It turns out that the animals will tend to *match* the rate of responding to the rate of available reinforcement. This is known as the _____ law. For example, if the animal is able to obtain twice as many reinforcers per unit time on Disk A as Disk B in a period of time, it will tend to make about twice as many responses on Disk ____. In other words, about two-thirds of the animal's responses per unit time will be on Disk A and one-third on Disk B.

11-5. The matching process isn't exact, but it is surprisingly close. Somehow, by using matching, animals are able to make choices that approximate optimal choices. In this way many animals are able to maximize nutrition gained in relation to energy expended, the major principle of optimal _____ theory. Clearly, being able to differentiate reinforcement in this way has _____ value for a species.

Answers: 11-1. reinforcement (consequences) **11-2.** concurrent **11-3.** A **11-4.** matching, Disk A **11-5.** foraging, survival.

12. Explain the distinction between positive and negative reinforcement.

12-1. Some Skinner boxes may be set up so that a mild electric shock can be delivered to the feet of the animal through the floor of the box. Suppose that just after the animal presses the bar, the shock is turned *off* for a period of time. Will the lever-pressing behavior be *strengthened* or *weakened*? _____

12-2. By definition, what effect does reinforcement have on behavior? What is the effect of positive reinforcement on behavior? Negative reinforcement?

12-3. With positive reinforcement, a stimulus is *presented* after the response. What is the procedure with negative reinforcement?

Answers: 12-1. strengthened **12-2.** Reinforcement strengthens (increases the frequency of) behavior. Both positive and negative reinforcement strengthen behavior. **12-3.** The stimulus (an aversive stimulus) is *removed* after the response.

13. Explain the role of negative reinforcement in avoidance behavior.

13-1. Once avoidance learning is established, the organism never experiences the aversive stimulus. For example, when a dog in a shuttle box jumps to the other side it never experiences shock. So, why doesn't the jumping response gradually extinguish? One explanation is that the dog isn't just avoiding the shock, it is also escaping something else as well. It is escaping the warning stimulus and the conditioned _____ that it produces.

13-2. Fear of the cue or warning stimulus is acquired through (<u>classical/operant</u>) conditioning, the association of the stimulus and shock. The jumping behavior, on the other hand, is maintained, by (<u>classical/operant</u>) conditioning, escape from the conditioned fear.

13-3. Escape increases the strength of a response through (<u>negative/positive</u>) reinforcement. The reason that phobic responses are so resistant to extinction is that when people (and other animals) come in contact with the feared stimulus (e. g., spiders, an elevator, heights, airplanes), they are negatively _____ for avoiding contact with these stimuli (leaving the room, taking the stairs, etc.). Thus, extinction tends not to occur.

Answers: 13-1. fear (conditioned to the cue light) **13-2.** classical, operant **13-3.** negative, reinforced.

14. Describe punishment and its effects.

14-1. Punishment involves *weakening* a response by presenting an aversive stimulus after the response has occurred. Review the concepts of reinforcement and punishment by labeling each of the following with one of these terms: *positive reinforcement, negative reinforcement,* or *punishment.*

(a) A stimulus is *presented* after the response; response rate *increases*:

_____

(b) A stimulus is *presented* after the response; response rate *decreases*:

_____

(c) A stimulus is *removed* after the response; response rate *increases*:

_____

14-2. Response rate *increases*. Which of the following procedures may have been used?

a. positive reinforcement

b. negative reinforcement

c. punishment

d. either a or b above

14-3. Response rate *decreases*. Which of the following procedures may have been used?

    a. positive reinforcement

    b. negative reinforcement

    c. punishment

    d. either *b* or *c* above

14-4. When a rat presses a bar in an operant chamber, the electric shock stops. Bar pressing increases. What procedure has been used?

    a. positive reinforcement

    b. negative reinforcement

    c. punishment

    d. extinction

14-5. When the dog ran after the car, his master immediately threw a bucket of water on him. This sequence of events was repeated only twice, and the dog stopped running after the car. What has occurred?

    a. positive reinforcement

    b. negative reinforcement

    c. punishment

    d. extinction

14-6. When Randolph stepped out in his new outfit, everyone stared. If Randolph tends *not* to wear this outfit in the future, what has occurred?

    a. positive reinforcement

    b. negative reinforcement

    c. punishment

    d. extinction

14-7. In the space below list two negative side effects of punishment.

Answers: 14-1. (a) positive reinforcement (b) punishment (c) negative reinforcement **14-2.** d, because if response rate increases, *either* positive *or* negative reinforcement may be involved **14-3.** c. Not d, because negative reinforcement *increases* response rate. **14-4.** b **14-5.** c **14-6.** c **14-7.** Punishment may (1) produce unwanted emotional responses (e.g., fear and anger directed at the parent or teacher who is the source of the punishment), and (2) increase aggressive behavior.

15. **Discuss the implications of instinctive drift and conditioned taste aversion for traditional views of conditioning and learning.**

   15-1.   What is instinctive drift?

   15-2.   Why was the occurrence of instinctive drift surprising to operant psychologists? Discuss this question in terms of the supposed *generality* of the laws of learning.

   15-3.   What is conditioned taste aversion?

   15-4.   Why is the occurrence of conditioned taste aversion surprising? Discuss this question in terms of classical conditioning relating to (1) CS-UCS delays and (2) the sense of taste compared with other senses.

   Answers: 15-1. It is the tendency for instinctive or innate behavior to interfere with the process of conditioning. **15-2.** Before the 1960s, operant psychologists assumed that any response that animals could emit could readily be conditioned. This turned out not to be true. Animals may exhibit instinctive drift, the tendency to respond with certain innate behaviors that actually interfere with the process of conditioning. **15-3.** It is the fact that if the distinctive taste of a particular food is followed some hours later by sickness (nausea, vomiting, etc.), that taste will become aversive and will also elicit the response of nausea. **15-4.** It is surprising because (1) classical conditioning generally does not occur if there are long CS-UCS delays, and (2) taste is only one of several senses stimulated in this situation. Garcia concluded that animals have an innate tendency to associate taste (rather than sight, sound, etc.) with sickness even though the sickness may occur much later.

16. **Explain the evolutionary perspective on learning.**

   16-1.   Psychologists used to believe that there were highly general "laws" of learning. More recently, studies like those just referred to and the emerging field of evolutionary psychology indicate that there probably (are/are not) principles of learning that apply to all species.

   16-2.   Instead, the new viewpoint emerging among psychologists is that ways of learning have evolved along different paths in different species, so that classical and operant conditioning, for example, are to some extent (universal/specific-specific). Finding food, avoiding predators, and reproducing allow a species to survive, but the ways of learning that accomplish these outcomes depend on the _____ value of these processes.

   Answers: 16-1. are not. **16-2.** species-specific, adaptive (survival, evolutionary).

17. **Describe research on signal relations and response-outcome relations, and explain their theoretical importance.**

17-1.   In the example of a signal relations study described, the number of conditioning trials in which CS and UCS were paired was the same for two groups, 20 trials. The difference between the two treatment groups was that for one group the (CS/UCS) was presented *alone* for an additional series of 20 trials.

17-2.   Theorists originally assumed that classical conditioning is an automatic, reflexive phenomenon that does not depend at all on higher mental processes. If that actually were true, then what should have been the effect of presenting the UCS alone for additional trials? Remember that both groups received exactly the same number of conditioning trials (CS-UCS pairings).

   a. Extinction would occur.

   b. The UCS-alone trials would weaken conditioning.

   c. The UCS-alone trials would have no effect on conditioning.

17-3.   In fact, what did occur in the signal relations studies?

   a. Extinction.

   b. The UCS-alone trials weakened conditioning.

   c. The UCS-alone trials had no effect on conditioning.

17-4.   These results suggest that the CS *signals* the occurrence of the UCS and that additional trials with the UCS alone weaken the _____ value of the CS. What is surprising about these results? Rather than being an automatic, mechanical process, these studies suggest that classical conditioning involves _____ processes.

17-5.   Response-outcome relations refers to the connection between an operant response and its consequences. For example, for a rat in a Skinner box the relationship between the lever press (the response) and the food pellet (the outcome) is this: the rat gets the food *only if* it presses the lever. In other words, the reinforcer is (contingent/not contingent) on the response.

17-6.   But does the animal "know" the connection between the response and reinforcer, or is the connection stamped in automatically? That is the crux of the response-outcome relations issue. Evidence suggests that

   a. reinforcement and punishment are relatively automatic, mindless processes.

   b. cognition is not involved in an organism's responding in an operant chamber

   c. humans and other animals actively try to figure out the contingencies, the relationship between response and outcome

17-7.   Thus, research on signal relations and response-outcome relations has forced the development of new theories that emphasize a much more _____ explanation of conditioning, an explanation in which organisms actively attempt to detect the *relationship* between their behaviors and environmental events.

17-8. Why are the signal relations studies in classical conditioning and response-outcome relations studies in operant conditioning surprising and of theoretical importance?

Answers: **17-1.** UCS! (If the CS were presented alone, it would be extinction.) **17-2.** c **17-3.** b **17-4.** signaling, cognitive (higher mental) **17-5.** contingent **17-6.** c **17-7.** cognitive **17-8.** These studies indicate that conditioning is not, as assumed earlier, an automatic process but instead depends to a considerable degree on higher mental (cognitive) processes.

18. Discuss the nature and importance of observational learning.

18-1. Observational learning occurs when an organism learns by observing others, who are called _____. This type of learning occurs in (humans/animals/both).

18-2. Why is the concept of observational learning so important? For one thing the idea was surprising to theorists who assumed that all learning could be accounted for by operant and classical conditioning. For another, it extends classical and operant conditioning to include not only *direct* experience but _____ or vicarious experience. We learn not only when we behave but when we _____ the behavior of others.

18-3. Bandura's theory has helped explain some puzzling aspects of conditioning in human behavior. For example, what happens when parents physically punish aggressive behavior in their children? While punishment by definition (increases/decreases) the behavior it follows, a parent using physical punishment also serves as a _____ for aggressiveness. In this way events intended to decrease aggression may, in the longer run, _____ aggression through the process of _____ learning.

Answers: **18-1.** models, both **18-2.** indirect, observe **18-3.** decreases, model, increase, observational.

PUTTING IT IN PERSPECTIVE

19. Explain how this chapter highlighted two of the text's unifying themes.

19-1. Skinner emphasized the importance of *environmental* events (reinforcers, punishers, discriminative stimuli, schedules of reinforcement) as the determinants of behavior. One of our unifying themes, however, is that heredity and environment interact. In support of this theme list the names of three phenomena that show that *biology* has a powerful effect on *conditioning*.

19-2. The second theme well illustrated in this chapter is that psychology evolves in a sociohistorical context. Discuss one concept from operant psychology that appears to have influenced our everyday lives.

Answers: **19-1.** instinctive drift, conditioned taste aversion, preparedness **19-2.** Operant psychology has probably influenced the trend in our society toward relying more on the use of positive reinforcement than punishment in child-rearing, in educational settings (e.g., the use of programmed learning), and as a management technique in business.

20. List and discuss the five steps in a self-modification program.

20-1.   In the space below list the five steps of a self-modification program in the order in which they are performed. The letters at the left are the first letters of the key words in each phase.

T: Specify your _____ behavior.

B: Gather _____ data.

D: _____ your program.

E: Execute and _____ your program.

E: _____ your program.

20-2.   What behavior do you want to change? The question sounds simple, but the task of defining a _____ behavior is frequently quite tricky.

20-3.   The behavior that you select must be defined in terms of observable events so that you will know if and when it changes. For example, for the problem of anger control, which of the following would be the most *directly observable* definition of "anger"?

a. inner turmoil

b. intense hostility

c. loud voice and clenched fists

20-4.   Once you specify the target behavior you must gather _____ data on your behavior prior to the intervention. At this time you should also keep track of events that precede the target behavior, the _____ events, and also the positive and negative reinforcers that follow it, the _____ events.

20-5.   To increase a target behavior you would use _____. The reinforcer (can/can not) be something that you already are receiving. For example, you probably already watch T. V., go to movies, or buy things for yourself, so you could make one of these events _____ on an increased frequency of the target behavior.

20-6.   You would specify exactly what behavioral goals must be met before you receive the reinforcer; that is, you would arrange the _____. If your goal is to increase studying, you might specify that T. V. watching for one hour is _____ on having studied for two hours.

20-7.   Or, you might specify that for each hour you studied you would earn points that could be "spent" for watching T. V., or going to movies, or talking with friends, and so on. This type of arrangement is referred to as a _____ economy. In some cases you may want to approach the target response gradually, to reinforce successive approximations to the target behavior using the procedure known as shaping.

20-8. A fairly obvious way to decrease a target behavior is to use _____. The problem with this approach is that it is difficult to follow through with self-punishment. So, there are two guidelines to keep in mind when using punishment in a self-control program: (1) Use punishment only in conjunction with _____ reinforcement; and (2) use a relatively _____ punishment that you, or perhaps a third party, will be able to administer.

20-9. It is also possible to use reinforcement to decrease behavior. For example, if you want to gradually reduce the amount that you smoke, you could reinforce yourself whenever you smoke fewer than a particular number of cigarettes per day. Paradoxically, you are using _____ to decrease behavior.

20-10. For some situations you may be able to identify events that reliably *precede* the behaviors you are trying to stop. For example, for some people smoking is at least under partial control of certain types of social events. So, one strategy for decreasing a behavior is to identify the (antecedent/consequent) events that may control the behavior.

20-11. Successful execution of the program depends on several factors. To avoid "cheating" try creating a formal written behavioral _____. Or, make an arrangement so that (only you/someone else) delivers the reinforcers and punishments.

20-12. If your program isn't working, some small revision may turn it around. Try increasing the strength of the reinforcer or else try _____ the delay between the behavior and delivery of the reinforcer.

20-13. It is generally a good idea to specify in advance the conditions under which you would end the program. You may wish to phase it out by having a/an (gradual/immediate) reduction in the frequency or potency of reinforcers, although for some successful programs the new behaviors become self-maintaining on their own.

Answers: 20-1. target, baseline, design, evaluate, end **20-2.** target **20-3.** c, although even those behaviors would have to be further described in a behavior modification program. Alternative a is not really observable. Alternative b could be behaviorally defined, but as it stands it is hard to know precisely which behaviors intense hostility refers to. **20-4.** baseline, antecedent, consequences (reinforcers and punishers) **20-5.** reinforcement, can, contingent **20-6.** contingency, contingent **20-7.** token **20-8.** punishment, positive, mild **20-9.** reinforcement **20-10.** antecedent **20-11.** contract (agreement), someone else **20-12.** decreasing **20-13.** gradual.

CRITICAL THINKING APPLICATION • MANIPULATING EMOTIONS: PAVLOV AND PERSUASION

21. **Describe how classical conditioning is used to manipulate emotions.**

    21-1. It is easy to forget that Pavlovian conditioning involves more than salivating dogs. It involves emotion, and in that respect it is important for a range of reactions–from phobias to sexual arousal to the effects of advertising. For practice with conditioning concepts label each of the following:

(a) A glamorous woman is shown entering an automobile. Label each of the following with CS, UCS, CR, and UCR. (Assume, for the sake of this example, that the target audience is initially more attracted to the woman than the car! It could work the other way, too.)

_____ the woman

_____ the car

_____ attraction to the car

_____ attraction to the woman

(b) A politician stands in front of an American flag.

What is the CS? _____

the UCS? _____

(c) A salesman takes you to lunch.

What is the CS? _____

The UCS? _____

The CR? _____

21-2. Of course, there's more going on in these examples than just classical conditioning. When we receive a favor, we are not only being conditioned but may feel obliged to pay back or _____ the person's favor.

21-3. While the examples we've used involve liking or attraction, other emotions may be conditioned as well—such as feelings of masculinity and femininity. Want to be more masculine? Smoke these cigarettes ads may suggest. Not that we must be conscious of manipulation attempts, for conditioning (<u>does/ does not</u>) seem to require our awareness

21-4. How do we protect ourselves against attempts to manipulate our emotions? One suggestion from research on persuasion is that merely being _____ of the pervasiveness of conditioning will by itself provide some protections against manipulation strategies.

Answers: **21-1.** (a) UCS, CS, CR, UCR (b) the politician, the flag (c) the salesman (or his product), the lunch, liking for the salesman (or his product) **21-2.** reciprocate **21-3.** does not **21-4.** forewarned (aware).

REVIEW OF KEY TERMS

Acquisition
Antecedents
Avoidance learning
Behavioral contract
Behavior modification
Classical conditioning
Concurrent schedules of reinforcement
Conditioned reinforcer
Conditioned response (CR)
Conditioned stimulus (CS)
Continuous reinforcement
Cumulative recorder
Discriminative stimuli
Elicit
Emit
Escape learning

Extinction
Fixed-interval (FI) schedule
Fixed-ratio (FR) schedule
Higher-order conditioning
Intermittent reinforcement
Learning
Matching law
Negative reinforcement
Observational learning
Operant conditioning
Optimal foraging theory
Pavlovian conditioning
Positive reinforcement
Primary reinforcers
Punishment
Reinforcement

Reinforcement contingencies
Resistance to extinction
Schedule of reinforcement
Secondary reinforcers
Shaping
Skinner box
Spontaneous recovery
Stimulus contiguity
Stimulus discrimination
Stimulus generalization
Token economy
Trial
Unconditioned response (UCR)
Unconditioned stimulus (UCS)
Variable-interval (VI) schedule
Variable-ratio (VR) schedule

_____ 1. A relatively durable change in behavior or knowledge that is due to experience.

_____ 2. The most common name of a type of learning in which a neutral stimulus acquires the ability to evoke a response that was originally evoked by another stimulus.

_____ 3. Another name for classical conditioning derived from the name of the person who originally discovered the conditioning phenomenon.

_____ 4. A stimulus that evokes an unconditioned response.

_____ 5. The response to an unconditioned stimulus.

_____ 6. A previously neutral stimulus that has acquired the capacity to evoke a conditioned response.

_____ 7. A learned reaction to a conditioned stimulus that occurs because of previous conditioning.

_____ 8. To draw out or bring forth, as in classical conditioning.

_____ 9. Any presentation of a stimulus or pair of stimuli in classical conditioning.

_____ 10. The formation of a new response tendency.

_____ 11. Occurs when there is a temporal (time) association between two events.

_____ 12. The gradual weakening and disappearance of a conditioned response tendency.

_____ 13. The reappearance of an extinguished response after a period of nonexposure to the conditioned stimulus.

_____ 14. Occurs when an organism responds to new stimuli that are similar to the stimulus used in conditioning.

_____ 15. Occurs when an organism learns not respond to stimuli that are similar to the stimulus used in conditioning.

_____ 16. Occurs when a conditioned stimulus functions as if it were an unconditioned stimulus.

_____ 17. This term, introduced by Skinner, refers to learning in which voluntary responses come to be controlled by their consequences.

_____ 18. Occurs when an event following a response strengthens the tendency to make that response.

_____ 19. A standard operant chamber in which an animal's responses are controlled and recorded.

_____ 20. Production of voluntary responses in responding in operant conditioning.

_____ 21. The circumstances or rules that determine whether responses lead to presentation of a reinforcer; or, the relationship between a response and positive consequences.

_____ 22. Device that creates a graphic record of operant responding as a function of time.

_____ 23. The reinforcement of closer and closer approximations of the desired response.

_____ 24. Occurs when an organism continues to make a response after the delivery of the reinforcer for it has been terminated.

_____ 25. Cues that precede operant behavior and that influence the behavior by indicating the probable consequences (reinforcement or no reinforcement) of a response.

_____ 26. Stimulus events that are inherently reinforcing because they satisfy biological needs.

_____ 27. Stimulus events that acquire reinforcing qualities by being associated with primary reinforcers.

_____ 28. A specific pattern of presentation of reinforcers over time.

_____ 29. Occurs when every instance of a designated response is reinforced.

_____ 30. The name for all schedules of reinforcement in which a designated response is reinforced only some of the time.

_____ 31. The schedule in which the reinforcer is given after a fixed number of nonreinforced responses.

_____ 32. The schedule in which the reinforcer is given after a variable number of nonreinforced responses.

_____ 33. The schedule in which the reinforcer is given for the first response that occurs after a fixed time interval has elapsed.

_____ 34. The schedule in which the reinforcer is given for the first response that occurs after a variable time interval has elapsed.

_____ 35. Occurs when a response is strengthened because it is followed by the arrival of a rewarding (presumably pleasant) stimulus.

_____ 36. Occurs when a response is strengthened because it is followed by the removal of an aversive ("unpleasant") stimulus.

_____ 37. Occurs when an organism engages in a response that brings aversive stimulation to an end.

_____ 38. Occurs when an organism engages in a response that prevents aversive stimulation from occurring.

_____ 39. Occurs when an event that follows a response weakens or suppresses the tendency to make that response.

_____ 40. Occurs when an organism's responding is influenced by the observation of others, who are called models.

_____ 41. A systematic approach to changing behavior through the application of the principles of conditioning.

_____ 42. Events that typically precede your target behavior and may play a major role in governing your target response; also, another term for discriminative stimuli.

_____ 43. A system for distributing symbolic reinforcers that are exchanged later for a variety of genuine reinforcers.

_____ 44. A written agreement outlining a promise to adhere to the contingencies of a behavior modification program.

_____ 45. Another name for secondary reinforcer.

_____ 46. A type of reinforcement schedule involving two or more reinforcement schedules operating simultaneously and independently, each for a different response.

_____ 47. The finding that under concurrent schedules of reinforcement, organisms' relative rate of responding to each alternative tends to match each alternative's relative rate of reinforcement.

_____ 48. The observation that food-seeking behavior of many animals tends to maximize nutrition gained per energy expended to locate, secure, and consume the food.

Answers: 1. learning **2.** classical conditioning **3.** Pavlovian conditioning **4.** unconditioned stimulus (UCS) **5.** unconditioned response (UCR) **6.** conditioned stimulus (CS) **7.** conditioned response (CR) **8.** elicit **9.** trial **10.** acquisition **11.** stimulus contiguity **12.** extinction **13.** spontaneous recovery **14.** stimulus generalization **15.** stimulus discrimination **16.** higher-order conditioning **17.** operant conditioning **18.** reinforcement **19.** Skinner box **20.** emit **21.** reinforcement contingencies **22.** cumulative recorder **23.** shaping **24.** resistance to extinction **25.** discriminative stimuli **26.** primary reinforcers **27.** secondary reinforcers **28.** schedule of reinforcement **29.** continuous reinforcement **30.** intermittent reinforcement **31.** fixed-ratio (FR) schedule **32.** variable-ratio (VR) schedule **33.** fixed-interval (FI) schedule **34.** variable-interval (VI) schedule **35.** positive reinforcement **36.** negative reinforcement **37.** escape learning **38.** avoidance learning **39.** punishment **40.** observational learning **41.** behavior modification **42.** antecedents **43.** token economy **44.** behavioral contract **45.** conditioned reinforcer **46.** concurrent schedules of reinforcement **47.** matching law **48.** optimal foraging behavior.

REVIEW OF KEY PEOPLE

Albert Bandura   Robert Rescorla   John B. Watson
Ivan Pavlov   B. F. Skinner

_____ 1. The first to demonstrate the process of classical conditioning.

_____ 2. Founded behaviorism; examined the generalization of conditioned fear in a boy known as "Little Albert."

_____ 3. Elaborated the learning process known as operant conditioning; investigated schedules of reinforcement.

_____ 4. Asserted that environmental stimuli serve as signals and that some stimuli in classical conditioning are better signals than others.

_____ 5. Described and extensively investigated the process of observational learning.

Answers: 1. Pavlov **2.** Watson **3.** Skinner **4.** Rescorla **5.** Bandura.

SELF-QUIZ

1. In Pavlov's original demonstration of classical conditioning, salivation to the bell was the:
   a. conditioned stimulus
   b. conditioned response
   c. unconditioned stimulus
   d. unconditioned response

2. Sally developed a fear of balconies after almost falling from a balcony on a couple of occasions. What was the conditioned response?
   a. the balcony
   b. fear of the balcony
   c. almost falling
   d. fear resulting from almost falling

3. When the UCS is removed and the CS is presented alone for a period of time, what will occur?
   a. classical conditioning
   b. generalization
   c. acquisition
   d. extinction

4. Sally developed a fear of balconies from almost falling. Although she has had no dangerous experiences on bridges, cliffs, and the view from tall buildings, she now fears these stimuli as well. Which of the following would account for her acquiring a fear of these other stimuli?
   a. instinctive drift
   b. spontaneous recovery
   c. generalization
   d. discrimination

5. A researcher reinforces closer and closer approximations to a target behavior. What is the name of the procedure she is using?
   a. shaping
   b. classical conditioning
   c. discrimination training
   d. extinction

6. The telephone rings. John answers it and is reinforced by the voice on the other end. In operant conditioning terminology, the ringing of the phone is a:
   a. discriminative stimulus
   b. response
   c. positive reinforcer
   d. conditioned stimulus (CS)

7. A rat is reinforced for the first lever-pressing response that occurs, *on the average*, after 60 seconds. Which schedule is the rat on?
   a. FR
   b. VR
   c. FI
   d. VI

8. When the rat presses a lever, the mild electric shock on the cage floor is turned off. What procedure is being used?
   a. punishment
   b. escape
   c. discrimination training
   d. avoidance

9. Earlier learning viewpoints considered classical and operant conditioning to be automatic processes that did not depend at all on biological or cognitive factors. Research involving which of the following topics cast doubt on this point of view?
   a. signal relations
   b. instinctive drift and conditioned taste aversion
   c. response-outcome relations
   d. All of the above

10. Suppose that when a response occurs, a stimulus is presented that has the effect of *decreasing* response strength. What procedure is being used?
    a. positive reinforcement
    b. negative reinforcement
    c. punishment
    d. avoidance training

11. In terms of the traditional view of conditioning, research on conditioned taste aversion was surprising because:
    a. there was a long delay between CS and UCS, and cues other than taste did not condition
    b. the dislike of a particular taste was operantly conditioned whereas the non-taste cues were classically conditioned
    c. conditioning occurred to all stimuli present when the food was consumed
    d. the sense of taste seems to be relatively weak, especially in the Midwest

12. Animal trainers (the Brelands) trained pigs to put coins in a piggy bank for a food reward. The animals learned the response but, instead of depositing the coins immediately in the bank, the pigs began to toss them in the air, drop them, push them on the ground, and so on. What had occurred that interfered with conditioning?
    a. conditioned taste aversion
    b. negative reinforcement
    c. instinctive drift
    d. modeling

13. Which of the following produces strong resistance to extinction?
    a. a continuous reinforcement schedule
    b. an intermittent reinforcement schedule
    c. optimal foraging behavior
    d. discrimination and differentiation

14. Earlier learning viewpoints considered classical and operant conditioning to be automatic processes involving only environmental events that did not depend at all on biological or cognitive factors. Research on which of the following concepts cast doubt on this point of view?
    a. signal relations, instinctive drift, and conditioned taste aversion
    b. extinction, discrimination, and generalization
    c. CRF, ratio, and interval schedules
    d. escape, avoidance, and spontaneous recovery

15. In devising your own self-modification procedure, your first step should be to:
    a. gather baseline data
    b. specify your target behavior
    c. design your program
    d. execute and evaluate your program

Answers: 1. b 2. b 3. d 4. c 5. a 6. a 7. d 8. b 9. d 10. c 11. a 12. c 13. b 14. a 15. b.

INFOTRAC

Behavior Modification   Classical Conditioning   Operant Conditioning

7 HUMAN MEMORY

REVIEW OF KEY IDEAS

ENCODING • GETTING INFORMATION INTO MEMORY

1. List and describe the three basic human memory processes.

    1-1.   The three basic human memory processes are:

        (a) Putting information in, a process called _____.

        (b) Holding onto information, a process called _____.

        (c) Getting information back out, a process called _____.

    Answers: 1-1. (a) encoding (b) storage (c) retrieval.

2. Discuss the role of attention and levels of processing in encoding.

    2-1.   Attention requires both filtering out irrelevant information and attending to selected information. Thus if you are being introduced to a new person whose name you want to remember, you must _____ attend to her name and _____ out irrevelant sensory input.

    2-2.   The debate between early and late selection theories of attention is an argument over where this filtering takes place, before or after _____ is given to the arriving information.

    2-3.   Research evidence, as well as casual observations, seem to support (<u>both/neither</u>) arguments and intermediate selection as well. In fact, some theorists believe that the location of the filter is _____ rather than fixed.

    2-4.   Craik and Lockhart propose three levels for encoding incoming information, with ever increasing retention as the depth of processing increases. In their order of depth these three levels are:

        (a) _____   (b) _____   (c) _____

2-5. Below are three-word sequences. Tell which level of processing each sequence illustrates and why.

(a) cat   IN   tree _____

(b) car   BAR   czar _____

(c) CAN CAP CAR _____

2-6. If the levels-of-processing theory is correct then we would expect most persons to best remember the sequence in _____. This is because the words in this sequence have greater _____ than do the other two sequences. It has been found that processing time (<u>is/is not</u>) a reliable index of depth of processing, and thus what constitutes "levels" remains vague.

Answers: 2-1. selectively, filter **2-2.** meaning **2-3.** both, flexible **2-4.** (a) structural (b) phonemic (c) semantic **2-5.** (a) Semantic because we immediately give meaning to the words (b) Phonemic because the words sound alike (c) Structural because the words look alike **2-6.** cat in tree, meaning, is not.

3. Discuss two techniques for enriching the encoding process.

3-1. Identify which of the following situations illustrates either elaboration or visual imagery as techniques for enriching the encoding process.

(a) A cat owner who hears about a new drug for treating cats is more likely to remember the name of the drug than a person without a cat.

(b) It is easier to remember the word APPLE rather than the word PREVAIL.

3-2. According to Paivio's dual-coding theory, why is it easier to remember the word APPLE rather than the word PREVAIL?

Answers: 3-1. (a) elaboration (b) visual imagery **3-2.** Because it is easier to form a visual image of the word APPLE thus allowing for storage of both the word and image.

STORAGE • MAINTAINING INFORMATION IN MEMORY

4. Describe the role of the sensory store in memory.

4-1. Sensory memory allows for retention of information for a very (<u>brief/long</u>) period of time. The retention time for vision is _____, and appears to be the same for audition. In other words, sensory memory allows us to retain information long enough to allow for further processing.

Answers: 4-1. brief, ¹/₄ of a second.

5. **Describe the characteristics of short-term memory and contrast them with long-term memory.**

    5-1.   Indicate whether the following statements apply to short-term memory (STM) or long-term memory (LTM).

        _____ (a) Has a virtually unlimited storage capacity.

        _____ (b) Has a storage capacity of seven, plus or minus two, items.

        _____ (c) Requires continuous rehearsal to maintain information in store for more than 20 or 30 seconds.

        _____ (d) Stores information more or less permanently.

        _____ (e) Chunking can help to increase the capacity of this system.

        _____ (f) Alan Baddeley has proposed three components of this memory system that make it a "working memory."

Answers: 5-1. (a) LTM (b) STM (c) STM (d) LTM (e) STM (f) STM.

6. **Summarize the evidence on the hypothesis that all memories are stored permanently in long-term memory (LTM).**

    6-1.   There are two views regarding the durability of information in LTM. One is that no information is ever lost and the other is that _____. Those who favor the "no-loss" view explain forgetting as a failure of _____. The information is still there, we just cannot get it out.

    6-2.   How do the some-loss proponents counter the following three lines of evidence cited by the no-loss proponents?

    (a) Flashbulb memories of previous events?

    (b) The remarkable recall of hypnotized subjects?

Answers: 6-1. some information is lost, retrieval 6-2. (a) They often tend to be inaccurate and less detailed with the passage of time (b) Their recall of information is often found to be incorrect.

7. **Explain the issues in the debate about whether short-term and long-term memory are really separate.**

    7-1.   The traditional view is that short-term memory differs from long-term memory in that it depends on phonemic (sound) encoding while long-term memory depends on _____ (meaning) encoding. These two systems are also said to differ in the manner in which forgetting occurs. The loss of memory in STM is thought to result from time-related decay, while LTM forgetting is attributed to _____.

    7-2.   What research findings undermine the traditional view?

7-3. How do theorists who support a unitary "generic" memory store explain such phenomena as the constant repeating of a phone number in short-term memory?

Answers: **7-1.** semantic, interference **7-2.** Semantic encoding and interference have also been found in short-term memory. **7-3.** This is merely the generic memory store in an elevated state of activation.

8. **Describe schemas and semantic networks and their role in long-term memory.**

8-1. Group the following words into two groups or categories:

rose   dog   grass   cat   tree   rat

You probably grouped the words into plants and animals, which is the general idea behind _____ networks. If you understand the idea behind semantic networks and its related idea of spreading activation, you should be able to answer the questions below.

Person A attends an urban university and frequently studies while riding a bus to and from school.

Person B attends a university located in a rural area and frequently studies outside in one of the many park-like areas surrounding the school.

(a) When asked to think of words associated with the word STUDY, which of the above persons is most likely to think of the word GRASS? _____

(b) Which person is most likely to think of the word TRAFFIC? _____

(c) Which person is most likely to think of the word PEACEFUL? _____

8-2. Finally, it appears that LTM also stores information in organized clusters of knowledge about a particular object or sequence of events, such as a professor's office. Clusters of this nature are called _____.

Answers: **8-1.** semantic (a) person B (b) person A (c) person B **8-2.** schemas.

9. **Explain how parallel distributed processing (PDP) models view the representation of information in memory.**

9-1. PDP models assume that a piece of knowledge is represented by a particular _____ of activation across an entire system of interconnected neural networks. This approach is called "connectionism" because the information lies in the strengths of the _____. The PDP approach (agrees/disagrees) with the general findings from neurophysiological research.

Answers: **9-1.** pattern, connections, agrees.

RETRIEVAL • GETTING INFORMATION BACK OUT OF MEMORY

10. **Describe how retrieval cues and context cues are related to retrieval.**

10-1. In the following examples indicate whether retrieval cues or context cues are being used to retrieve information from long-term memory.

(a) In trying to recall the name of a high school classmate, you get the feeling that his first name began with an "L" and begin saying names like Larry, Leroy, Lionel, etc.

(b) Or you may attempt to recall the high school classmate by imagining the history class in which he sat in the row next to you.

Answers: 10-1. (a) retrieval cues (b) context cues.

11. Summarize evidence on the misinformation effect and discuss source-monitoring and its implication.

11-1. The recalled memory of an event is actually a (replication/reconstruction) of the original event. Events following the original event can intrude into the memory and produce a misinformation effect. For example, Elizabeth Loftus found that subjects were much more likely to falsely recall seeing broken glass on a videotaped scene when they were originally asked, "How fast were the cars going when they (hit/smashed) into each other?" In this case the word "smashed" resulted in a different _____ than did the word "hit." The distortion of memory by the word "smashed" is an example of the post-event _____ effect.

11-2. Another factor that can contribute to the misinformation effect occurs when a memory from one source is misattributed to another source, an error that results from faulty _____ monitoring. Thus persons who remember seeing something that was only verbally suggested may simply be making a _____ _____ error.

Answers: 11-1. reconstruction, smashed, schema, misinformation **11-2.** source, source monitoring.

FORGETTING • WHEN MEMORY LAPSES

12. Describe the various measures of forgetting.

12-1. Which of the three different methods of measuring forgetting (*recall*, *recognition*, or *relearning*) is illustrated in each of the following situations?

(a) You are asked to identify a suspect in a police lineup.

(b) You time yourself while learning 20 new French words. After a week you find you have forgotten some of the words, and you again time yourself while learning the list a second time.

(c) You are asked to draw a floor plan of your bedroom from memory.

Answers: 12-1. (a) recognition (b) relearning (c) recall.

13. Explain how forgetting may be due to ineffective encoding.

13-1. Why are most people unable to recognize the correct penny shown at the beginning of this chapter in the text?

13-2. What is another name for information loss due to ineffective coding of this kind?

13-3. Why is semantic coding better than phonemic coding for enhancing future recall of written material?

Answers: **13-1.** They never encoded the correct figure in their memories **13-2.** pseudoforgetting **13-3.** Semantic coding will lead to deeper processing and more elaborate associations.

14. Discuss how much decay, interference, and retrieval failure contribute to forgetting.

14-1. Three other theories of forgetting propose additional factors that may be involved in retrieval failure. One theory holds that retrieval failure may be due to the impermanence of the memory storage itself. This is the notion behind the _____ theory of forgetting. Decay theory is best able to explain retrieval failure in sensory and _____ memory, but there is no evidence that decay interferes with long-term memory.

14-2. Another theory attributes retrieval failure to other information already in the memory or to information arriving at a later time. This is the notion behind the _____ theory of forgetting. According to interference theory, the failure may be caused by interference from information already in the memory, a phenomenon called _____ interference, or the failure may be caused by interference occurring after the original memory was stored, a phenomenon called _____ interference. Interference is most likely to occur when the materials being stored are very (similar/different).

14-3. Breakdowns in the retrieval process can also occur when the encoding specificity principle is violated. This means there has been a mismatch between the _____ cue and the _____ code. A common instance of this violation is seen when one attempts to retrieve a semantically coded word with (semantic/phonetic) retrieval cues.

Answers: **14-1.** decay, short-term (STM) **14-2.** interference, proactive, retroactive, similar **14-3.** retrieval, memory, phonemic.

15. Summarize both sides of the repressed memories controversy.

15-1. Sigmund Freud felt that some breakdowns in the retrieval process could be attributed to purposeful suppression of information by unconscious forces, a phenomenon called _____ forgetting. Freud called motivated forgetting _____.

15-2. Those who argue that the recovered memories of early childhood abuse are genuine believe that these recovered memories are examples of _____ and that the frequency of sexual abuse in childhood is (less/more) widespread than most people realize.

15-3. How do the skeptics of these recovered memories of childhood sexual abuse explain their origin?

15-4. What is the best way to tell determine if a recovered memory is genuine or a false memory?

Answers: **15-1.** motivated, repression **15-2.** repression, more **15-3.** Some suggestible people are convinced by persuasive therapists (that these events must have happened). **15-4.** through independent corroborative evidence.

IN SEARCH OF THE MEMORY TRACE • THE PHYSIOLOGY OF MEMORY

16. Distinguish between two types of amnesia and identify the anatomical structures implicated in memory.

16-1. Amnesia cases due to head injury provide clues about the anatomical basis of memory. There are two basic types of head-injury amnesia. When the memory loss is for events prior to the injury, it is called _____ amnesia. When the memory loss is for events following the injury, it is called _____ amnesia.

16-2. What two general regions in the brain have been found to be critical for storing and retrieving long-term memories?

16-3. The hypothesized consolidation process assumes that the consolidation of memories begins in the _____ system. These memories are then stored in the same areas that were originally involved in processing the sensory input in the cerebral _____.

Answers: **16-1.** anterograde, retrograde **16-2.** hippocampal and parahippocampal **16-3.** hippocampal, cortex.

17. Summarize evidence on the biochemistry and neural circuitry underlying memory.

17-1. Research evidence indicates that specific neural circuits related to specific memories (may/may not) exist. So far, however, such a circuit has only been found for the conditioned _____ response of a rabbit.

17-2. Which of the following biochemical processes are now thought to be implicated in the formation of memories?

(a) Alterations in neurotransmitter secretions at specific sites.

(b) Hormonal fluctuations that can facilitate or impair memory.

(c) Protein synthesis in the brain.

(d) Changes in RNA in the brain.

Answers: **17-1.** may, eye blink **17-2.** a, b, and c are correct.

18. Distinguish between implicit versus explicit memory and their relationship to declarative versus procedural memory.

18-1.   Label the two following situations as to whether they are examples of implicit or explicit memory.

(a) After studying for your history test, you were able to easily recall the information during the exam.

_____

(b) While studying for your history exam, you unexpectedly recall an incident from the previous summer. _____

18-2.   Another division of memory systems has been hypothesized for declarative memory and procedural memory. Identify these two divisions from their descriptions given below.

_____ (a) This system allows you to drive a car or play a piano with minimal attention to the execution of movements that are required.

_____ (b) This system allows you to explain how to drive a car or play a piano to a friend.

18-3.   It has been suggested that there is an apparent relationship between implicit memory and _____ memory and between explicit memory and _____ memory.

Answers: 18-1. (a) explicit (b) implicit **18-2.** (a) procedural (b) declarative **18-3.** procedural, declarative.

19. Explain the distinction between episodic versus semantic memory.

19-1.   It has also been hypothesized that declarative memory can be further subdivided into semantic and episodic memory. Identify these two kinds of memory from the following descriptions:

_____ (a) This kind of memory acts like an encyclopedia, storing all of the factual information you possess.

_____ (b) This kind of memory acts like an autobiography, storing all of your personal experiences.

Answers: 19-1. (a) semantic (b) episodic.

PUTTING IT IN PERSPECTIVE

20. Explain how this chapter highlighted the subjectivity of experience and the multifactorial causation of behavior.

20-1.   The text mentions two areas in which subjectivity may influence memory. Identify them below.

(a) What we see in the world around us depends on where we focus our _____ .

(b) Every time we tell about a particular experience, details are added or subtracted because of the _____ nature of memory.

20-2. Since the memory of a specific event can be influenced by many factors, operating in each of the three memory stores, it is obvious that memory, like most behavior, has _____ _____.

Answers: 20-1. (a) attention (b) reconstructive **20-2.** multifactorial causation.

PERSONAL APPLICATION • IMPROVING EVERYDAY MEMORY

21. Outline strategies by which everyday memory can be improved.

21-1. The text lists some general strategies for improving everyday memory. Identify which strategy is being employed in the following examples.

(a) Most persons can remember their phone number because of extensive _____.

(b) Willie Nurd the bookworm always takes breaks between study periods when changing subject matter. Willie must realize the importance of _____ practice.

(c) Ajax never studies any other material besides mathematics on the day of his math exams in order to minimize _____.

(d) Answering questions such as these is much better than simply underlining the same material in the text because it forces you to engage in _____ processing.

(e) Various procedures, such as rearranging material into meaningful groupings, may aid memory because of the improvement in _____.

21-2. Specific strategies for enhancing memory are called _____ devices. Examples of strategies that do not employ visual images are listed below. See if you can identify which strategy is being employed in each illustration.

(a) Using the phrase "My Very Excellent Mother Just Sells Nuts Under Protest" to remember the names and positions of the planets illustrates the use of an _____.

(b) International Business Machines is easily identified by its _____ IBM.

(c) Since you are going to the store your roommate asks you to bring her a bar of Ivory soap, a box of Kleenex and a Snickers bar. You then make up a story that begins, "On my way to the Ivory Coast to check on the latest shipment of Kleenex, I . . ." Here you're making use of a _____ method as a mnemonic device.

21-3. Two techniques involving visual imagery, the link method and the method of loci, can also serve as helpful mnemonic devices. Identify them in the examples below.

(a) You want to remember to buy bananas, eggs, milk, and bread. You visualize walking in your front door and tripping on a bunch of bananas. Stumbling forward into the hallway you notice broken eggs on the table. _____.

(b) You imagine yourself using a banana to break eggs, which you then pour into a bowl of milk and bread. _____.

Answers: 21-1. (a) rehearsal (b) distributed (c) interference (d) deep (e) organization **21-2.** mnemonic (a) acrostic (b) acronym (c) narrative **21-3.** (a) method of loci (b) link method.

22. **Explain how hindsight bias and overconfidence contribute to the frequent inaccuracy of eyewitness testimony.**

22-1. The frequent inaccuracy of eyewitness testimony is due in part to the reconstructive nature of memory, source monitoring, and the misinformation effect. In addition, the text points out that still another factor is our tendency to mold our interpretation of the past to fit how events actually turned out. This is called the _____ _____.

22-2. The failure to seek disconfirming evidence can often lead to the _____ effect, which is still another reason for the frequent inaccuracy of eyewitness testimony.

Answers: **22-1.** hindsight bias **22-2.** overconfidence.

REVIEW OF KEY TERMS

Anterograde amnesia
Attention
Chunk
Connectionist models
Consolidation
Decay theory
Declarative memory system
Dual-coding theory
Elaboration
Encoding
Encoding specificity principle
Episodic memory system
Explicit memory
Flashbulb memories
Forgetting curve
Hindsight bias

Implicit memory
Interference theory
Levels of processing theory
Link method
Long-term memory (LTM)
Method of loci
Misinformation effect
Mnemonic devices
Nonsense syllables
Overlearning
Parallel distributed processing (PDP) models
Proactive interference
Procedural memory system
Recall
Recognition
Rehearsal

Relearning
Repression
Retention
Retrieval
Retroactive interference
Retrograde amnesia
Schema
Semantic memory system
Semantic network
Sensory memory
Serial-position effect
Short-term memory (STM)
Source monitoring
Source monitoring error
Storage
Tip-of-the-tongue phenomenon

_____ 1. Putting coded information into memory.

_____ 2. Maintaining coded information in memory.

_____ 3. Recovering information from memory stores.

_____ 4. The process of focusing awareness on a narrowed range of stimuli or events.

_____ 5. Memory that involves the intentional recollection of previous experiences.

_____ 6. A theory that proposes that deeper levels of processing result in longer-lasting memory codes.

_____ 7. Involves linking a stimulus to other information at the time of encoding.

_____ 8. A theory that memory is enhanced by forming both semantic and visual codes since either can lead to recall.

_____ 9. Preserves information in the original sensory form for a very brief time.

_____ 10. A limited capacity memory store that can maintain unrehearsed information for 20 to 30 seconds.

_____ 11. The process of repetitively verbalizing or thinking about new information.

_____ 12. A group of familiar stimuli stored as a single unit.

_____ 13. An unlimited capacity memory store that can hold information over lengthy periods of time.

_____ 14. Unusually vivid and detailed recollections of momentous events.

_____ 15. Occurs when subjects show better recall of items at the beginning and end of a list than for items in the middle.

_____ 16. Models that assume cognitive processes depend on patterns of activation in highly interconnected computational networks that resemble neural networks.

_____ 17. The general term given to PDP models of cognitive processing wherein the information lies in the strength of the connections.

_____ 18. Memory for factual information.

_____ 19. Memory for actions, skills, and operations.

_____ 20. Memory made up of chronological, or temporally dated material.

_____ 21. Memory that contains general knowledge that is not tied to the time when the information was learned.

_____ 22. The process of making attributions about the origins of memories.

_____ 23. These consist of concepts joined together by links that show how the concepts are related.

_____ 24. An organized cluster of knowledge about a particular object or sequence of events.

_____ 25. A temporary inability to remember something you know accompanied by the feeling that it's just out of reach.

_____ 26. Consonant-vowel-consonant letter combinations that do not correspond to words (NOF, KER, etc.).

_____ 27. A curve graphing retention and forgetting over time.

_____ 28. The proportion of material remembered.

_____ 29. The ability to remember information without any cues.

_____ 30. Requires the selection of previously learned information from an array of options (e.g., multiple-choice tests).

_____ 31. Requires the memorization of information a second time to determine how much time or effort is saved.

_____ 32. Attributes forgetting to the impermanence of memory storage.

_____ 33. Attributes forgetting to competition from other material.

_____ 34. Occurs when new information impairs the retention of previously learned information.

_____ 35. Occurs when previously learned information impairs the retention of new information.

_____ 36. States that the value of a retrieval cue depends on how well it corresponds to the memory code.

_____ 37. Involves purposeful (motivated) suppression of memories.

_____ 38. A theoretical process involving the gradual conversion of information into durable memory codes stored in long-term memory.

_____ 39. The loss of memory for events that occurred prior to a brain injury.

_____ 40. The loss of memory for events that occur after a brain injury.

_____ 41. Strategies for enhancing memory.

_____ 42. The continued rehearsal of material after it has apparently been mastered.

_____ 43. Involves forming a mental image of items to be remembered in a way that connects them together.

_____ 44. A mnemonic device that involves taking an imaginary walk along a familiar path.

_____ 45. Is apparent when retention is exhibited on a task that does not require intentional remembering.

_____ 46. Occurs when a memory derived from one source is misattributed to another source.

_____ 47. Results from people putting too much faith in their estimates, beliefs and decisions, even when they should know better.

_____ 48. The tendency to mold our interpretations of the past to fit how events actually turned out.

Answers: 1. encoding **2.** storage **3.** retrieval **4.** attention **5.** explicit memory **6.** levels of processing theory **7.** elaboration **8.** dual-coding theory **9.** sensory memory **10.** short-term memory (STM) **11.** rehearsal **12.** chunk **13.** long-term memory (LTM) **14.** flashbulb memories **15.** serial position effect **16.** parallel distributed processing (PDP) models **17.** connectionist models **18.** declarative memory system **19.** procedural memory system **20.** episodic memory system **21.** semantic memory system **22.** source monitoring **23.** semantic networks **24.** schema **25.** tip-of-the-tongue phenomenon **26.** nonsense syllables **27.** forgetting curve **28.** retention **29.** recall **30.** recognition **31.** relearning **32.** decay theory **33.** interference theory **34.** retroactive interference **35.** proactive interference **36.** encoding specificity principle **37.** repression **38.** consolidation **39.** retrograde amnesia **40.** anterograde amnesia **41.** mnemonic devices **42.** overlearning **43.** link method **44.** method of loci **45.** implicit memory **46.** source-monitoring error **47.** overconfidence effect **48.** hindsight bias.

REVIEW OF KEY PEOPLE

Richard Atkinson & Richard Shiffrin   Herman Ebbinghaus   George Miller
Fergus Craik & Robert Lockhart   Elizabeth Loftus   Endel Tulvig

_____ 1. Proposed three progressively deeper levels for processing incoming information.

_____ 2. Influential in the development of the model of three different kinds of memory stores (sensory, STM and LTM).

_____ 3. Demonstrated that the reconstructive nature of memory can distort eyewitness testimony.

_____ 4. Used nonsense syllables to become famous for his forgetting curve.

_____ 5. One of his many contributions was the encoding specificity principle.

_____ 6. Proposed the concept of chunking for storing information in short-term memory.

Answers: 1. Craik & Lockhart **2.** Atkinson & Shiffrin **3.** Loftus **4.** Ebbinghaus **5.** Tulvig **6.** Miller.

SELF-QUIZ

1. Which of the following is not one of the three basic human memory processes?
   a. storage
   b. retrieval
   c. decoding
   d. encoding

2. Which one of the three levels of processing would probably be employed when attempting to memorize the following three-letter sequences WAB WAC WAD?
   a. structural
   b. semantic
   c. phonemic
   d. chunking

3. Retrieval from long-term memory is usually best when the information has been stored at which level of processing?
   a. structural
   b. semantic
   c. phonemic
   d. chunking

4. According to Paivio's dual-coding theory:
   a. words are easier to encode than images
   b. abstract words are easier to remember than concrete words
   c. visual imagery may hinder the retrieval of words
   d. concrete words are easier to remember than abstract words

5. Chunking can increase the capacity of:
   a. sensory memory
   b. short-term memory
   c. long-term memory
   d. declarative memory

6. Which of the following statements is the most accurate evaluation as to the authenticity of the recall of repressed memories?
   a. Research confirms that they are authentic.
   b. Research confirms that they are not authentic.
   c. Researchers cannot confirm or deny their authenticity.
   d. I have no idea what you're talking about.

7. You recall being lost in a shopping mall at the age of five but your parents assure you that it never happened. Errors like this are most likely due to:
   a. ineffective encoding
   b. a reality monitoring error
   c. a source monitoring error
   d. the misinformation effect

8. Which of these appear to be intimately related?
   a. implicit and procedural memory
   b. implicit and semantic memory
   c. explicit and procedural memory
   d. implicit and declarative memory

9. When you attempt to recall the name of a high school classmate by imagining yourself back in the English class with her, you are making use of:
   a. retrieval cues
   b. context cues
   c. schemas
   d. recognition cues

10. Taking this particular self-test measures your:
    a. relearning ability
    b. reconstructive ability
    c. recall ability
    d. recognition ability

11. Ineffective encoding of information may result in:
    a. the primacy effect
    b. the recency effect
    c. pseudoforgetting
    d. chunking

12. Decay theory is best able to explain the loss of memory in:
    a. sensory store
    b. long-term memory
    c. short-term memory
    d. both sensory store and short-term memory

13. When you violate the encoding specificity principle, you are likely to experience an inability to:
    a. encode information
    b. store information
    c. retrieve information
    d. connect the verbal and visual images of an experience

14. It is very easy to recall the name of your high school because it has been subjected to extensive:
    a. deep processing
    b. overlearning
    c. chunking
    d. clustering

15. Failure to seek out disconfirming evidence can often lead to:
    a. the overconfidence effect
    b. reconstructive bias
    c. hindsight bias
    d. a source monitoring error

Answers: 1. c **2.** a **3.** b **4.** d **5.** b **6.** c **7.** d **8.** a **9.** b **10.** d **11.** c **12.** d **13.** c **14.** b **15.** a.

INFOTRAC

Attention   Flashbulb Memories   Misinformation Effect

8 LANGUAGE AND THOUGHT

REVIEW OF KEY IDEAS

LANGUAGE • TURNING THOUGHTS INTO WORDS

1. **Describe the key properties of language.**

   1-1. Language is characterized by four properties: its symbolic, semantic, generative, and structured. Identify each of these properties in the following statements.

   (a) Applying rules to arrange words into phrases and sentences illustrates the _____ property of language.

   (b) Using words or geometric forms to represent objects, actions, or events illustrates the _____ property of language.

   (c) Making different words out of the same letters, such as NOW and WON, illustrates the _____ property of language.

   (d) Giving the same meaning to different words, such as chat, Katz, and cat, illustrates the _____ property of language.

   1-2. Identify the following parts (units) of language.

   (a) With around 40 of these basic sounds you can say all of the words in the English language. _____

   (b) Phonemes are combined into these smallest units of meaning in a language, which may include root words as well as prefixes and suffixes. _____

   (c) These rules specify how words can be combined into phrases and sentences. _____

   Answers: 1-1. (a) structured (b) symbolic (c) generative (d) semantic **1-2.** (a) phonemes (b) morphemes (c) syntax.

2. **Outline the development of human language during the first year.**

    2-1. Answer the following question regarding the development of language during the first year of life.

        (a) What arc a child's three major vocalizations during the first 6 months of life?

        (b) What two gradual changes occur with respect to the sounds being made during the babbling stage of language development?

        (c) What is the range in months for the babbling stage of language development?

Answers: 2-1. (a) Crying, laughing, and cooing (b) They become more complex and they increasingly resemble spoken language (c) 6 to l8 months.

3. **Describe children's early use of single words and word combinations.**

    3-1. What does the text mean when it states that the receptive vocabulary of toddlers is much larger than their productive vocabulary?

    3-2. Identify the following phenomenon observed in children's early use of language.

        (a) What phenomenon is illustrated when a child calls all four-legged creatures "doggie"?_____

        (b) What phenomenon is illustrated when a child complains to her mother, "doggie eat cookie"?_____

        (c) What phenomenon is illustrated when a child says, "doggie runned away"? _____

        (d) What phenomenon is illustrated when a child puns, "I love your "I's"?_____

        (e) Solve the following anagram that best describes how children acquire language skills. FWSYLIFT_____

Answers: 3-1. They can understand more spoken words than they can reproduce themselves. **3-2.** (a) overextensions (b) telegraphic speech (c) overregularization (d) metalinguistic awareness (e) SWIFTLY.

4. **Summarize the effect of bilingualism on language and cognitive development and the factors that influence the learning of a second language.**

    4-1. What does research comparing monolingual and bilingual children show with respect to their language and cognitive development?

4-2. What factor positively influences the learning of a second language?

Answers: 4-1. They are largely similar in their rate of development (in both areas) **4-2.** starting at an early age.

5. Compare and contrast the behaviorist, nativist, and interactionist perspectives on the development of language.

5-1. Identify the following perspectives on the development of language.

(a) This perspective places great emphasis on the role of reinforcement and imitation.

(b) This perspective assumes that children make use of an innate language acquisition device (LAD) that biologically equips them to acquire language skills.

(c) This perspective argues that while language development has a biological basis, it is also aided by social exchanges with parents and others.

5-2. Which perspective places greatest emphasis on:

(a) nature _____

(b) nurture _____

(c) nature interacting with nurture _____

Answers: 5-1. (a) nativist (b) behaviorist (c) interactionist **5-2.** (a) behaviorist (b) nativist (c) interactionist.

6. Discuss the possible evolutionary bases of language.

6-1. While it seems apparent that the ability to communicate has adaptive value, what must be demonstrated to show that evolutionary factors are at work?

Answers: 6-1. It must increase reproductive fitness (the Neanderthals became extinct and we're still here).

7. Discuss culture and language and the status of the linguistic relativity hypothesis.

7-1. According to Benjamin Whorf's linguistic relativity hypothesis, does thought determine language or does language determine thought?

7-2. What did Eleanor Rosch's experiment show when she compared the color recognition ability of English-speaking people and Dani people, who have only two words for "color"?

7-3. While language does not appear to invariably determine thought, it does appear to exert some influence over the way we approach an idea. In other words, one's language may make it either _____ or more _____ to think along certain lines.

Answers: 7-1. Language determines thought **7-2.** She found no difference (in the ability to deal with colors) **7-3.** easier, difficult.

PROBLEM SOLVING • IN SEARCH OF SOLUTIONS

8. List and describe the three types of problems proposed by Greeno.

8-1. Greeno has proposed three types of problems (*arrangement, inducing structure*, and *transformation*). Identify each of these types from their descriptions given below.

(a) This type of problem requires the problem solver to discover the relations among the parts of the problem.

(b) This type of problem requires the problem solver to place the parts in a way that satisfies some specific criterion.

(c) This type of problem requires the problem solver to carry out a sequence of changes or rearrangements in order to reach a specific goal.

8-2. Which types of Greeno's problems are represented in the following situations?

(a) What two three-letter English words can be made from the letters TBU?

(b) Fill in the missing word in, "grass is to green as snow is to _____."

(c) You need to take your child to a pediatrician, your dog to the veterinarian, and your mother to the hairdresser all within a limited time period. You think to yourself, "I'll take the kid and the dog and pick up Mom. Mom can stay with the kid at the doctor's office while I take the dog to the vet. Then I'll . . ."

Answers: 8-1. (a) arrangement (b) inducing structure (c) transformation **8-2.** (a) inducing structure (b) arrangement (c) transformation.

9. **Describe four common barriers to effective problem solving.**

   9-1. Which of the barriers to effective problem solving (*functional fixedness, unnecessary constraints, mental set,* and *irrelevant information*) are you overcoming when you:

   (a) make a financial decision without first consulting your horoscope?

   (b) teach an old dog a new trick?

   (c) use a page of newspaper as a wedge to keep a door open?

   (d) color outside the lines to make a more interesting picture?

   Answers: 9-1. (a) irrelevant information (b) mental set (c) functional fixedness (d) unnecessary constraints.

10. **Describe a variety of general problem-solving strategies.**

   10-1. The text describes several different problem-solving strategies. One of these strategies simply involves sequentially trying every possible solution, a strategy called _____ and _____.

   10-2. However, when there are a large number of potential solutions, then people often turn to a quicker "rule of thumb" approach called a _____. Which of these heuristics (*forming subgoals, working backward, searching for analogies,* or *changing the representation of the problem*) would be most applicable for solving the following problems?

   (a) While opening your car door you drop the keys. The keys hit your foot and bounce underneath the car, too far to reach. It has stopped raining so you close your umbrella and ponder how to get your keys.

   (b) You have accepted the responsibility for chairing the homecoming celebration at your school.

   (c) Alone at night in the office you observe that the ribbon is missing from a printer you want to use. After obtaining a new ribbon you can't figure out how to install it correctly. Glancing around you observe a similar printer with the ribbon installed.

   (d) You have agreed to become the campaign chairwoman of a friend who wants to run for student body president. Obviously your goal is to make your friend look like a good choice to students, but which heuristic do politicians often employ here?

Answers: 10-1. trial, error **10-2.** heuristic (a) search for analogies (the umbrella can be used as a rake) (b) form subgoals (c) work backward (see how the ribbon comes out of the intact printer) (d) change the representation of the problem (make the opponent look like a bad choice).

11. **Discuss cultural variations in cognitive style as they relate to problem solving.**

   11-1.   Answer the following true-false questions regarding the distinctions between field dependent and field independent persons and cultures.

   _____ (a) Field dependent persons are more likely to use internal cues to orient themselves in space.

   _____ (b) Field independent persons tend to analyze and restructure the physical environment rather than accepting it as it is.

   _____ (c) Persons living in cultures that depend on hunting and gathering for their subsistence are generally more field dependent than persons living in more stable agricultural societies.

   _____ (d) Persons raised in cultures with lenient child-rearing practices and an emphasis on personal autonomy tend to be more field independent.

   Answers: 11-1. (a) false (b) true (c) false (d) true.

DECISION MAKING • CHOICES AND CHANCES

12. **Compare the additive and elimination by aspects approaches to selecting an alternative.**

   12-1.   Which of these two approaches to decision making would probably be best when:

   (a) The task is complex and there are numerous alternatives?

   (b) You want to weight attributes differently based on their importance?

   Answers: 12-1. (a) elimination by aspects (b) additive.

13. **Explain the factors that individuals typically consider in risky decision making.**

   13-1.   What differentiates risky decision making from other kinds of decision making?

   13-2.   What is the most you can know when making a risky decision?

   13-3.   What two things must be known in order to calculate the expected value of making a risky decision when gambling with money?

13-4. How does the concept of subjective utility explain why some persons still engage in risky decision making when the expected value indicates the probability of a loss?

Answers: 13-1. The outcome is uncertain **13-2.** The probability of a particular outcome **13-3.** The average amount of money you could expect to win or lose with each play and the probability of a win or loss **13-4.** The personal worth of the outcome may outweigh the probability of losing.

14. Describe the availability and representativeness heuristics.

14-1. Estimating the probability of an event on the basis of how often one recalls it has been experienced in the past is what Tversky and Kahneman call a (an) _____ heuristic.

14-2. When most people are asked if there are more words that begin with N or words that have N as the third letter, they apply the availability heuristic and guess incorrectly. Explain why they do this.

14-3. Estimating the probability of an event on the basis of how similar it is to a particular model or stereotype of that event is what Tversky and Kahneman call a _____ heuristic.

14-4. "Steve is very shy. He has a high need for structure and likes detail. Is Steve more likely to be a salesperson or a librarian?" When persons are given this problem, they usually guess that he is a librarian even though there are many more salespersons than there are librarians. Explain why they do this.

Answers: 14-1. availability **14-2.** Because they can immediately recall many more words that begin with N than words having N as the third letter **14-3.** representativeness **14-4.** Because they employ the representativess heuristic and Steve fits the stereotype of a librarian.

15. Describe base rate neglect and the conjunction fallacy and their causes.

15-1. Identify which example of flawed reasoning, base rate neglect or the conjunction fallacy, is being described below.

(a) Estimating that the odds of two uncertain events happening together are greater than the odds of either event happening alone.

(b) Guessing that "Steve" is a librarian and not a salesperson.

(c) Which one of these two errors in judgment illustrates a misapplication of the representativeness heuristic?

Answers: **15-1.** (a) the conjunction fallacy (b) base rate neglect (c) base rate neglect.

16. **Explain evolutionary theorists' evaluation of cognitive research on flaws in human decision strategies.**

    16-1.   According to evolutionary theorists' is the human mind better wired to deal with:

        (a) base rates and probabilities or raw frequencies?

        (b) whole actions or parts of actions?

    16-2.   What happens when problems are reformulated in ways that resemble problems ancient humans had to face?

Answers: **16-1.** raw frequencies (b) whole actions **16-2.** the irrationality decreases (or the rationality increases).

PUTTING IT IN PERSPECTIVE

17. **Explain how this chapter highlighted four of the text's themes.**

    17-1.   Indicate which one of the four unifying themes (*the interaction of heredity and the environment, behavior is shaped by cultural heritage, the empirical nature of psychology, and the subjectivity of experience*) are best represented by the following statements.

        (a) Psychologists developed objective measures for higher mental processes thus bringing about the cognitive revolution.

        (b) Human decision making strategies are often flawed.

        (c) Neither pure nativist theories nor pure nurture theories appear to adequately explain the development of language.

        (d) Cultural variations shaped by the ecological demands of one's environment appear to somewhat affect one's cognitive style.

Answers: **17-1.** (a) the empirical nature of psychology (b) the subjectivity of experience (c) the interaction of heredity and the environment (d) behavior is shaped by cultural heritage.

18. Explain some common flaws in reasoning about decisions.

18-1. Identify which example of the flawed reasoning, the gambler's fallacy or the law of small numbers, is being described below.

(a) The belief that a small sampling of cases can be as valid as a large sampling of cases.

(b) The belief that the odds of a chance event increases if the event hasn't occurred recently.

18-2. What flaw in reasoning often results from intense media coverage of dramatic, vivid, but infrequent events.

18-3. What omission leads to the confirmation bias when making decisions?

18-4. How is the confirmation bias related to belief perseverance?

18-5. Answer the following true/false questions regarding the overconfidence effect.

_____(a) We are much less subject to this effect when making decisions about ourselves as opposed to more worldly matters.

_____(b) Scientists are not generally prone to this effect when making decisions about information in their own fields.

_____(c) In the study of college students cited by the text it was observed that the gap between personal confidence and actual accuracy of decisions increased as the confidence level increased.

Answers: **18-1.** (a) the law of small numbers (b) the gambler's fallacy **18-2.** The propensity to overestimate the improbable **18-3.** Failure to seek out disconfirming evidence **18-4.** Disconfirming evidence is subjected to little or skeptical evaluation **18-5.** (a) false (b) false (c) true.

CRITICAL THINKING APPLICATION • SHAPING THOUGHT WITH LANGUAGE: "ONLY A NAÏVE MORON WOULD BELIEVE THAT"

19. **Describe some language manipulation strategies that people use to shape others' thought.**

    19-1.   State which language manipulation strategy is being used in each of the following situations.

        (a) A politician says that his opponent "has an IQ somewhat below room temperature."

        (b) Pet owners have their pets "put to sleep" when they become terminally ill.

        (c) Only someone unbelievably stupid would be against more gun control legislation.

        (d) Insurance companies sell "life insurance" policies rather than "death benefits" policies.

    19-2.   Organizations generally prefer to slant their objectives so as to be (for/against) something when attempting to accomplish their goal.

    Answers: **19-1.** (a) name calling (b) semantic slanting (c) anticipatory name calling (d) semantic slanting **19-2.** for.

REVIEW OF KEY TERMS

Availability heuristic
Belief perseverance
Bilingualism
Cognition
Confirmation bias
Conjunction fallacy
Decision making
Fast mapping
Field dependence-independence
Functional fixedness

Gambler's fallacy
Heuristic
Insight
Language
Language acquisition device (LAD)
Linguistic relativity
Mean length of utterance (MLU)
Mental set
Metalinguistic awareness
Morphemes

Overextension
Overregularization
Phonemes
Problem solving
Representativeness heuristic
Risky decision making
Syntax
Telegraphic speech
Trial and error
Underextension

_____   1.   A collection of symbols, and rules for combining those symbols, that can be used to create an infinite variety of messages.

_____   2.   The smallest units of sound in a spoken language.

_____   3.   The smallest units of meaning in a language.

_____   4.   The rules that specify how words can be combined into phrases and sentences.

_____   5.   Using a word incorrectly to describe a wider set of objects or actions than it is meant to.

_____   6.   Occurs when a child incorrectly uses a word to describe a narrower set of objects or actions than it is meant to.

_____   7.   Consists mainly of content words with articles, prepositions, and other less-critical words omitted.

126   CHAPTER EIGHT

_____	8. The ability to reflect on the use of language.
_____	9. Basing the estimated probability of an event on the ease with which relevant instances come to mind.
_____	10. Basing the estimated probability of an event on how similar it is to the typical prototype of that event.
_____	11. The mental processes involved in acquiring knowledge.
_____	12. The tendency to perceive an item only in terms of its most common use.
_____	13. The sudden discovery of a correct solution to a problem following incorrect attempts.
_____	14. A strategy for solving problems.
_____	15. The process by which children map a word on an underlying concept after only one exposure to the word.
_____	16. The average of youngsters' spoken statements (measured in morphemes).
_____	17. Generalizing grammatical rules to irregular cases where they do not apply.
_____	18. Making decisions under conditions of uncertainty.
_____	19. A hypothetical innate mechanism or process that facilitates the learning of language.
_____	20. Persisting in using problem-solving strategies that have worked in the past.
_____	21. The theory that one's language determines one's thoughts.
_____	22. The active efforts to discover what must be done to achieve a goal that is not readily attainable.
_____	23. Trying possible solutions sequentially and discarding those that are in error until one works.
_____	24. Evaluating alternatives and making choices among them.
_____	25. The acquisition of two languages that use different speech sounds, vocabulary, and grammatical rules.
_____	26. The tendency to hang onto beliefs in the face of contradictory evidence.
_____	27. The tendency to seek information that supports one's decisions and beliefs while ignoring disconfirming evidence.
_____	28. Refers to individuals' tendency to rely primarily on external versus internal frames of reference when orienting themselves in space.
_____	29. The belief that the odds of a chance event increase if the event hasn't occurred recently.
_____	30. Occurs when people estimate the odds of two uncertain events happening are greater than either event happening alone.

Answers: 1. language **2.** phonemes **3.** morphemes **4.** syntax **5.** overextensions **6.** underextensions **7.** telegraphic speech **8.** metalinguistic awareness **9.** availability heuristic **10.** representativeness heuristic **11.** cognition **12.** functional fixedness **13.** insight **14.** heuristic **15.** fast mapping **16.** mean length of utterances (MLU) **17.** overregularization **18.** risky decision making **19.** language acquisition device (LAD) **20.** mental set **21.** linguistic relativity **22.** problem solving **23.** trial and error **24.** decision making **25.** bilingualism **26.** belief perseverance **27.** confirmation bias **28.** field dependence-independence **29.** gambler's fallacy **30.** conjunction fallacy.

REVIEW OF KEY PEOPLE

Noam Chomsky   Herbert Simon   B. F. Skinner
Daniel Kahneman and Amos Tversky

_____   1.   Won the Nobel Prize for his research on decision making and artificial
                                  intelligence.

_____   2.   Proposed that children learn language through the established principles of
                                  learning.

_____   3.   Proposed that children learn language through a biologically built-in language
                                  acquisition device.

_____   4.   Performed research that showed people base probability estimates on
                                  heurestics that do not always yield reasonable estimates of success.

Answers: 1. Simon **2.** Skinner **3.** Chomsky **4.** Kahneman and Tversky.

SELF-QUIZ

1. The word SLOWLY would be an example of a:
    a. metalinguistic
    b. phoneme
    c. syntactical unit
    d. morpheme

2. Which of the following words best describes the speed at which children acquire language skills?
    a. slowly
    b. swiftly
    c. haltingly
    d. grudgingly

3. When a child says that TUB and BUT are constructed of the same three letters, she is showing an awareness of:
    a. morphemes
    b. phonemes
    c. metalinguistics
    d. syntax

4. The fact that children appear to learn rules, rather than specific word combinations, when acquiring language
    skills argues most strongly against which theory of language development?
    a. cognitive
    b. behaviorist
    c. nativist
    d. interactionist

5. Which of the following is not one of the basic properties of language?
    a. generative
    b. symbolic
    c. structured
    d. alphabetical

6. According to the text, which factor positively influences the learning of a second language?
   a. beginning only after mastering one's native language
   b. being a good listener
   c. beginning at an early age
   d. being wealthy

7. Which barrier to problem solving are you overcoming when you use a piece of paperclip as a temporary replacement for the screw that fell out of your glasses?
   a. irrelevant information
   b. functional fixedness
   c. mental set
   d. unnecessary constraints

8. Which of the following heuristics would you probably employ if assigned the task of carrying out a school election?
   a. work backward
   b. representativeness
   c. search for analogies
   d. form subgoals

9. Which one of Greeno's problems is exemplified by the anagram?
   a. arrangement
   b. inducing structure
   c. transformation
   d. chunking

10. When faced with having to choose among numerous alternatives, most persons will opt for:
    a. an elimination by aspects approach
    b. an additive approach
    c. a means/end analysis
    d. a subjective-utility model

11. As compared to field dependent persons, field independent persons are more likely to come from cultures that:
    a. discourage lenient child-rearing practices
    b. depend on a stable agricultural base
    c. encourage personal autonomy
    d. encourage group cohesiveness

12. Most persons mistakenly believe that more people die from tornadoes than from asthma. This is because they mistakenly apply:
    a. a means/end analysis
    b. a compensatory decision model
    c. an availability heuristic
    d. a representativeness heuristic

13. Failure to actively seek out contrary evidence may lead to:
    a. overestimating the improbable
    b. the conjunction fallacy
    c. the gambler's fallacy
    d. the confirmation bias

14. Owners of automobile junkyards prefer to use the term automobile recycling centers. This is an example of the use of:
    a. framing
    b. semantic slanting
    c. anticipatory name calling
    d. subjective utility

15. Which of the following perhaps best illustrates the interaction effect of both heredity and environment on behavior?
    a. the development of language skills in a child
    b. the development of field independence in nomadic cultures
    c. the development of problem-solving skills in experts
    d. the development of the overconfidence effect in all of us

Answers: **1.** d **2.** b **3.** c **4.** b **5.** d **6.** c **7.** b **8.** d **9.** a **10.** a **11.** c **12.** c **13.** d **14.** b **15.** a.

INFOTRAC

Bilingualism   Mental Set   Risky Decision Making

INTELLIGENCE AND PSYCHOLOGICAL TESTING

REVIEW OF KEY IDEAS

KEY CONCEPTS IN PSYCHOLOGICAL TESTING

1. **List and describe the principle categories of psychological tests.**

   1-1. Most psychological tests can be placed into one of two very broad categories. These two categories are: _____ _____ tests and _____ tests.

   1-2. There are three categories of mental abilities tests. Below are examples of each of these categories. Identify them.

       (a) The ACT and SAT tests you may have taken before entering college are examples of _____ tests.

       (b) The exams you frequently take in your introductory psychology class are examples of _____ tests.

       (c) Tests used to demonstrate general intellectual giftedness are examples of _____ tests.

   1-3. Personality tests allow an individual to compare himself or herself to other persons with respect to particular personality _____. Personality tests generally (<u>do/do not</u>) have right and wrong answers.

   Answers: **1-1.** mental ability, personality **1-2.** (a) aptitude (b) achievement (c) intelligence **1-3.** characteristics or traits, do not.

2. **Discuss the concepts of standardization and test norms.**

   2-1. Developing test norms and uniform procedures for use in the administration and scoring of a test is the general idea behind test _____.

2-2. In order to interpret a particular score on a test it is necessary to know how other persons score on this test. This is the purpose of test _____. An easy method for providing comparisons of test scores is to convert the raw scores into _____ scores.

Answers: 2-1. standardization 2-2. norms, percentile.

3. Explain the meaning of test reliability and validity and how they are estimated.

3-1. The ability of a test to produce consistent results across subsequent measurements of the same persons is known as its _____. The ability of a test to actually measure what it claims to measure is known as its _____.

3-2. Readministering the same test to the same group of persons in a week or two following the original testing allows one to estimate the _____ of a test. If a test is highly reliable, then a person's scores on the two different administrations will be very similar. The amount of similarity can be assessed by means of the _____ coefficient.

3-3. There are three general kinds of validity (*content, criterion-related, and construct*). Identify each of these kinds from the descriptions given below.

(a) This kind of validity will tend to be high when, for example, scores on the ACT and SAT actually predict success in college.

(b) This kind of validity will be of particular importance to you when taking your exams for this class. It will be high if the exam sticks closely to the explicitly assigned material.

(c) This kind of validity is more vague than the other two kinds and refers to the ability of a test to measure abstract qualities, such as intelligence.

3-4. As with the estimation of reliability, the estimation of validity often makes use of the _____ _____.

Answers: 3-1. reliability, validity 3-2. reliability, correlation 3-3. (a) criterion-related validity (b) content validity (c) construct validity 3-4. correlation coefficient.

THE EVOLUTION OF INTELLIGENCE TESTING

4. Summarize the contributions of Galton, Binet, Terman, and Wechsler to the evolution of intelligence testing.

4-1. Identify each of the above men from the descriptions of their contributions given below.

(a) This man developed the first useful intelligence test. His tests were used to predict success in school, and scores were expressed in terms of mental age. _____

(b) This man revised Binet's tests to produce the Stanford-Binet Intelligence Scale, the standard for all future intelligence tests. _____

(c) This man began the quest to measure intelligence. He assumed that intelligence was mainly inherited and could be measured by assessing sensory acuity. _____

(d) This man developed the first successful test of adult intelligence, the WAIS. He also developed new intelligence tests for children. _____

(e) In developing his new intelligence tests, this man added many non-verbal items, which allowed for the separate assessment of both verbal and non-verbal abilities. He also replaced the IQ score with one based on the normal distribution. _____

Answers: 4-1. (a) Binet (b) Terman (c) Galton (d) Wechsler (e) Wechsler.

BASIC QUESTIONS ABOUT INTELLIGENCE TESTING

5. **Explain the meaning of an individual's score on a modern intelligence test.**

   5-1.   Answer the following questions regarding intelligence test scores.

   (a) In what manner is human intelligence assumed to be distributed?

   (b) What percentage of people have an IQ score below 100?

   (c) What percentage of persons would score two or more standard deviations above the mean? (see Fig. 9.6 in the text)

   Answers: 5-1. (a) It forms a normal distribution (bell curve) (b) 50 percent (c) approximately 2 percent.

6. **Describe the reliability and validity of modern intelligence tests.**

   6-1.   Answer the following questions about the reliability of modern intelligence tests.

   (a) What kind of reliability estimates (correlation coefficients) are found with most modern intelligence tests?

   (b) What might be a problem here with respect to an individual's test score?

6-2. Answer the following questions with respect to the validity of modern intelligence tests.

    (a) What is the correlation between IQ tests and grades in school?

    (b) What is the correlation between IQ tests and the number of years of schooling that people complete?

    (c) What might be a general problem with assuming intelligence tests are a valid measure of general mental ability?

Answers: **6-1.** (a) They are in the low .90's (b) Temporary conditions could lower the score **6-2.** (a) .50 to .60 (b) .60 to .80 (c) They principally focus on academic/verbal intelligence and ignore other kinds of intelligence.

7. Discuss how well IQ scores predict vocational success.

7-1. Is the ability of intelligence tests to predict vocational success much higher or much lower than their ability to predict academic success?

7-2. What kind of tests are psychologists now trying to develop to aid employers in their hiring decisions?

Answers: **7-1.** much lower **7-2.** tests of practical intelligence.

HEREDITY AND ENVIRONMENT AS DETERMINANTS OF INTELLIGENCE

8. Summarize evidence from twin studies and adoption studies on whether heredity affects intelligence and discuss the concept of heritability.

8-1. Below are the mean correlations for the intelligence of three different groups of children: *fraternal twins reared together, identical twins reared apart, and identical twins reared together.* Match the group with the appropriate correlation.

.86 _____   .60 _____

.72 _____

8-2. What do the above correlations tell us about the role of heredity on intelligence?

8-3. What relationship has been found between the intelligence of children adopted out at birth and their biological parents?

8-4. The consensus estimate of experts is that the heritability ratio for human intelligence hovers around 60 percent. What does this mean?

8-5. Why can you not use a heritability ratio to explain a particular individual's intelligence?

Answers: **8-1.** (.86) identical twins reared together (.72) identical twins reared apart (.60) fraternal twins reared together **8-2.** That heredity plays a significant role in intelligence **8-3.** There is a significant correlation in intelligence **8-4.** The variation in intelligence in a particular group is estimated to be 60% due to heredity, leaving 40% for environmental factors **8-5.** It is a group statistic and may give misleading results when applied to particular individuals.

9. Summarize evidence from research on adoption, environmental deprivation or enrichment, and home environment showing how experience shapes intelligence.

9-1. Complete the statements below that list three findings from adoption studies indicating that environment influences intelligence.

(a) There is (no/some) relationship between the intelligence of adopted children and their foster parents.

(b) Siblings reared together are more alike than siblings _____ _____.

(c) Unrelated children reared together show a significant positive relationship with respect to their _____.

9-2. What effects on intelligence have been found among children reared in deprived environments?

9-3. What effects on intelligence have been found among children moved from deprived environments to more enriched environments?

Answers: **9-1.** (a) some (b) reared apart (c) intelligence **9-2.** There is a gradual decrease in intelligence across time **9-3.** There is a gradual increase in intelligence across time .

10. **Using the concept of reaction range, explain how heredity and the environment interact to affect intelligence.**

   10-1. The notion behind the concept of reaction range is that heredity places an upper and lower _____ on how much an individual can vary with respect to a characteristic such as intelligence. The reaction range for human intelligence is said to be around _____ IQ points.

   10-2. This means that a child with an average IQ of 100 can vary between 90 and 110 IQ points, depending on the kind of _____ he or she experiences.

   10-3. The major point here is that the limits for intelligence are determined by _____ factors and the movement within these limits is determined by _____ factors.

   Answers: **10-1.** limit, 20-25 **10-2.** environment **10-3.** genetic or hereditary, environmental.

11. **Discuss proposed explanations for cultural differences in IQ scores.**

   11-1. Three explanations for the cultural differences in IQ scores are listed below. Tell what each of these explanations means.

   (a) Jensen's heritability explanation.

   (b) Cultural disadvantage.

   (c) Cultural bias in IQ tests.

   11-2. Which of these theories is best supported by research?

   Answers: **11-1.** (a) The cultural differences are due to heredity (b) The cultural differences are due to environmental factors (c) IQ tests are biased in favor of persons from white middle-class backgrounds **11-2.** cultural disadvantage.

NEW DIRECTIONS IN THE ASSESSMENT AND STUDY OF INTELLIGENCE

12. **Describe new trends in the assessment and study of intelligence.**

   12-1. Answer the following questions regarding new trends in the assessment and study of intelligence.

   (a) One trend is that two kinds of tests are replacing intelligence tests in many school districts. What kinds of tests are these?

(b) A second trend concerns the search for biological correlates of intelligence. What biologically oriented approach to assessing intelligence, measuring reaction times or inspection times, appears to be the more promising?

Answers: 12-1. (a) achievement and aptitude tests (b) measuring inspection times.

13. **Describe Sternberg's and Gardner's theories of intelligence.**

    13-1. Sternberg's triarchic theory proposes that intelligence is composed of three basic parts. Match these parts with their individual functions:

        _____ Contextual subtheory   (a) Emphasizes the role played by society.

        _____ Experiential subtheory   (b) Emphasizes the cognitive processes underlying intelligence.

        _____ Componential subtheory   (c) Emphasizes the interplay between intelligence and experience.

    13-2. Gardner has proposed seven relatively distinct human intelligences. What does his research show with respect to a general ("g") factor among these separate intelligences?

Answers: 13-1. contextual (a), experiential (c), componential (b) **13-2.** There does not appear to be a general ("g") factor; rather, people display a mix of strong, weak, and intermediate abilities.

PUTTING IT IN PERSPECTIVE

14. **Discuss how the chapter highlighted three of the text's unifying themes.**

    14-1. Answer the following questions about the three unifying themes (*cultural factors shape behavior, heredity and environment jointly influence behavior, and psychology evolves in a sociohistorical content*).

    (a) What theme is exemplified by the continuing involvement of psychologists in the debate about the roots of racial and ethnic differences in intelligence?

    (b) What theme is exemplified by the different views about the nature of intelligence held by Western and non-Western cultures.

    (c) What theme is exemplified by the extensive research using twin studies, adoption studies, and family studies?

Answers: 14-1. (a) Psychology evolves in a sociohistorical context. (b) Cultural factors shape behavior. (c) Heredity and environment jointly influence behavior.

PERSONAL APPLICATION • MEASURING AND UNDERSTANDING CREATIVITY

15. **Discuss the nature of creativity and summarize how well creativity tests predict creative achievement.**

   15-1.   In addition to being original and novel, what other characteristic must a creative idea have?

   15-2.   Popular notions about creativity would have us believe that creative ideas arise from nowhere, occur in a burst of insight, and are not related to hard work or intelligence. What does the text say about these notions?

   15-3.   Creativity tests are rather (<u>good/mediocre</u>) predictors of creativity in the real world. One reason for this is that they attempt to treat creativity as a (<u>specific/general</u>) trait while research evidence seems to show it is related to quite _____ domains.

   Answers: 15-1. It must be useful (appropriate to the situation and problem). **15-2** They are all false. **15-3.** mediocre, general, specific.

16. **Discuss associations between creativity and personality, intelligence, and mental illness.**

   16-1.   What two traits appear to be at the core of the personality characteristics common to creative people?

   16-2.   What is the intelligence level of most highly creative people?

   16-3.   What form of mental illness appears to be associated with creative achievement?

   Answers: 16-1. autonomy and independence **16-2.** average to above average **16-3.** mood disorders.

CRITICAL THINKING APPLICATION • THE INTELLIGENCE DEBATE, APPEALS TO IGNORANCE, AND REIFICATION

17. **Explain how appeals to ignorance and reification have cropped up in numerous debates about intelligence.**

   17-1.   Tell whether the following statements represent examples of appeals to ignorance or to reification.

(a) He doesn't do very well in college because he's lacking in intelligence.

(b) Since educational enrichment programs like Head Start have failed to produce substantial long-term gains in IQ, then intelligence must be mostly inherited.

(c) More money should be spent on research to find the accurate heritability coefficient of intelligence.

Answers: 17-1. (a) reification (b) appeals to ignorance (c) reification.

REVIEW OF KEY TERMS

Achievement tests
Aptitude tests
Construct validity
Content validity
Convergent thinking
Correlation coefficient
Creativity
Criterion-related validity
Deviation IQ scores
Divergent thinking

Heritability ratio
Intelligence quotient (IQ)
Intelligence tests
Mental age
Normal distribution
Percentile score
Personality tests
Psychological test

Reaction range
Reification
Reliability
Standardization
Test norms
Test-retest reliability
Validity

_____ 1. A standardized measure of a sample of a person's behavior.

_____ 2. Tests that measure general mental ability.

_____ 3. Tests that measure various personality traits.

_____ 4. Tests that assess talent for specific kinds of learning.

_____ 5. Tests that gauge the mastery and knowledge of various subject areas.

_____ 6. The development of uniform procedures for administering and scoring tests, including the development of test norms.

_____ 7. Data that provides information about the relative standing of a particular test score.

_____ 8. Number indicating the percentage of people who score above or below a particular test score.

_____ 9. The measurement consistency of a test.

_____ 10. Estimated by comparing subjects' scores on two administrations of the same test.

_____ 11. The ability of a test to measure what it was designed to measure.

_____ 12. The degree to which the content of a test is representative of the domain it is supposed to measure.

_____ 13. The degree to which the scores on a particular test correlate with scores on an independent criterion (test).

_____ 14. The degree to which there is evidence that a test measures a hypothetical construct.

_____ 15. A score indicating the mental ability typical of a chronological age group.

_____	16.	Mental age divided by chronological age and multiplied by 100.
_____	17.	A symmetrical, bell-shaped curve that describes the distribution of many physical and psychological attributes.
_____	18.	Scores that translate raw scores into a precise location in the normal distribution.
_____	19.	An estimate of the percentage of variation in a trait determined by genetic inheritance.
_____	20.	Genetically determined limits on intelligence.
_____	21.	The generation of ideas that are original, novel, and useful.
_____	22.	Thinking that attempts to narrow down a list of alternatives to a single best solution.
_____	23.	Thinking that attempts to expand the range of alternatives by generating many possible solutions.
_____	24.	A numerical index of the degree of relationship between two variables.
_____	25.	Occurs when a hypothetical, abstract concept is given a name and then treating it as though it were a concrete, tangible object.

Answers: 1. psychological tests **2.** intelligence tests **3.** personality tests **4.** aptitude tests **5.** achievement tests **6.** standardization **7.** test norms **8.** percentile score **9.** reliability **10.** test-retest reliability **11.** validity **12.** content validity **13.** criterion-related validity **14.** construct validity **15.** mental age **16.** intelligence quotient (IQ) **17.** normal distribution **18.** deviation IQ scores **19.** heritability ratio **20.** reaction range **21.** creativity **22.** convergent thinking **23.** divergent thinking **24.** correlation coefficient **25.** reification.

REVIEW OF KEY PEOPLE

Alfred Binet
Sir Francis Galton
Howard Gardner

Arthur Jensen
Sandra Scar
Robert Sternberg

Lewis Terman
David Wechsler

_____	1.	Developed the Standford-Binet Intelligence Scale.
_____	2.	Developed the first successful test of adult intelligence.
_____	3.	Postulated a cognitive triarchic theory of intelligence.
_____	4.	Proposed a reaction range model for human intelligence.
_____	5.	Developed the first useful intelligence test.
_____	6.	Postulated a heritability explanation for cultural differences in intelligence.
_____	7.	Began the quest to measure intelligence.
_____	8.	Has proposed the existence of a number of autonomous human intelligences.

Answers: 1. Terman **2.** Wechsler **3.** Sternberg **4.** Scarr **5.** Binet **6.** Jensen **7.** Galton **8.** Gardner.

SELF-QUIZ

1. This self-test you are now taking is an example of:
   a. an aptitude test
   b. an achievement test
   c. an intelligence test
   d. a criterion-related test

2. Which of the following statistics is generally used to estimate reliability and validity?
   a. the correlation coefficient
   b. the standard deviation
   c. the percentile score
   d. the median

3. What kind of validity do tests such as the SAT and ACT particularly strive for?
   a. content validity
   b. construct validty
   c. absolute validity
   d. criterion-related validity

4. If a psychologist readministers the same test to the same individuals following a two-week interval, she is probably interested in the test's:
   a. reliability
   b. standardization
   c. validity
   d. norms

5. With respect to modern intelligence tests:
   a. reliability is generally higher than validity
   b. validity is generally higher than reliability
   c. reliability and validity are about the same
   d. I have no idea what you are talking about

6. If the heritability ratio for intelligence is 80%, this means that for you as an individual 80% of your intelligence is determined by heredity and 20% is determined by your environment. This statement is:
   a. true
   b. false

7. Perhaps the strongest evidence for a heredity factor for intelligence comes from studies of:
   a. unrelated children reared together
   b. deprived home environments
   c. enriched home environments
   d. identical twins reared apart

8. If the reaction range concept of human intelligence is correct, then a child with exactly normal intelligence will probably not exceed an IQ of:
   a. 107
   b. 112
   c. 122
   d. 130

9. IQ tests are fairly good predictors of:
   a. academic success
   b. vocational success
   c. creativity
   d. social success

10. What effect has been found among children moved from deprived to enriched environments?
    a. they abruptly increase in intelligence
    b. they gradually increase in intelligence
    c. they show no change in intelligence
    d. they gradually decrease in intelligence

11. Which of the following groups shows the highest correlation with respect to intelligence?
    a. fraternal twins reared together
    b. fraternal twins reared apart
    c. identical twins reared apart
    d. adoptive children and their biological parents

12. Which of the following explanations for the racial differences in intelligence is best supported by research evidence?
    a. Jensen's heritability theory
    b. cultural bias in IQ tests
    c. cultural disadvantage
    d. Watson's differential conditioning theory

13. Which of the following statements regarding creativity is correct?
    a. Creativity appears to be a general trait.
    b. Divergent thinking is the key ingredient of creativity.
    c. Creativity tests are excellent predictors of future creativity.
    d. Creativity appears to be related to specific domains.

14. What form of mental illness has been frequently found to be associated with outstanding creative ability?
    a. anxiety disorders
    b. mood disorders
    c. schizophrenia
    d. antisocial personality

15. Which of the following statements is an example of reification?
    a. Birds of a feather flock together.
    b. Creative people are born not raised.
    c. She gets good grades in school because she is intelligent.
    d. Intelligence tests are only moderate predictors of vocational success.

Answers: 1. b 2. a 3. d 4. a 5. a 6. b 7. d 8. b 9. a 10. b 11. c 12. c 13. d 14. b 15. c.

INFOTRAC

Achievement Tests   Aptitude Tests   Intelligence Tests

10 MOTIVATION AND EMOTION

REVIEW OF KEY IDEAS

MOTIVATIONAL THEORIES AND CONCEPTS

1. **Distinguish between the two major categories of motives found in humans.**

   1-1. Most theories of motivation distinguish between _____ motives (e.g., for food, water, sex, warmth) and _____ motives. In general biological needs are essential for the _____ of the group or individual.

   1-2. Social motives (e.g., for achievement, autonomy, affiliation) are acquired as a result of people's experiences. While there are relatively few biological needs, people theoretically may acquire an unlimited number of _____ needs.

   Answers: 1-1. biological, social, survival **1-2.** social.

THE MOTIVATION OF HUNGER AND EATING

2. **Summarize evidence on the areas of the brain implicated in the regulation of hunger.**

   2-1. Within the brain the major structure implicated in eating behavior is the _____.

   2-2. Researchers used to think that eating was controlled by "on" and "off" centers in the hypothalamus. When the lateral hypothalamus (LH) was destroyed, animals stopped eating, as if hunger had been turned off like a switch. When the ventromedial hypothalamus (VMH) was destroyed, animals started to eat. While these structures are still considered important in hunger regulation, researchers now believe that eating is controlled to a greater extent by complex (neural circuits/anatomical centers) rather than (neural circuits/anatomical centers) in the brain.

   Answers: 2-1. hypothalamus **2-2.** neural circuits, anatomical centers.

3. **Summarize evidence on how fluctuations in blood glucose and insulin affect hunger.**

   3-1.   Much of the food we consume is converted into _____, a simple sugar that is an important source of energy.

   3-2.   Based on research findings about glucose, Mayer proposed the theory that there are specialized neurons, which he called _____, that function to monitor glucose levels in the blood. Lower levels of glucose are associated with a/an (<u>increase/decrease</u>) in hunger. (While glucostats were originally thought to be in the brain, their location and exact nature remain obscure.)

   3-3.   For cells to extract glucose from the blood, the hormone _____ must be present. Insulin will produce a/an (<u>increase/decrease</u>) in the level of sugar in the blood, with the result that the person experiences a (an) (<u>increase/decrease</u>) in the sensation of hunger. Thus, insulin is another factor contributing to hunger.

   Answers: **3-1.** glucose **3-2.** glucostats, increase **3-3.** insulin, decrease, increase.

4. **Summarize evidence how culture, learning, food cues, and stress influence hunger.**

   4-1.   Although we have some innate taste preferences (e.g., for fat), it is also clear that _____ affects some of our food choices and even influences the amounts that we eat. For example, taste preferences and aversions may be learned by pairing a taste with pleasant or unpleasant experiences, the process of _____ conditioning.

   4-2.   In addition, we are more likely to eat food that we see others eating, especially if the others are parents or friends. Thus, food preferences are acquired indirectly through the process of _____ learning as well as directly through conditioning.

   4-3.   Most people also experience hunger based on the appearance, taste, and smell of food and the effort involved in securing food. These and other food-related _____ in our environments clearly affect when and what we eat.

   4-4.   Besides affecting eating habits and providing cues to eating, the environment may also provide unpleasant or frustrating events that produce emotional _____, a factor that may also trigger eating in many people. Although stress and increased eating are linked, recent evidence suggests that the important factor may be heightened physiological _____ accompanying stress rather than the stress itself.

   Answers: **4-1.** learning (environment, culture), classical **4-2.** observational **4-3.** cues **4-4.** stress, arousal.

5. **Outline the four phases of the human sexual response.**

   5-1.   Write the names of the four phases of the human sexual response in the order in which they occur. (Hint: I made up a mnemonic device that's hard to forget. The first letter of each phase name produces EPOR, which happens to be ROPE spelled backward.)

(a) _____

(b) _____

(c) _____

(d) _____

5-2. In the blanks below write the first letter of each phase name that correctly labels the descriptions below.

_____ Rapid increase in arousal (respiration, heart rate, blood pressure, etc.)

_____ Vasocongestion of blood vessels in sexual organs; lubrication in female

_____ Continued arousal, but at a slower place

_____ Tightening of the vaginal entrance

_____ Pulsating muscular contractions and ejaculation

_____ Physiological changes produced by arousal subside

_____ Includes a refractory period for men

Answers: 5-1. (a) excitement (b) plateau (c) orgasm (d) resolution **5-2.** E, E, P, P, O, R, R.

6. Discuss parental investment theory and findings on human gender differences in sexual activity.

6-1. Triver's parental investment theory is the idea that a species' mating patterns are determined by the *investment* each sex must make to produce and nurture offspring. Since human females are the ones who are pregnant for nine months and subsequently breast feed the offspring, their _____ in the child is, by this analysis, greater than that of human males.

6-2. Parental investment theory is that idea that the sex that makes the smaller investment will compete in order to have mating opportunities with the sex that makes the larger investment, and that the sex that makes the larger investment will be more selective of partners. Thus, males of many mammalian species, including human beings, seek to maximize their reproductive potential by mating with (<u>as many/as few</u>) females as possible. Females, on the other hand, optimize their reproductive potential by being (<u>selective/ unrestricted</u>) in mating.

6-3. In line with predictions from parental investment theory and evolutionary theory in general, several studies have found that in comparison to women, men will show (1) (<u>more/less</u>) interest in sexual activity in general, (2) desire for a greater _____ of sexual partners, and (3) more willingness to engage in (<u>casual/committed</u>) sex.

Answers: 6-1. investment **6-2.** as many, selective **6-3.** more, variety (number), casual.

7. Discuss evolutionary analyses of gender differences in mating preferences and relationship jealousy.

7-1. To test their hypotheses about mating preferences, evolutionary theorists tend to emphasize research done (in <u>the United States/cross-culturally</u>).

7-2.   The cross-cultural data tend to support the evolutionary theory, although there are viable alternative explanations. According to the evolutionary research, what characteristics do human females look for in a male partner? What do males look for in a female partner?

7-3.   Evolutionary psychologists explain gender differences in jealousy as follows. Paternity (who the father is) is not always certain. Maternity is certain. Thus, if males want to make sure that they pass on their genes, they must be concerned with paternity, and their jealousy relates to (sexual/emotional) infidelity. For females, on the other hand, certain that the child is theirs, the continued availability of the male partner's resources and, hence, his (sexual/emotional) commitment, is the more important factor. Again, cross-cultural data are available that support the evolutionary case.

7-4.   What conclusions can reasonably be drawn from the data obtained from the evolutionary theorists? Place T or F in the blanks.

   _____ Differences in mating preferences and jealousy tended to be universal across cultures.

   _____ The data are consistent with evolutionary theories of sexual motivation.

   _____ The data may be explained by alternative interpretations that do not derive from evolutionary theory.

Answers: 7-1. cross-culturally 7-2. According to the evolutionary theory, women want men who will be able to acquire resources that can be invested in children, men with education, money, status, and ambition. Men, on the other hand, want women who have good breeding potential, women who are beautiful, youthful, and in good health (as summed up in the song *Summertime* from Gerschwin's *Porgy and Bess*, "Oh, your daddy's rich, and your ma is good looking."). 7-3. sexual, emotional 7-4. All of these statements are true or represent reasonable inferences. Some differences were universal, and the data are consistent with evolutionary theories. At the same time there are alternative explanations involving the fact of discrimination against women in virtually all societies.

8.   Summarize evidence on the nature of sexual orientation and on how common homosexuality is.

8-1.   Sexual orientation refers to a person's preference for emotional and sexual relationships with individuals of the other sex, the same sex, or either sex. Those who prefer relationships with the other sex are termed _____ , with the same sex _____ , and with either sex _____ .

8-2.   Because people may have experienced homosexuality in varying degrees, it seems reasonable to consider sexual orientation as a/an (continuum/all-or-none distinction). In part because of this definitional problem and in part due to prejudice against homosexuals, it is difficult to determine precisely the proportion of homosexuals in the population. A frequently cited statistics is 10%, but recent survey place the proportion somewhere between _____ .

Answers: 8-1. heterosexuals (straights), homosexuals (gays or lesbians), bisexuals 8-2. continuum, 5-8%. See Figure 10.12 in your text for more detailed information.

9. Summarize evidence on the determinants of sexual orientation.

9-1. What factors determine sexual orientation? Psychoanalysts thought the answer involved some aspect of the parent-child relationship. Behaviorists assumed that it was due to the association of same-sex stimuli with sexual arousal. Thus, both psychoanalytic and behavioral theorists proposed (environmental/ biological) explanations of homosexuality.

9-2. Extensive research on the upbringing of homosexuals has (supported/not supported) the idea that homosexuality is largely explainable in terms of environmental factors.

9-3. Recent studies have produced evidence that homosexuality is in part genetic. Which of the following types of studies have supported this conclusion? (Place Y for yes or N for no in the blanks.)

_____ Studies of hormonal differences between heterosexuals and homosexuals.

_____ Studies of twins and adopted children.

_____ Autopsy studies of the hypothalamus.

_____ Differences in genetic material on the X chromosome.

9-4. Subjects in one of the studies described were gay men who had either identical twin brothers, fraternal twin brothers, or adopted brothers. For each of the categories what percent of the brothers of the subjects were also gay? Place the appropriate percentages in the blanks: 22%, 11%, 52%.

_____ Identical twins

_____ Fraternal twins

_____ Adopted brothers

9-5. LeVay (1991) has reported that a cluster of neurons in the anterior _____ is (smaller/ larger) in gay men than in straight men. Since all of the gay men in this study had died of AIDS, which itself may produce changes in brain structure, these findings should be interpreted with caution. Nonetheless, these data support the idea that there are (environmental/biological) factors that are related to sexual orientation.

9-6. Many theorists also suspect that secretions of _____ during prenatal development may be involved.

9-7. While much of the evidence points toward biological factors, the fact that identical twins turn out to share sexual orientation only half of the time suggests that _____ factors are involved in some way. Exactly what those factors might be is unknown, however.

Answers: 9-1. environmental **9-2.** not supported **9-3.** N, Y, Y, Y **9-4.** 52%, 22%, 11%. Note that a companion study for lesbians found similar results. **9-5.** hypothalamus, smaller, biological **9-6.** hormones **9-7.** environmental.

10. **Describe the achievement motive and discuss how individual differences in the need for achievement influence behavior.**

   10-1. People with high achievement motivation have a need to:

   a. master difficult challenges

   b. outperform others

   c. excel and compete

   d. all of the above

   10-2. What is the relationship between estimates of achievement motive in a country and the economic growth of that county?

   10-3. The procedure used for measuring need for achievement is the same as that used to measure need for affiliation: subjects tell stories about pictures shown in the _____.

   10-4. How do people who score high on need for affiliation differ from those who score low?

   Answers: 10-1. d **10-2.** Countries with estimated high achievement motivation have higher economic growth (and greater productivity in general). **10-3.** TAT **10-4.** They tend to work hard, compete, be persistent, delay gratification, and be successful in their careers.

11. **Explain how situational factors and fear of failure affect achievement strivings.**

   11-1. According to Atkinson's elaboration of McClelland's views, achievement-oriented behavior is deter-mined not only by (1) achievement motivation but by (2) the _____ that success will occur and (3) the incentive _____ of success.

   11-2. As the difficulty of a task increases, the _____ of success at the task decreases. At the same time, success at harder tasks may be more satisfying, so the _____ value of the task is likely to increase. Thus, when both the incentive value and probability of success are weighed together, people with a high need for achievement would tend to select tasks of (<u>extreme/moderate</u>) difficulty.

   11-3. What motivates you, is it the desire for success or the fear of failure? Atkinson has included another factor in the equation. In some situations people are driven to achieve not only because they want success but because they are motivated to avoid _____.

   Answers: 11-1. probability, value **11-2.** probability, incentive, moderate **11-3.** failure.

12. **Describe the cognitive component of emotion.**

    12-1.   The word *cognition* refers to thoughts, beliefs, or conscious experience. When faced with an ugly-looking insect (or, for some people, being on the edge of a cliff or having to make a speech in public), you might say to yourself, "This is terrifying (or maybe disgusting)." This thought or cognition has an *evaluative* aspect: we assess our emotions as pleasant or unpleasant. Thus, one component of emotion is the _____ component, which includes _____ in terms of pleasantness-unpleasantness.

    Answers: 12-1. cognitive, evaluation.

13. **Describe the physiological underpinnings of emotion.**

    13-1.   The second component of emotion is the _____ component, primarily actions of the _____ nervous system. Your encounter with the insect might be accompanied by changes in heart rate, breathing, or blood pressure–or by increased electrical conductivity of the skin known as the _____ skin response (GSR).

    13-2.   Lie detectors don't actually detect lies, they detect _____ reflected by changes in heart rate, respiration, and GSR. Emotion does not necessarily reflect lying, however. Because of (<u>relatively high/very low</u>) error rates, polygraph results (<u>can/cannot</u>) be used as evidence in most courtrooms.

    13-3.   Recent evidence suggests that the brain structure known as the _____ plays a central role in emotion. For example, research has found that animals who have their amygdala's destroyed cannot learn classically conditioned _____ responses.

    13-4.   The amygdala doesn't process emotion by itself but is at the core of a complex set of neural circuits. Sensory information relating to fear arrives at the thalamus and from there is relayed along two pathways, to the nearby _____ and also to areas in the _____.

    13-5.   The amygdala processes information extremely rapidly, which has clear _____ value for the organism in threatening situations. The cortex responds more slowly but in greater detail and relays potentially moderating information to the amydala. While the hub of this vigilance system seems to be the _____, both pathways are useful in assessing threat.

    Answers: 13-1. physiological, autonomic, galvanic **13-2.** emotion (autonomic arousal), relatively high, cannot **13-3.** amygdala, fear **13-4.** amygdala, cortex **13-5.** survival (adaptive), amygdala.

14. **Discuss the body language of emotions and the facial feedback hypothesis.**

    14-1.   We communicate emotions not only verbally but _____, through our postures and gestures and, especially, in our facial _____.

    14-2.   Ekman and Friesen found that there are at least _____ fundamental facial expressions of emotion and perhaps as many as ten. Since children who have been blind since birth show the same expressions as sighted children, it seems reasonable to believe that basic facial expressions are largely (<u>learned/innate</u>).

14-3. According to some researchers facial expressions not only reflect emotions but help create them. This viewpoint, known as the _____ hypothesis, asserts that facial muscles send signals to the brain that help produce the subjective experience of emotion. For example, turning up the corners of your mouth will tend to make you feel _____.

Answers: 14-1. nonverbally (through body language), expressions **14-2.** six, innate **14-3.** facial-feedback, happy.

15. Discuss cross-cultural similarities and variations in emotional experience.

15-1. Ekman and Friesen asked people in different cultures to label the emotion shown on photographs of faces. What did they find?

15-2. Different cultures show striking similarities in other aspects of emotional experience as well. For example, regardless of culture, meeting with friends tends to trigger one emotion and encountering failure another. Thus, certain types of _____ trigger the same emotions across cultures.

15-3. While there are similarities in emotional expression across cultures, there are also striking differences. For example, certain word labels for emotion (e.g., sadness, anxiety, remorse) that exist in some cultures (also occur/do not occur) in others.

15-4. Although people in different cultures tend to show the same basic expressions of emotion, *when* they do so is governed by different cultural norms. What emotions are you "supposed to" show at a funeral, or when watching a sporting event? The unwritten rules that regulate our display of emotion, known as _____ rules, vary considerably across cultures.

Answers: 15-1. People from very different cultures, including cultures that have had virtually no contact with the West, tended to respond with considerable agreement in labeling photographs of facial expressions with approximately six basic emotions. These data support the idea that emotional expression is largely universal. **15-2.** events (experiences, situations) **15-3.** do not occur **15-4.** display.

THEORIES OF EMOTION

16. Describe the James-Lange and Cannon-Bard theories of emotion.

16-1. Suppose you saw a rat in your room (and assume that you are afraid of rats). Why would you be afraid? One would think that the process would be as follows: first you would be consciously aware of your fear of the rat, then you would experience the autonomic or visceral arousal that accompanies fear. The James-Lange theory reverses this process: we first experience the (visceral arousal/conscious fear) and then we experience (visceral arousal/conscious fear).

16-2. According to the James-Lange theory, then, fear and other emotions occur not as a result of different conscious experiences but as a result of different patterns of _____ activation.

16-3. The Cannon-Bard theory argued that a subcortical structure in the brain (they thought it was the thalamus) simultaneously sends signals to both the cortex and the autonomic nervous system. According to this theory:

a. conscious fear would precede autonomic arousal

b. autonomic arousal would precede conscious fear

c. autonomic arousal and conscious fear would occur at the same time

16-4. According to Cannon-Bard, emotion originates in:

a. subcortical structures

b. the autonomic nervous sytem

c. conscious awareness

16-5. The Cannon-Bard theory contends that different emotions (e.g., fear, joy, love, anger) are accompanied by:

a. different patterns of autonomic arousal

b. nearly identical patterns of autonomic arousal

c. neither of the above

Answers: 16-1. visceral arousal, conscious fear **16-2.** autonomic (visceral) **16-3.** c **16-4.** a **16-5.** b.

17. Describe the two-factor and evolutionary perspectives on emotion.

17-1. Schachter's two-factor view is similar to the James-Lange theory in that (visceral arousal/conscious experience) is thought to precede the mental awareness of an emotion. The theory is similar to the Cannon-Bard theory in that (general autonomic arousal is/different autonomic responses are) assumed to account for a wide variety of emotions.

17-2. Since arousal is in large part the same regardless of the emotion, according to Schachter, we feel different emotions as a result of inferences we make from events in the environment. Hence, the two factors in Schachter's theory are _____ (roughly the same for all emotions) and _____ (people's interpretation of the arousal based on the situation).

17-3. For review of these three theories, label the following with the name of the theory:

(a) The subjective experience of emotion is caused by different patterns of autonomic arousal.
_____

(b) Emotions can not be distinguished on the basis of a autonomic arousal; general autonomic arousal causes one to look for an explanation or label. _____

(c) Love is accompanied by a different autonomic pattern from hate. _____

(d) The subjective experience of emotion is caused by two factors, by arousal and by cognition.
_____

(e) Emotions originate in subcortical brain structures; different emotions produce almost identical patterns of autonomic arousal. _____

(f) Ralph observes that his heart pounds and that he becomes a little out of breath at times. He also notices that these signs of arousal occur whenever Mary is around, so he figures that he must be in love. _____

17-4. By preparing an organism for aggression and defense, the emotion of anger helps an organism survive. From an evolutionary perspective, anger as well as the other emotions have _____ value for a species.

17-5. Evolutionary theorists view emotions primarily as a group of (<u>innate/learned</u>) reactions that have been passed on because of their survival value. They also believe that emotions originate in subcortical areas, parts of the brain that evolved before the cortical structures associated with higher mental processes. In the view of the evolutionary theorists, emotion evolved before thought and is largely (<u>dependent on/independent of</u>) thought.

17-6. How many basic, inherited emotions are there? The evolutionary writers assume that the wide range of emotions we experience are blends or different levels of approximately _____ innate or prewired primary emotions.

Answers: **17-1.** visceral arousal, general autonomic arousal **17-2.** arousal, cognition **17-3.** (a) James-Lange
(b) Schachter's two-factor (c) James-Lange (d) Schachter's two-factor (e) Cannon-Bard (f) Schachter's two-factor
17-4. survival (adaptive) **17-5.** innate, independent of **17-6.** eight to ten.

PUTTING IT IN PERSPECTIVE

18. Explain how this chapter highlighted five of the text's unifying themes.

18-1. Five of the text's organizing themes were prominent in this chapter. Indicate which themes fit the following examples by writing the appropriate abbreviations in the blanks below: C for cultural contexts, SH for sociohistorical context, T for theoretical diversity, HE for heredity and environment, and MC for multiple causation.

(a) Achievement behavior is affected by achievement motivation, the likelihood of success, the likelihood of failure, and so on. ____

(b) Display rules in a culture tell us when and where to express an emotion. ____

(c) Changing attitudes about homosexuality have produced more research on sexual orientation; in turn, data from the research has affected societal attitudes. ____

(d) Body weight seems to be influenced by set point, blood glucose, and inherited metabolism. It is also affected by eating habits and acquired tastes, which vary across cultures. ____, ____, and ____.

(e) The James-Lange theory proposed that different emotions reflected different patterns of physiological arousal; Cannon-Bard theory assumed that emotions originate in subcortical structures; Schachter viewed emotion as a combination of physiological arousal and cognition ____.

Answers: **18-1.** (a) MC (b) C (c) SH (d) HE, MC, C (e) T.

19. Summarize information on factors that do and do not predict happiness.

19-1. Indicate whether each of the following statements is true or false.

(a) _____ There is very little correlation between income and happiness.

(b) _____ Younger people tend to be happier than older people.

(c) _____ People who have children tend to be happier than those without children.

(d) _____ People with high IQ scores tend to be happier than those with low IQ scores.

(e) _____ There is a negligible correlation between physical attractiveness and happiness.

19-2. List five factors discussed in your text that have little or no relationship to happiness.

19-3. Indicate whether each of the following statements is true or false.

(a) _____ One of the strongest predictors of happiness is good health.

(b) _____ Social support and friendship groups are moderately related to happiness.

(c) _____ Religious people tend to be somewhat happier than nonreligious people.

(d) _____ Marital status is strongly related to happiness; married people tend to be happier than single people.

(e) _____ Job satisfaction tends to be strongly related to general happiness; people who like their jobs tend to be happy.

(f) _____ Differences in personality have a negligible relationship to happiness; introverts, on the average, are just as happy as extraverts.

19-4. List three factors that are moderately correlated with happiness and three that are strongly correlated.

Answers: **19-1.** (a) T (b) F (c) F (d) F (e) T **19-2.** money (income), age, parenthood (either having or not having children), intelligence, physical attractiveness **19-3.** (a) F (People adapt, so there is only a moderate relationship between health and happiness.), (b) T (c) T (d) T (e) T (f) F (People who are extraverted, optimistic, and have high self-esteem tend to be happier.) **19-4.** Moderately related: health, social activity (friendship), and religion. Strongly related: marriage, work (job satisfaction), and personality.

20. Explain four conclusions that can be drawn about the dynamics of happiness.

20-1. One conclusion about happiness is that how we feel about our health, wealth, job, and age are more important than the facts of our situation. In other words, the objective realities are less important than our _____ reactions.

20-2. In addition, the extent of our happiness depends on the comparison group. Generally, people compare themselves to others who are similar in some dimension, such as friends or neighbors. In the final analysis, however, our happiness is *relative* to the _____ to which we compare ourselves.

20-3. A third conclusion is that our baseline for judging pleasantness and unpleasantness constantly changes. When good things happen, we shift our baselines (what we feel we "need" or want) upward; when bad things happen, we shift down. In other words, people _____ to changing circumstances by changing their baselines of comparison, a process termed _____ adaptation.

20-4. Finally, many people find happiness despite seemingly insurmountable problems. We adapt and change our perspectives, which make the quest for happiness never completely _____.

Answers: 20-1. subjective **20-2.** group (people) **20-3.** adapt (adjust), hedonic **20-4.** hopeless.

CRITICAL THINKING APPLICATION • ANALYZING ARGUMENTS: MAKING SENSE OUT OF CONTROVERSY

21. Describe the key elements in arguments.

21-1. In logic, an *argument* is a series of statements that claims to prove something (whether it does or not). Arguments are comprised of two major parts, a *conclusion* and one or more *premises*. The _____ are statements intended to present evidence or proof. The _____ supposedly derives from or is proved by the premises.

21-2. Consider this logical argument: "Any field of study that uses the scientific method is a science. Psychology uses the scientific method. Thus, psychology is a science." Label the parts of the argument below (C or conclusion and P form premise).

___ Any field of study that uses the scientific method is a science.

___ Psychology uses the scientific method.

___ Thus, psychology is a science.

Answers: 21-1. premises, conclusion **21-2.** P, P, C. Note that this is an example of a logically valid argument. One may or may not agree with the premises (e.g., they may define science differently), but the conclusion logically follows from the premises.

22. Explain some common fallacies that often show up in arguments.

22-1. Read over the section on common logical fallacies described in your text. Then match the examples with the appropriate terms. (Suggestion: Use the abbreviations in parentheses for matching. Note that there are five fallacies and seven examples; two fallacies are used twice.)

irrelevant reasons (IR)

circular reasoning (CR)

slippery slope (SS)

weak analogies (WA)

false dichotomy (FD)

(a) ____ Trouble sleeping causes great difficulty in our lives because insomnia is a major problem for people. (Hint: Is the conclusion different from the premise?)

(b) ____ People with insomnia should use the herb melatonin because insomnia is an enormous problem in our country. (Hint: Is the premise really related to the conclusion?)

(c) _____ Vitamin C is extremely effective in slowing the aging process. I know it is effective because Vitamin C functions to reduce aging.

(d) _____ If we don't stop communism in Vietnam now, it will spread next to Laos, then to Cambodia, and then to the entire Southeast Asian Peninsula.

(e) _____ We saw what happened when Chamberlain gave in to Hitler. The same thing will happen again unless we stand up to the tyranny in the Middle East. (Hint: Are the two situations the same?)

(f) _____ We can fight in the Balkans now, or we can prepare for World War III. (Hint: Are these our only choices?)

(g) _____ Ralph bought a mixmaster on a Tuesday in Peoria and it lasted a long time. If I buy a mixmaster on a Tuesday in Peoria, it should also last a long time.

Answers: 22-1. (a) CR. The premise and conclusion are the same. (b) IR. Insomnia may be a problem but that does not lead to the conclusion that the herb melatonin should be taken. (c) CR. The conclusion, the first statement, is simply a restatement of the premise, which is the last statement. (d) SS. The argument is that if you allow one thing to happen, then a series of other things will inevitably happen. In fact, there may be no necessary connection between the events. (e) WA. While the two situations may have a degree of similarity, they are also likely to be sufficiently dissimilar to make the argument invalid. (f) FD. The choice seems to be between the two options, but, logically, these are not the only choices. We may also do both, or neither. (g) WA. While the situations share some elements in common, this does not mean that they share all elements or that some elements cause others.

REVIEW OF KEY TERMS

Achievement motive
Affiliation motive
Androgens
Aphrodisiac
Argument
Assumptions
Bisexuals
Body Mass Index (BMI)
Display rules
Emotion
Estrogens

Galvanic skin response (GSR)
Glucose
Glucostats
Hedonic Adaptation
Heterosexuals
Homeostasis
Homosexuals
Individualism
Lie detector
Motivation

Subjective-Being
Obesity
Orgasm
Pheromone
Polygraph
Premise
Refractory period
Set point
Sexual orientation
Vasocongestion

_____ 1. Goal-directed behavior that may be affected by needs, wants, interests, desires, and incentives.

_____ 2. Cultural norms that regulate the expression of emotions.

_____ 3. One or more premises that are used to provide support for a conclusion.

_____ 4. The reasons presented in an argument to persuade someone that a conclusion is true.

_____ 5. Premises in an argument which are assumed but for which no proof or evidence is offered.

_____ 6. Blood sugar.

_____ 7. Neurons that are sensitive to glucose.

_____ 8. Occurs when one's baseline of comparison for judging happiness shifts to a higher of lower level.

_____ 9. Engorgement of the blood vessels.

_____ 10. Sexual climax.

_____ 11. A time following orgasm during which males are unresponsive to sexual stimulation.

_____ 12. Whether a person prefers emotional-sexual relationships with members of the same sex, the other sex, or either sex.

_____ 13. People who seek emotional-sexual relationships with members of the same sex.

_____ 14. People who seek emotional-sexual relationships with members of the other sex.

_____ 15. People who seek emotional-sexual relationships with members of either sex.

_____ 16. Individuals' personal perceptions of their overall happiness and life satisfaction.

_____ 17. The need to master difficult challenges and to excel in competition with others.

_____ 18. An increase in the electrical conductivity of the skin related to an increase in sweat gland activity.

_____ 19. A reaction that includes cognitive, physiological, and behavioral components.

_____ 20. The technical name for the "lie detector."

_____ 21. The informal name for polygraph, an apparatus that monitors physiological aspects of arousal (e.g., heart rate, GSR).

Answers: 1. motivation **2.** display rules **3.** argument **4.** premises **5.** assumptions **6.** glucose **7.** glucostats **8.** hedonic adaptation **9.** vasocongestion **10.** orgasm **11.** refractory period **12.** sexual orientation **13.** homosexuals **14.** heterosexuals **15.** bisexuals **16.** subjective well-being **17.** achievement motive **18.** galvanic skin response (GSR) **19.** emotion **20.** polygraph **21.** lie detector.

REVIEW OF KEY PEOPLE

David Buss   William James   Henry Murray
Walter Cannon   William Masters & Virginia Johnson   Stanley Schachter
Paul Ekman & Wallace Friesen   David McClelland

_____ 1. Proposed that emotions arise in subcortical areas of the brain.

_____ 2. Compiled an influential catalogue of common social needs; also devised the TAT.

_____ 3. Prominent evolutionary theorist who explored, among many other topics, gender differences in human mate preferences.

_____ 4. Originated the two-factor theory of emotion.

_____ 5. Did the ground-breaking work on the physiology of the human sexual response.

_____ 6. Is responsible for most of the early research on achievement motivation.

_____ 7. In a series of cross-cultural studies found that people can identify six or so basic emotions from facial expressions.

_____ 8. Thought that one's cognitive awareness of emotion arose from variations in autonomic arousal.

Answers: 1. Cannon **2.** Murray **3.** Buss **4.** Schachter **5.** Masters & Johnson **6.** McClelland **7.** Ekman & Friesen **8.** James.

SELF-QUIZ

1. What generally happens when a rat's ventromedial hypothalamus (VMH) is lesioned?
    a. It starts eating.
    b. It looks for a sexual partner.
    c. It becomes aggressive.
    d. It loses bladder and bowel control.

2. The subjective feeling of hunger is influenced by:
    a. the amount of glucose in the bloodstream
    b. secretion of insulin by the pancreas
    c. external cues, including odor and appearance of food
    d. all of the above

3. What is the effect of insulin on blood glucose?
    a. Glucose level increases.
    b. Glucose level decreases.
    c. Glucose changes to free fatty acids.
    d. CCK increases.

4. According to this theory, the sex that makes the larger investment in offspring (bearing, nursing, etc.) will be more selective of partners than the sex that makes the smaller investment.
    a. adaptation level theory
    b. parental investment theory
    c. investment differentiation theory
    d. social learning theory

5. According to data from the evolutionary theorists, which of the following is true concerning jealousy in human beings?
    a. in general, females tend to be more jealous than males
    b. females tend to be more jealous than males about sexual infidelity
    c. males tend to be more jealous than females about emotional infidelity
    d. females tend to be more jealous than males about emotional infidelity

6. Which of the following would best reflect the James-Lange theory of emotion?
    a. The subjective experience of emotion is caused by thinking about the cause of autonomic arousal.
    b. The conscious experience of emotion is caused by different patterns of autonomic arousal.
    c. Emotion originates in subcortical structures, which send signals to both the cortex an autonomic nervous system.
    d. Cognitive awareness of emotion precedes autonomic arousal.

7. The fact that identical twins are more likely to share sexual orientation than fraternal twins suggests that sexual orientation is in part:
    a. environmental
    b. genetic
    c. chemical
    d. hormonal

8. Cultural norms that indicate which facial expressions of emotion are appropriate on what occasions are termed:
    a.. display rules
    b. parental investments
    c. investment differentiations
    d. social scripts

9. According to the evolutionary theories, men seek as partners women who:
   a. are similar to them in important attitudes
   b. have a good sense of humor
   c. are beautiful, youthful, and in good health
   d. have good financial prospects

10. What test is generally used to measure need for achievement?
    a. the TAT
    b. the GSR
    c. the Rorschach
    d. the MMPI

11. Evidence regarding facial expression in different cultures suggests that:
    a. two-factor theory accounts for nonverbal behavior
    b. facial expression of emotion is to some extent innate
    c. emotions originate in the cortex
    d. learning is the major factor in explaining basic facial expressions

12. Which of the following proposed that emotion arises from one's perception or interpretation of autonomic arousal?
    a. Schachter
    b. Cannon-Bard
    c. LeDoux
    d. McClelland

13. Which of the following theories assert that thinking or cognition plays a relatively small role in emotion?
    a. two-factor theory
    b. James-Lange theory
    c. achievement theory
    d. evolutionary theory

14. Of the following, which has been found to be most strongly associated with happiness?
    a. physical attractiveness
    b. health
    c. job satisfaction
    d. general intelligence

15. Someone exhorts people to take action against company policy, as follows: "We can oppose these changes, or we can live out our lives in poverty." While the intent of the argument may be appropriate and persuasive, logically it would reflect which of the following fallacies?
    a. slippery slope
    b. weak analogy
    c. false dichotomy
    d. circular reasoning

Answers: 1. a **2.** d **3.** b **4.** b **5.** d **6.** d **7.** b **8.** a **9.** c **10.** a **11.** b **12.** a **13.** d **14.** c **15.** c.

INFOTRAC

Bisexuals   Galvanic Skin Response   Lie Detector   Motivation

11 HUMAN DEVELOPMENT ACROSS THE LIFE SPAN

REVIEW OF KEY IDEAS

PROGRESS BEFORE BIRTH: PRENATAL DEVELOPMENT

1. **Outline the major events of the three phases of prenatal development.**

   1-1.   Each box below represents one month in the typical pregnancy; each short line at the top of the boxes represents one week. Indicate the beginning and end of each phase of prenatal development by placing the appropriate capital letters from the diagram in the blanks below.

   ```
   A   B   C       D       E              F                                          G
   ```

   (a) The germinal stage begins at conception, represented by point _____ in the diagram, and ends at point _____.

   (b) The embryonic stage begins at point _____ and ends at point _____.

   (c) The fetal stage begins at point _____ and ends at point _____.

   1-2.   List the names of the three phases of prenatal development in the order in which they occur. In the parentheses at the right indicate the age ranges encompassed by each stage.

   (a) _____   (   )

   (b) _____   (   )

   (c) _____   (   )

   1-3.   Match the letter identifying each stage in the previous question with the descriptions below.

   _____   The placenta begins to form.

   _____   At the end of this stage the organism begins to have a human appearance; it is about an inch in length.

_____ The zygote begins to implant in the uterine wall; about one in five are rejected.

_____ Muscles and bones develop and physical movements occur.

_____ Most major birth defects probably have their origins in this stage.

_____ The age of viability (about 22 to 26 weeks after conception) occurs during this stage.

Answers: 1-1. (a) A, B (b) B, D (c) D, G **1-2.** (a) germinal (birth to two weeks) (b) embryonic (two weeks to two months) (c) fetal (two months to nine months) **1-3.** a, b, a, c, b, c.

2. **Summarize the impact of environmental factors on prenatal development.**

   2-1. Indicate whether the following statements concerning environmental factors and fetal development are true (T) or false (F).

   _____ Severe malnutrition increases the risk of birth complications and neurological deficits.

   _____ Studies consistently indicate that moderate malnutrition does not have a harmful effect on infant development.

   _____ Few if any drugs consumed by a pregnant woman are able to pass through the placental barrier.

   _____ Relative to its affluence the U. S. has a high infant mortality rate.

   _____ Recent studies indicate that moderate drinking during pregnancy produces no risk for the developing fetus.

   _____ Heavy drinking of alcohol by a pregnant woman may produce microencephaly, heart defects, and retardation in her child.

   _____ Smoking during pregnancy is related to increased risk of miscarriage and other birth complications.

   _____ The placenta screens out many but not all infectious diseases.

   _____ Genital herpes is usually transmitted during the birth process, when newborns come into contact with their mothers' lesions.

   _____ AIDS is transmitted primarily during the birth process, when newborns come into contact with their mothers' blood cells.

   _____ Good quality prenatal care is associated with fewer premature births and higher infant survival rates.

Answers: 2-1. T, F, F, T, F, T, T, T, T, T, T.

3. **Describe general trends and cultural variations in motor development**

3-1. In the space below, list and describe the two basic trends in motor development described in the text.

Cephalocaudal trend:

Proximodistal trend:

3-2. The average ages at which children display various behaviors and abilities are referred to as developmental _____. While these averages provide useful information they don't reflect variability, and the age at which children display certain behaviors or abilities varies (<u>enormously/very little</u>) across children.

3-3. Thus, with regard to the behavior of walking up steps, for example, which of the following is true?

a. children walk up steps at approximately the same age.

b. many normal children don't walk up steps until well after or well before the average age indicated.

3-4. The process that underlies the developmental norms is *maturation*. What is maturation? (Be specific with regard to the factors of hereditary and environment.)

3-5. Cross-cultural research has revealed a considerable degree of consistency between cultures in terms of when and in what order motor skills appear. In general, early motor development is much more dependent on (<u>maturation/culture</u>) than is later motor development. As children in a culture grow older, however, the motor skills that they acquire depend to a greater extent on (<u>maturation/culture</u>).

Answers: 3-1. Head to foot: children tend to gain motor control of the upper body before the lower body. Center outward: the tendency to gain control of the torso before the limbs. **3-2.** norms, enormously **3-3.** b **3-4.** Maturation refers to developmental changes that occur in an organism as a result of *genetic*, as opposed to environmental, factors. **3-5.** maturation, culture.

4. **Summarize the findings of Thomas and Chess's longitudinal study of infant temperament.**

4-1. Identify the following designs by indicating whether they are longitudinal or cross-sectional.

(a) _____ In this experimental design researchers compare groups of subjects of differing ages at a single point in time.

(b) _____ This design measures a single group of subjects over a period of time.

4-2. Thomas and Chess identified three basic temperaments, described below. Place the names of these temperamental styles in the appropriate blanks.

(a) _____ Happy, regular in sleep and eating, adaptable, not readily upset.

(b) _____ Less cheery, less regular in sleep and eating, slower in adapting to change, more wary of new experiences, moderate in reactivity.

(c) _____ Glum, erratic in sleep and eating, resistant to change, irritable.

4-3. The largest group of children (about 40%) were of the _____ temperament, another 15% were _____, and 10% were in the _____ category. The remaining 35% showed mixtures of these three temperaments.

4-4. What is the major from the Thomas and Chess study?

Answers: 4-1. (a) cross-sectional (b) longitudinal 4-2. (a) easy (b) slow-to-warm-up (c) difficult 4-3. easy, slow-to-warm-up, difficult 4-4. Temperament seems to be very stable across time: A child's temperament at 3 months tended to be a fair predictor of his or her temperament at 10 years of age. This stability suggests that temperament has a strong biological basis.

5. **Summarize research on infant-mother attachment, including cultural variations and evolutionary views.**

5-1. Newborn babies do not form attachments to their mothers immediately. They begin to show a strong preference for their mothers, often crying when they are separated, when they are about _____ months of age.

5-2. The emotional distress that occurs when some infants are separated from their caregivers is called _____ anxiety. This distress peaks at about _____ months of age and then begins to decline.

5-3. Research by Ainsworth and her colleagues indicates that attachments between mothers and their infants tend to fall into three categories. Label each of the following with the pattern of attachment described: *secure, anxious-ambivalent,* or *avoidant.*

(a) _____ The infant is anxious even when the mother is near, becomes very agitated when she leaves, and is not comforted when the mother returns.

(b) _____ The infant seeks little contact with the mother and is not distressed when she leaves.

(c) _____ The infant plays comfortably when the mother is present, is upset when the mother leaves, but is quickly calmed by her when she returns.

5-4. Although one cannot assume a causal relationship, attachment in infancy has been found to be related to behavior in later childhood. For a number of desirable characteristics, including social skills, persistence, curiosity, leadership, and cognitive development, it appears that children who experienced a _____ attachment have the advantage.

5-5. Does day care affect infant-mother attachment? Belsky found that day care for more than 20 hours per week increases the likelihood that a/an (<u>insecure</u>/secure) attachment will form between mother and infant.

5-6. Belsky's findings must be put in perspective, however. Which of the following statements are/is true (T) or false (F)?

_____ The proportion of insecure attachments found in the Belsky studies is only slightly higher than the US norm.

_____ The preponderance of other studies suggests that day care is not harmful to children's attachment relationships.

_____ Considering the deprived childrearing conditions in many homes, day care can have beneficial effects on some children's social development

5-7. Separation anxiety occurs at roughly the same ages across different cultures. There are some interesting cross-cultural differences, however, shown in Table 11.1 in your text.

(a) Which cultural sample (USA, Germany, or Japan) showed the highest proportion of *avoidant* attachments? _____

(b) Which cultural sample evidenced *no avoidant attachments* at all? _____

(c) Which sample showed the highest levels of *anxious ambivalent* attachments?

_____

(d) Which two countries had the highest proportion of *secure* attachments?

_____ and _____

5-8. Belsky proposed that in our evolutionary past the relative harshness of the environment affected parent-child attachment style, which in turn affected the later _____ strategy of the sexually mature offspring.

5-9. For example, a harsh, unsafe environment with scarce resources would cause parents to have little time for the child, which would produce a/an (secure/<u>insecure</u>) attachment. When the child reached sexual maturity, the earlier attachment style would yield a sexually (<u>opportunistic</u>/enduring) mating strategy. Such a strategy would maximize reproductive potential in environments where long-term survival is (ensured/<u>precarious</u>).

5-10. In contrast, a safe environment rich in resources would allow parents the time and energy to be responsive to an infant's needs, which would produce a/an _____ attachment. Belsky asserts that such an attachment is associated with (<u>quality</u>/quantity) in later mating relationships with relatively (<u>few</u>/many) sexual partners and a strong romantic bond.

5-11. In short, Belsky proposed that the local _____ affected parent-child _____ which influenced the child's later _____ strategy, which in turn had _____ value for the environment in which it occurred.

Answers: 5-1. 6 to 8. 5-2. separation, 14 to 18. 5-3. (a) anxious-ambivalent (b) avoidant (c) secure 5-4. secure
5-5. insecure 5-6. true, true, true 5-7. (a) Germany (b) Japan (c) Japan (d) USA, Japan. 5-8. reproductive 5-9. insecure,
opportunistic, precarious 5-10. secure, quality, few 5-11. environment, attachment, reproductive, adaptive (survival,
reproductive fitness).

6. Outline Erikson's stages of childhood personality development and critique Erikson's theory.

6-1. Erikson's theory is clearly derived from Freudian psychoanalytic theory. Freud asserted that there are five childhood stages that determine the adult's personality. In contrast, Erikson proposed that there are

_____ stages that influence personality across an individual's (childhood/entire lifespan).

6-2. Erikson described four childhood stages and four adult stages. In the spaces below write the names of the crises that mark the four *childhood* stages, and indicate in the parentheses the approximate ages at which the crises are supposed to occur.

(a) _____ vs. _____   (   )

(b) _____ vs. _____   (   )

(c) _____ vs. _____   (   )

(d) _____ vs. _____   (   )

6-3. Below are descriptions of several individuals. In what childhood stage would they have acquired the characteristics described, according to Erikson? Use the letters from the question above to indicate the stages.

_____ Jack has trouble functioning effectively in the world outside his family; he is unproductive, and he lacks a sense of competence.

_____ Kristi is insecure and suspicious of everyone.

_____ Larry was torn between being independent of his family and avoiding conflict; as an adult he feels guilty and lacks self-esteem.

_____ From an early age Maureen's parents never seemed satisfied with what she did. Maureen is plagued by a sense of shame and self-doubt.

6-4. As you may have noted in responding to the previous item, a weakness of Erikson's theory is that it attempts to account for very (few/many) aspects of personality. Thus, the theory cannot explain the enormous individual _____ between people.

Answers: 6-1. 8, entire lifespan 6-2. (a) trust vs. mistrust (first year) (b) autonomy vs. shame and doubt (second year)
(c) initiative vs. guilt (ages 3 to 6) (d) industry vs. inferiority (age 6 through puberty) 6-3. d, a, c, b 6-4. few, differences
(variation).

7. Outline Piaget's stages of cognitive development and critique Piaget's theory.

7-1. The diagram below represents Piaget's four main stages of development. Write the names of the stages in the appropriate blanks.

```
    |   '   |
    |   '   |
11 |-------|         (d) _____
   |       |
 7 |-------|         (c) _____
   |       |
   |       |         (b) _____
 2 |-------|
Birth|_____|         (a) _____
    Ages
```

7-2.   Following is a list of characteristics of children's thinking during various stages. Identify the stage by placing the correct letter (from the diagram above) in the blanks.

_____   At the end of this stage the child is beginning to develop the capacity for symbolic thought (to think terms of mental images).

_____   At the beginning of this stage the child's behavior is dominated by reflexes and the ability to coordinate sensory input and movement.

_____   The child understands conservation and can handle hierarchical classification but tends not to use abstractions.

_____   The child's thought processes are abstract and systematic.

_____   Object permanence occurs toward the end of this stage.

_____   During the first part of this stage, "out of sight, out of mind" might describe the child's reaction to hidden objects.

_____   When water is poured from a wide beaker into a taller beaker, children say there is now more water in the taller beaker.

_____   The child demonstrates a lack of understanding of conservation.

_____   The child shows the shortcomings of centration, irreversibility, egocentrism, and animism.

_____   For the first time the child in this stage is mentally able to undo an action and also is able focus on more than one feature of a problem at the same time.

7-3.   When my (R. S.'s) daughter Vanessa was about 5, I placed two rows of stones on the grass, as illustrated below. Each row contained the same number of stones.

Row A: • • • • • • •

Row B: • • • • • • •

I then spread out one row so that it took up more space:

Row A: • • • • • • •

Row B: • • • • • • •

(a) I then asked Vanessa to point to the row that now had more stones. If Vanessa behaved like other *preoperational* children, which row would she point to? _____

(b) The preoperational child has not yet mastered the principle that physical quantities remain constant in spite of changes in their shape or, in this case, arrangement. What is the name of this principle? _____

7-4. Some research has demonstrated that certain aspects of Piaget's theory may be incorrect in detail. For example, there is some evidence that object permanence and some aspects of conservation may develop (earlier/later) than Piaget had thought.

7-5. Piaget also had little to say about individual _____ in development or about so-called _____ of stages in which elements of an earlier stage may appear in a later one.

7-6. Piaget thought that people of all cultures would pass through the stages at the same time; subsequent research has found that this (is/is not) the case. While the *sequence* of stages appears to be relatively invariant across cultures, the _____ that children follow in passing through these stages varies considerably across cultures. Nonetheless, Piaget's brilliance, the novelty of his approach, and the wealth of research that his theory inspired assure his place in history.

Answers: **7-1.** (a) sensorimotor (b) preoperational (c) concrete operations (d) formal operations **7-2.** a, a, c, d, a, a, b, b, b, c **7-3.** (a) Row A (at which point Samantha, then 8 and in the stage of concrete operations, was astonished by her sister's choice and informed her that there were the same number in both!) (b) conservation **7-4.** earlier **7-5.** differences, mixing **7-6.** is not, timetable (age, time).

8. Summarize evidence which suggests that some cognitive abilities could be innate.

8-1. When infants look at a stimulus that is presented repeatedly, the strength of their responses gradually decreases. They spend less and less time looking at the stimulus, and their heart and respiration rates decrease. This reduction in response strength is known as _____. When a new stimulus is presented, response strength increases, a process known as _____.

8-2. By using the habituation-dishabituation technique, researchers can tell when a child is able to discriminate between different events. For example, at 3 to 4 months of age, infants understand that (write T or F for each of the following):

____ Objects on slopes roll down rather than up.

____ One solid object cannot pass through another.

____ Objects move in continuous paths.

8-3. In another demonstration of the cognitive abilities of young children, 5-month-old infants were shown a display in which an object was added to or subtracted from others behind a screen. Remarkably, the children exhibited surprise, indicated by the response of (habituation/dishabituation), when the expected number of objects was not there. This result suggests that infants (are/are not) able to add and subtract small numbers.

8-4. Because these cognitive abilities occur at such an early age, before infants would have had much chance to learn them, some theorists have concluded that these capacities are largely (acquired/innate).

8-5. Two groups of theorists favor an explanation in terms of innate cognitive abilities: the *nativists* and the *evolutionary* psychologists. Of these theoretical positions it is primarily the (nativists/evolutionary theorists) who are interested in explaining why these abilities are innately programmed.

8-6. Why would we be pre-wired to understand addition and subtraction? The (nativists/evolutionary theorists), assert that basic addition and subtraction abilities had clear _____ value in a hunting, foraging, and social-bargaining society.

Answers: 8-1. habituation, dishabituation **8-2.** T, T, T **8-3.** dishabituation, are **8-4.** innate **8-5.** evolutionary theorists **8-6.** evolutionary theorists, survival.

9. Outline Kohlberg's stages of moral development and critique Kohlberg's theory.

9-1. Kohlberg's theory includes three moral levels, each with two stages for a total of six stages. Indicate which of the three moral levels is described in each of the following statements.

    (a) Acts are considered wrong because they are punished or right because they lead to positive consequences. _____

    (b) Individuals at this level conform very strictly to society's rules, which they accept as absolute and inviolable. _____

    (c) This level is characterized by situational or conditional morality, such that stealing might be considered wrong in one circumstance but permissible in another. _____

9-2. The central ideas of Kohlberg's theory have received a fair amount of support. Research has found that children (do/do not) tend to progress through Kohlberg's stages in the order that he indicated. As children get older, stages 1 and 2 reasoning tend to decrease while stages 3 and 4 reasoning tend to

_____.

9-3. There have also been several criticisms of Kohlberg's theory. First, individuals may show characteristics of several different stages at the same time. In other words, as was true of other stage theories, there tends to be a "_____" of stages.

9-4. Second, some critics assert that Kohlberg's theory reflects the liberal, individualistic values that characterize modern _____ societies rather than human beings in general. In other words, Kohlberg's dilemmas may not reflect disparities in moral development that exist across cultures. Thus, Kohlberg's theory may be much more (cross-cultural/culture-specific) than he realized.

Answers: 9-1. (a) preconventional (b) conventional (c) postconventional **9-2.** do, increase **9-3.** mixing **9-4.** Western, culture-specific.

10. **Describe the major events of puberty and discuss the problem of unusually early or late maturation.**

   10-1.   Read over the section on <u>Puberty and the Growth Spurt</u> in your text. Then fill in the blanks below with the appropriate terms.

   (a) _____ The approximately two-year span preceding puberty that is marked by rapid growth in height and weight.

   (b) _____ The period of time during which secondary sex characteristics appear.

   (c) _____ Physical features that distinguish one sex from another but that are not essential for reproduction (e.g., facial hair in males, breasts in females).

   (d) _____ The stage during which sexual functions essential for reproduction reach maturity.

   (e) _____ The stage that includes menarche in females and the first production of sperm in males.

   (f) _____ The first occurrence of menstruation.

   (g) _____ The transitional period between childhood and adulthood that includes early physical changes (puberty) and later cognitive and social changes.

   10-2.   Adolescents who mature especially early or especially late may be subjected to stresses brought about by their appearance. This is particularly true of girls who mature (<u>early/late</u>), since they may be subjected to pressures and temptations brought about by their grown-up appearances, and of boys who mature (<u>early/late</u>). Early maturation is associated with difficulties in both sexes (e.g., alcohol use, trouble with the law), but the problems encountered by early-maturing (<u>females/males</u>) are likely to be more severe.

Answers: 10-1. (a) pubescence (b) pubescence (c) secondary sex characteristics (d) puberty (e) puberty (f) menarche (g) adolescence **10-2.** early, late, females.

11. **Evaluate the assertion that adolescence is a time of turmoil.**

   11-1.   How tumultuous is adolescence? With regard to suicide and other indicants of stress, current data indicate that: (Mark T or F for each of the following statements.)

   _____ Suicide rates among adolescents are higher than for any other age group.

   _____ The frequency of attempted suicide is much higher for adolescents than for any other age group.

   _____ Adolescence does bring an increase in volatile and risky behaviors and conflict between parents and children.

   _____ In general, adolescents may encounter somewhat more, but not much more, turmoil than do people in other periods of life.

Answers: 11-1. F, T, T, T.

12. **Explain why the struggle for a sense of identity is particularly intense during adolescence and discuss some common patterns of identity formation.**

    12-1. Adolescence is a period of change, so it is readily understandable that adolescents tend to focus on the struggle for _____, the question of "Who am I?"

    12-2. Recall that Erik Erikson described four crises that mark childhood. What is the crisis that marks adolescence, according to Erikson? _____ vs. _____

    12-3. Marcia (1966, 1980) has described four orientations that people may adopt in attempting to resolve the identity crisis. These are not stages that people pass through in an orderly manner but statuses that they may adopt on either a relatively permanent or temporary basis. One possible status is simply to take on the values and roles prescribed by one's parents; this is termed _____. While this may temporarily resolve the crisis, in the long run the individual may not be comfortable with the adopted identity. A second orientation involves a period of experimentation with various ideologies and careers and a delay in commitment to any one; this is termed _____. If the experimentation and lack of commitment become permanent, the individual is said to be in a status of _____ _____. On the other hand, if the consideration of alternatives leads to conviction about a sense of self, one takes on the status referred to as _____ _____.

Answers: **12-1.** identity **12-2.** identity, confusion **12-3.** foreclosure, moratorium, identity diffusion, identity achievement.

THE EXPANSE OF ADULTHOOD

13. **Summarize evidence on the stability of personality and the prevalence of the mid-life crisis.**

    13-1. Do people's personalities change throughout their lifetimes? Research evidence supports the conclusion that:

        a. personality is stable across one's lifetime

        b. personality changes across one's lifetime

        c. both of the above are true

        d. neither of the above is true

    13-2. The explanation for these apparently contradictory findings is that some personality traits do appear to _____ as people grow older while others remain _____.

    13-3. Two influential studies conducted in the 1970s asserted that people experience a period of emotional turmoil some time between ages 35 and 45, a transitional phase known as the _____ _____.

    13-4. The mid-life crisis, described as a period of reappraisal and assessment of time left, was thought by both Gould and Levinson to be a transitional phase that affected (a minority/most) adults. More recently, a large number of other investigators, using more objective research methods, have found that (very few/most) people go through a mid-life crisis.

Answers: **13-1.** c **13-2.** change, stable (the same) **13-3.** mid-life crisis **13-4.** most, very few.

14. **Outline Erikson's stages of development in adulthood.**

14-1. In the spaces below write the names of the crises that mark Erikson's three stages of adulthood. In the parentheses indicate the approximate period of adulthood during which the crises are supposed to occur.

(a)_____ vs. _____   (   )

(b)_____ vs. _____   (   )

(c)_____ vs. _____   (   )

14-2. Following are descriptions of the crises occurring in each of the above stages. Indicate the stages by placing the appropriate letters (from the previous question) in the blanks.

_____ Concern for helping future generations versus a self-indulgent concern for meeting one's own desires.

_____ Concern to find meaning in the remainder of one's life versus a preoccupation with earlier failures and eventual death.

_____ Concern for developing a capacity for intimacy with others versus a strategy in which others are manipulated as a means to an end.

Answers: **14-1.** (a) intimacy vs. isolation (early adulthood) (b) generativity vs. self-absorption (middle adulthood) (c) integrity vs. despair (aging years) **14-2.** b, c, a.

15. **Describe typical transitions in family relations during the adult years.**

15-1. In part as a result of economic factors and in part due to an increased emphasis on personal autonomy, remaining single or postponing marriage is a much more acceptable option today than it was a few decades ago. Nonetheless, over _____ percent of adults eventually marry.

15-2. In general the level of happiness in marriage tends to be U-shaped. That is, spouses overall satisfaction with marital life tends to reach a low point toward the (beginning/middle/end) of the family cycle.

15-3. What causes the drop in marital satisfaction during the middle years? To some degree it coincides with the burdens of child-rearing. The decline begins to occur (only after/even before) the first child is born, however, so other factors appear to be involved as well

15-4. Although most couples rate parenthood as a very positive experience, the birth of a child is frequently quite stressful. Adolescence, while not as contentious a period as previously believed, does bring an increase in parent-child conflict, especially for the (mother/father).

15-5. Marital satisfaction tends to (decrease/increase) as the children grow up and leave home. While the "empty nest" syndrome may briefly occur, it seems to have little lasting negative impact.

Answers: **15-1.** 90 **15-2.** middle **15-3.** even before **15-4.** mother **15-5.** increase.

16. **Describe the physical and cognitive changes associated with aging.**

16-1. As we age, our physical and cognitive characteristics change. Indicate which of the following physical traits increase and which decrease by placing checkmarks in the appropriate blanks.

	INCREASES	DECREASES
Physical changes		
Proportion of body fat:	_____	_____
Overall weight:	_____	_____
Number of neurons in the brain:	_____	_____
Visual acuity:	_____	_____
Ability to see close:	_____	_____
Hearing:	_____	_____

16-2. An abnormal condition marked my memory loss and loss of other cognitive abilities is termed a _____. Dimentia occurs in approximately _____ % of individuals over age 65.

16-3. With regard to changes in *general intelligence* and in *memory* that may accompany aging, which of the following is/arc truc? (Mark T or F.)

_____ Average test scores in cognitive ability show some decline after age 60.

_____ For the majority of people the decline in cognitive ability that occurs in later years is relatively slight.

_____ The memory loss that accompanies aging is relatively severe.

_____ The type of memory loss is thought to involve working memory or processing speed.

16-4. Despite the decline in physical and cognitive capacities, aging is not so bad as it may at first seem. With regard to loss of brain cells, it's not so much a matter of "who needs 'em" as that the gradual loss appcars to have (little/a strong) effect on functioning.

16-5. Intellectual performance and memory decline modestly with advancing age and are not universal. Speed of problem solving generally (does/does not) decrease with age, but problem solving ability (is/is not) impaired if time is not a factor.

Answers: 16-1. Body fat and overall weight increase (except that overall weight may decrease somewhat after the mid-50s); the rest decrease **16-2.** dementia, 15 **16-3.** T, T, F, T **16-4.** little **16-5.** does, is not.

PUTTING IT IN PERSPECITVE

17. Explain how this chapter highlighted the text's unifying theme about the importance of heredity and environment.

17-1. The behavior of a child is the result of the child's genetic inheritance and its environment, which includes the behavior of the child's parents. In turn, the behavior of the parents toward the child is affected both by their inherited characteristics and by the behavior of the child. Thus, behavior is the result not of heredity or environment operating separately but of an _____ between the two factors.

17-2. To understand the concept of *interaction* consider this problem: There is a form of mental retardation that results from phenylketonuria, an inherited inability to metabolize a common amino acid in milk. When fed milk, children born with phenylketonuria become mentally retarded. Is this type of retardation an inherited disorder?

a. Yes, it's genetic.

b. No, it's caused by the environment.

c. A certain proportion of the causal factors are hereditary and the remainder due to the environment.

d. The disorder results from heredity and environment operating jointly.

17-3. This chapter has been concerned with changes in human behavior across the life span. The theme being stressed here is that these changes result from an *interaction* of heredity and environment. In your own words, explain how the interaction operates.

Answers: 17-1. interaction **17-2.** d. (This disorder might at first seem to be inherited, since there is a genetic trait involved. But the retardation does not occur if the infant is not fed milk products, which involves the environment. The point is that this disorder, like behavior in general, cannot be attributed solely to nature or to nurture or even to relative weights of each: It is a function of an *interaction* between the two. **17-3.** Heredity and environment don't operate separately. The interaction of heredity and environment refers to the joint influence of these two factors. Interaction means that the genetic factors affect the operation of the environment and that environmental factors affect genetic predispositions. The influence of one factor *depends on* the effects of the other.

PERSONAL APPLICATION • UNDERSTANDING GENDER DIFFERENCES

18. **Summarize evidence on gender differences in behavior and discuss the significance of these differences.**

18-1. Which gender tends to show more of (or score higher on tests of) the following abilities or traits? Circle the correct answer at the right.

Cognitive

verbal skills	MALES	FEMALES	NEITHER
mathematical skills	MALES	FEMALES	NEITHER
visual-spatial skills	MALES	FEMALES	NEITHER

Social

aggression	MALES	FEMALES	NEITHER
sensitivity to nonverbal cues	MALES	FEMALES	NEITHER
risk-taking	MALES	FEMALES	NEITHER
sexually permissive attitudes	MALES	FEMALES	NEITHER
assertiveness	MALES	FEMALES	NEITHER
anxiety	MALES	FEMALES	NEITHER
nurturance	MALES	FEMALES	NEITHER

18-2. There is an enormous overlap between the genders with regard to these traits. There are, of course, many females who are more aggressive than the average male and many males who are more sensitive to nonverbal cues than the average female. Thus, it is important to note that the differences referred to in this section are differences between group _____ and that the size of the differences is relatively _____.

Answers: 18-1. cognitive: females, males, males; social: males, females, males, males, males, females, females
18-2. averages (means), small.

19. Explain how biological and environmental factors contribute to existing gender differences.

19-1. For evolutionary theorists, the relative invariance of gender differences found across cultures reflects natural selection. From this perspective males are more sexually active and permissive than females because reproductive success for males is maximized by seeking (few/many) sexual partners. Greater aggressiveness has survival value for males because it enhances their ability to acquire material _____ sought by females selecting a mate.

19-2. Evolutionary theorists also assert that ability differences between the genders reflect the division of labor in our ancestral past. Males were primarily the hunters and females the gatherers, and the adaptive demands of hunting may have produced males' superiority at most _____ tasks.

19-3. The evolutionary view of gender is certainly an interesting and plausible explanation of the remarkable similarity in gender differences across cultures. The viewpoint has its critics, however. For one thing, there are reasonable _____ theories of gender differences; for another, the evolutionary explanation is relatively (easy/difficult) to test empirically.

19-4. Concerning other biological factors, several studies indicate that hormones contribute to shaping gender differences. For example, females exposed prenatally to high levels of an _____-like drug given their mothers during pregnancy tend to show more male-typical behavior than do other females.

19-5. Other biological evidence indicates that males depend more heavily on the left hemisphere for verbal processing and the right for spatial processing than is the case with females. That is, males may tend to exhibit more cerebral _____ than females. This finding has been linked to another finding, that females have larger _____ callosums (the connecting sheath of axons between hemispheres) than do males.

19-6. Results from studies of specialization and of gender differences in the corpus callosum have not been consistent, however. In addition, it would be difficult to see how gender differences in *specialization* could account for gender differences in *ability*, that is, the superiority of males on _____ tasks and the superiority of females on _____ tasks.

19-7. Many researchers remain convinced that gender differences are largely shaped by the environment. One of the ways that children learn gender roles is from the consequences for their behavior, the rewards and punishments that they receive in the process known as _____ conditioning.

19-8. Children also acquire information by seeing what others do, the process of _____ learning. While children imitate both males and females, they are more likely to imitate the behavior of (same-sex/opposite-sex) models.

19-9. In addition to operant conditioning and observational learning, children are active participants in their own gender-role socialization, the process referred to as _____-socialization. First, once they discover (at age 5 or 6) that being a boy or girl is a permanent condition, they will then _____ themselves as boys or girls. Second, following classification in terms of gender children will _____ characteristics and behaviors associated with their gender. Third, they will bring their _____ in line with their values by engaging in "sex-appropriate" behaviors.

19-10. Whether through operant conditioning, observational learning, or self-socialization, the major forces for gender-role socialization occur in three main aspects of the child's environment: in their _____, in _____, and in the _____.

Answers: **19-1.** many, resources **19-2.** spatial (visual-spatial) **19-3.** alternative, difficult **19-4.** androgen **19-5.** specialization, corpus **19-6.** visual-spatial, verbal. **19-7.** operant **19-8.** observational (modeling), same-sex **19-9.** self, classify (categorize), value, behavior **19-10.** families, schools, media.

CRITICAL THINKING APPLICATION • ARE FATHERS ESSENTIAL TO CHILDREN'S WELL-BEING?

20. **Explain the argument that fathers are essential for healthy development and some criticism of this line of reasoning.**

20-1. Over the past several decades the percentage of children brought up without fathers in the home has steadily increased, from about 17% in 1960 to more than 35% today. During the same period there has also been a dramatic (decrease/increase) in teen pregnancy, juvenile delinquency, violent crime, drug abuse, eating disorders, and family dysfunction in general.

20-2. Further, fatherless children are two to three times more likely than fathered children to drop out of high school, become a teenage parent, or become a juvenile delinquent. In other words, father absence (causes/is correlated with) a host of unfortunate cultural trends.

20-3. Based on the association between father absence and social problems, some writers have asserted that the presence of a father is essential for a child's well-being. As you are by now well aware, however, one (can/cannot) infer causation on the basis of correlational data alone.

20-4. Among the reasonable alternative explanations for the correlational relationship described are the following. Father absence frequently occurs when the parents _____, so it is possible that this factor, rather than father absence, may cause the negative effects referred to.

20-5. Or, since father absence is much more frequent in (low-income/high-income) families, it is possible that poverty, rather than father absence, may cause some (or all) of the negative effects.

20-6. In your continued critical thinking about the assertions discussed, recall also the fallacies in reasoning introduced in Chapter 10: irrelevant reasons, circular reasoning, slippery slope, weak analogies, and false dichotomy. Which of these apply to the following assertions? Use the abbreviations IR, CR, SS, WA, or FD.

(a) _____ "To tolerate the trend of fatherlessness is to accept the inevitability of continued societal recession."

(b) _____ "If present trends continue, our society could be on the verge of social suicide."

Answers: 20-1. increase **20-2.** is correlated with **20-3.** cannot **20-4.** divorce **20-5.** low-income **20-6.** (a) FD. The quote may have elements of more than one fallacy, but the author really is posing a dichotomy: Either we reduce father absence, or else we will face social decline. Of course, we could do both (reduce father absence and face social decline) or neither. (b) SS. The argument is that if we allow one event to happen, then other events will inevitably follow on this slippery slope that will lead to disaster.

REVIEW OF KEY TERMS

Age of viability
Animism
Attachment
Centration
Cephalocaudal trend
Cognitive development
Conservation
Cross-sectional design
Dementia
Development
Developmental norms
Dishabituation
Egocentrism
Embryonic stage

Fetal alcohol syndrome
Fetal stage
Gender
Gender differences
Gender roles
Gender stereotypes
Germinal stage
Irreversibility
Longitudinal study
Maturation
Menarche
Motor development
Object permanence

Placenta
Prenatal period
Primary sex characteristics
Proximodistal trend
Puberty
Pubescence
Secondary sex characteristics
Separation anxiety
Infant mortality
Sex
Stage
Temperament
Zygote

_____ 1. The sequence of age-related changes that occurs as a person progresses from conception to death.

_____ 2. The period of pregnancy, extending from conception to birth.

_____ 3. The first two weeks after conception.

_____ 4. The structure that connects the circulation of the fetus and the mother but that blocks passage of blood cells.

_____ 5. The second stage of prenatal development, lasting from two weeks after conception until the end of the second month.

_____ 6. The third stage of prenatal development, lasting from two months after conception through birth.

_____ 7. The age at which the baby can first survive in the event of a premature birth.

_____ 8. A collection of congenital problems associated with a mother's excessive use of alcohol during pregnancy.

_____ 9. The death rate in the first year of life per 1000 births.

_____ 10. Developmental changes in muscular coordination required for physical movement.

_____ 11. The head-to-foot direction of motor development.

_____ 12. The center-outward direction of motor development.

_____ 13. The average ages at which people display certain behaviors and abilities.

_____ 14. Characteristic mood, energy level, and reactivity.

_____ 15. One group of subjects is observed over a long period of time.

_____ 16. Investigators compare groups of subjects of differing ages at a single point in time.

_____ 17. Emotional distress displayed by an infant when separated from a person with whom it has formed an attachment.

_____ 18. Culturally constructed distinctions between femininity and masculinity.

_____ 19. Widely held beliefs about females' and males' abilities, personality traits, and social behavior.

_____ 20. Development of thinking, reasoning, remembering, and problem solving.

_____ 21. A mental capacity that involves recognizing that objects continue to exist even when they are no longer visible.

_____ 22. Piaget's term for the awareness that physical quantities remain constant in spite of changes in their shape or appearance.

_____ 23. The Piagetian term for the tendency to focus on just one feature of a problem and neglect other important features.

_____ 24. The inability to cognitively visualize reversing an action.

_____ 25. Thinking characterized by a limited ability to share another person's viewpoint.

_____ 17. The attribution of lifelike qualities to inanimate objects.

_____ 27. A developmental period during which certain behaviors and capacities occur.

_____ 28. The biologically based categories of male and female.

_____ 29. Expectations concerning what the appropriate behavior is for each sex.

_____ 30. An abnormal deterioration in mental faculties that accompanies aging in about 15 percent of people over age 65.

_____ 31. A close, emotional bond of affection between an infant and its caregiver.

_____ 32. Physical features associated with gender that are not directly needed for reproduction.

_____ 33. The physical structures necessary for reproduction.

_____ 34. The two-year span preceding puberty marked by the appearance of secondary sex characteristics and by rapid growth.

_____ 35. The first occurrence of menstruation.

_____ 36. The stage during which reproductive functions reach maturity.

_____ 37. Occurs if a new stimulus elicits an increase in strength of a previously habituated response.

_____ 38. Developmental changes that reflect one's genetic blueprint rather than environment.

_____ 39. A one-celled organism created by the process of fertilization, the union of sperm and egg.

_____ 40. Behavioral differences between females and males.

Answers: 1. development **2.** prenatal period **3.** germinal stage **4.** placenta **5.** embryonic stage **6.** fetal stage **7.** age of viability **8.** fetal alcohol syndrome **9.** infant mortality **10.** motor development **11.** cephalocaudal trend **12.** proximodistal trend **13.** developmental norms **14.** temperament **15.** longitudinal design **16.** cross-sectional design **17.** separation anxiety **18.** gender **19.** gender stereotypes **20.** cognitive development **21.** object permanence **22.** conservation **23.** centration **24.** irreversibility **25.** egocentrism **26.** animism **27.** stage **28.** sex **29.** gender roles **30.** dementia **31.** attachment **32.** secondary sex characteristics **33.** primary sex characteristics **34.** pubescence **35.** menarche **36.** puberty **37.** dishabituation **38.** maturation **39.** zygote **40.** gender differences.

REVIEW OF KEY PEOPLE

Mary Ainsworth   Lawrence Kohlberg   Alexander Thomas & Stella Chess
Erik Erikson   Jean Piaget

_____   1. Conducted a major longitudinal study which identified three basic styles of children's temperament.

_____   2. Partitioned the life span into eight stages, each accompanied by a psychosocial crisis.

_____   3. Pioneered the study of children's cognitive development.

_____   4. Developed a stage theory of moral development.

_____   5. Described three categories of infant-mother attachment.

Answers: 1. Thomas & Chess **2.** Erikson **3.** Piaget **4.** Kohlberg **5.** Ainsworth.

SELF-QUIZ

1. Which prenatal period begins at the second week and ends at the second month of pregnancy?
   a. germinal stage
   b. embryonic stage
   c. fetal stage
   d. seminal stage

2. In which prenatal stage do most major birth defects probably have their origins?
   a. germinal stage
   b. embryonic stage
   c. fetal stage
   d. seminal stage

3. Some research have found that very young children (e.g., 5 months old) appear to be aware of the addition or subtraction of objects from behind a screen. The technique used in these studies was:
   a. sensory preconditioning
   b. self-socialization
   c. classical conditioning
   d. habituation-dishabituation

4. According to Belsky's evolutionary viewpoint, the current harshness of an environment affects parent-child attachment, which in turn affects the offspring's later:
   a. accommodation and assimilation
   b. adaptation to traumatic events
   c. reproductive or mating strategy
   d. expression of discomfort and alienation

5. What is the major conclusion from Thomas and Chess's longitudinal study of temperament?
   a. Children's temperaments tend to go through predictable stages.
   b. The temperament of the child is not a good predictor of the temperament of the adult.
   c. Opposites attract.
   d. Children's temperaments tend to be consistent over the years.

6. The crisis occurring in the first year, according to Erikson, is one involving:
   a. trust versus mistrust
   b. initiative versus guilt
   c. industry versus inferiority
   d. identity versus conformity

7. During which stage in Piaget's system is the child first able to handle conservation problems and hierarchical classification problems?
   a. sensorimotor
   b. preoperational
   c. concrete operations
   d. formal operations

8. A child in the early sensorimotor period is shown a ball, which she watches intensely. The ball is then hidden under a pillow. What will the child do?
   a. ask, "Where is the pillow?"
   b. stare at the pillow but not pick it up
   c. move the pillow and pick up the ball
   d. ignore the pillow, as if the ball didn't exist

9. Who developed a stage theory of moral development?
   a. Piaget
   b. Kohlberg
   c. Gould
   d. Bowlby

10. Which of the following cognitive capacities is most likely to decline as a function of aging?
    a. speed of processing
    b. crystallized intelligence
    c. problem-solving ability
    d. specialized intelligence

11. Suicide in the 15–23 age group (adolescents and young adults) occurs:
    a. more frequently than in all other age groups
    b. more frequently than in the 25-44 age groups
    c. more frequently than in the 65–73 age group
    d. at about the same rate as or less frequently than in older age groups

12. Which of the following factors tends to be accompanied by a drop in ratings of marital satisfaction?
    a. childlessness during early married life
    b. the birth of the first child
    c. the first child's departure for college
    d. when the last child leaves home

13. Females tend to score slightly higher than males on tests of:
    a. verbal ability
    b. mathematical ability
    c. visual-spatial ability
    d. specialized ability

14. Females exposed to high levels of — during prenatal development tend to have masculine interests and preferences for male playmates.
    a. estrogen
    b. androgen
    c. lithium chloride
    d. insulin

15. Once children discover that their gender is permanent, they are likely to want to engage in behavior that is "sex appropriate" as defined by the culture. This process is referred to as:
    a. operant conditioning
    b. observational learning
    c. self-socialization
    d. classical conditioning

Answers: 1. b **2.** b **3.** d **4.** c **5.** d **6.** a **7.** c **8.** d **9.** b **10.** a **11.** d **12.** b **13.** a **14.** b **15.** c.

INFOTRAC

Dementia

Fetal Alcohol Syndrome

Gender Stereotypes

Puberty

Temperament

12 PERSONALITY: THEORY, RESEARCH, AND ASSESSMENT

REVIEW OF KEY IDEAS

THE NATURE OF PERSONALITY

1. **Define the construct of personality in terms of consistency and distinctiveness.**

   1-1. I could always tell when my colleague across the hall (now retired) had finished for the day because I could hear squeaking as he carefully moved his computer table under his bookcase. And I knew what followed: He closed and reshelved his books, sorted the papers on his desk into two piles, and slid the pens and pencils into his desk drawer bin. The fact that my colleague engaged in the *same behaviors* every day illustrates the feature of personality termed _____.

   1-2. When I'm done, on the other hand, I usually just stand up and walk out, leaving my somewhat (some would say very) messy desk behind. The fact that my colleague and I *differ* with respect to office neatness illustrates the feature of personality termed _____.

   Answers: 1-1. consistency (stability) **1-2.** distinctiveness (behavioral differences).

2. **Explain what is meant by a personality trait and describe proposed systems for organizing traits.**

   2-1. A consistent or durable disposition to behave in particular way is referred to as a personality _____. Personality trait descriptions frequently consist of a series of _____ (e.g., anxious, excitable, shy, aggressive, etc.).

   2-2. There are an enormous number of trait words that could be used to describe people. For example, Gordon Allport came up with a system that included 4500 personality traits. Raymond Cattell reduced Allport's list to just _____ traits, and more recently McCrae and Costa have described yet a simpler model involving only _____ traits.

   2-3. Some researchers maintain that more than five factors are needed to describe personality. Others contend that fewer than five factors are needed. Of the various models, however, the dominant conception of personality structure is currently the _____-factor model.

   Answers: 2-1. trait, adjectives **2-2.** 16, five **2-3.** five.

3. **List and describe the three components into which Freud divided personality and his three levels of awareness.**

    3-1. Below is a schematic illustration of the three Freudian structures of personality. Label each.

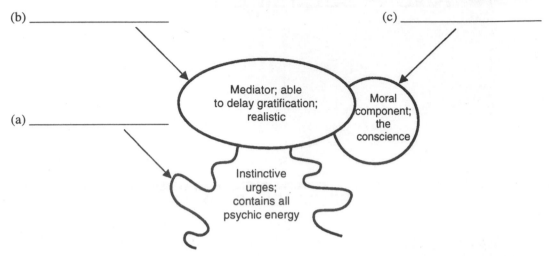

(b) _____

(c) _____

(a) _____

Mediator; able to delay gratification; realistic

Moral component; the conscience

Instinctive urges; contains all psychic energy

    3-2. Freud superimposed levels of consciousness on the psychic structures. The following illustration makes clear that two of the structures exist at all three levels while one is entirely unconscious. Label the levels.

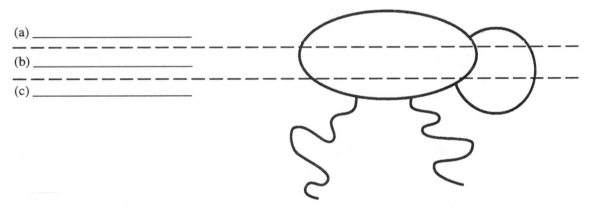

(a) _____

(b) _____

(c) _____

Answers: 3-1. (a) id (b) ego (c) superego **3-2.** (a) conscious (b) preconscious (c) unconscious (The diagram shows that the ego emerges from the id and that the superego grows out of the ego.)

4. **Explain the preeminence of sexual and aggressive conflicts in Freud's theory and describe various defense mechanisms.**

    4-1. Freud believed that most of our conflicts arise from _____ and _____ urges. Conflicts relating to these areas were preeminent in his mind because (1) they are subject to subtle social _____ and, for that reason, are a source of confusion; and (2) they are more apt to be _____ than other urges.

    4-2. Following is a list of the defense mechanisms. Match each with the correct description by placing the appropriate letters in the blanks.

A. rationalization   D. displacement   F. regression
B. repression   E. reaction formation G. identification
C. projection

_____ A return to an earlier, less mature stage of development.

_____ Forming an imaginary or real alliance with a person or group; becoming like them.

_____ Creating false but reasonable-sounding excuses.

_____ Pushing distressing thoughts into the unconscious.

_____ Attributing ones own thoughts, feelings, or conflicts to another.

_____ Expressing an emotion that is the exact opposite of the way one really, but unconsciously, feels.

_____ Diverting emotional feelings from their original source to a substitute target.

4-3. Using the letters from the previous question, match the defense mechanisms with the following examples.

_____ After John and Marsha break up, John says he hates Marsha; this statement helps him defend against his real feelings of affection.

_____ "Society is filled with perverts," says the preacher; but later evidence suggests that he is the one with the sexual conflicts.

_____ In reaction to the stress of entering college, Alice started acting like a grade-school kid.

_____ Bruce acts like John Wayne, and he owns tapes of all the Duke's movies.

_____ Mary is angry at her mother, so she kicks her baby brother.

Answers: 4-1. sexual, aggressive, norms (rules, controls), frustrated (thwarted, unfulfilled) **4-2.** F, G, A, B, C, E, D
4-3. E, C, F, G, D.

5. Outline Freud's psychosexual stages of development and their theorized relations to adult personality.

5-1. List Freud's stages of psychosexual development, in the order in which they are supposed to occur, in the blanks below. Place the approximate ages (Table 12.3) in the parentheses.

(a) _____ (   )

(b) _____ (   )

(c) _____ (   )

(d) _____ (   )

(e) _____ (   )

5-2. The following behaviors or personality characteristics were thought to result from fixation at a particular psychosexual stage. Place the names of the correct stages in the blanks.

(a) She has problems with anger control, is hostile toward people in authority, and defies any attempt at regulation of her behavior. _____

(b) He eats too much, drinks too much, and smokes. _____

(c) He has occasional outbursts of hostility toward his father that he can't understand. In family arguments he sides with his mother. _____

5-3. The Oedipus complex occurs during the _____ stage, at about age four or five. This complex theoretically involves an erotically tinged attraction toward the (<u>same-sex/opposite-sex</u>) parent and a strong hostility toward the (<u>same-sex/opposite-sex</u>) parent. Resolution of the Oedipus complex involves (<u>increasing/stopping</u>) both the child's erotic attraction and the child's hostility.

Answers: 5-1. (a) oral (0-1) (b) anal (2-3) (c) phallic (4-5) (d) latency (6-12) (e) genital (puberty on) **5-2.** (a) anal (b) oral (c) phallic **5-3.** phallic, opposite-sex, same-sex, stopping.

6. Summarize the revisions of Freud's theory proposed by Jung and Adler.

6-1. Freud devised the theory and method of treatment termed *psychoanalysis*. To differentiate his approach from Freud's, Jung called his theory _____ _____. Like Freud, Jung emphasized the unconscious determinants of personality. Unlike Freud, he proposed that the unconscious consists of two layers, a _____ unconscious and a _____ unconscious. The personal unconscious is similar to Freud's unconscious. The collective unconscious is a repository of inherited, ancestral memories that Jung termed _____.

6-2. Jung's major contribution to psychology is considered by many to be his description of two major personality types: _____, reserved, contemplative people who tend to be concerned with their own internal world of thoughts; and _____, outgoing people who are more interested in the external world of others.

6-3. For Freud, the driving energy behind the human personality was sexuality; for Jung it may have been the collective unconscious. For Adler, it was striving for _____ and the attempt to overcome childhood feelings of inferiority. Efforts to overcome imagined or real inferiorities involve _____ through development of one's abilities. While Adler considered compensation to be a normal mechanism, he saw _____ as an abnormal attempt to conceal feelings of inferiority.

6-4. Adler is associated with the term _____ _____, an exaggerated feeling of inadequacy supposedly caused by parental pampering or neglect in early childhood. To a greater extent than either Freud or Jung, Adler emphasized the effects of the social context on personality development. For example, he thought that _____ _____ (that is, whether one is an only child, first-born, second-born, etc.) had a major effect on personality. Although the concept created considerable interest, birth order has turned out to be a (<u>weaker/ stronger</u>) and (<u>more/less</u>) consistent factor than he had supposed.

Answers: 6-1. analytical psychology, personal, collective, archetypes **6-2.** introverts, extraverts **6-3.** superiority, compensation, overcompensation **6-4.** inferiority complex, birth order, weaker, less.

7. **Summarize the strengths and weaknesses of the psychodynamic approach to personality.**

    7-1.   Psychoanalytic formulations have had a major impact on the field of psychology. List the three contributions discussed in your text.

    7-2.   Psychoanalytic formulations have also been extensively criticized. After each of the following statements list the particular criticism, from the discussion in your text, that the statement represents.

        (a) Freud proposed that females develop weaker superegos and that they have a chronic sense of inferiority caused by penis envy. _____

        (b) Although he discussed some characteristics associated with the psychosexual stages, Freud didn't really specify which events, occurring during which childhood stages, produce which sets of personality traits. _____

        (c) Claims of support for the theories are based largely on clinical case studies and clinical intuition. _____

Answers: 7-1. the discovery that *unconscious forces* can influence behavior, that *internal conflict* may generate psychological distress, and that *early childhood experiences* influence the adult personality **7-2.** (a) sexism (male-centered) (b) vague (untestable ideas) (c) inadequate or weak evidence.

BEHAVIORAL PERSPECTIVES

8. **Discuss how Skinner's principles of operant conditioning can be applied to the understanding of personality.**

    8-1.   Which of the following processes plays an important part in Skinner's ideas about human behavior?

        a. mental conflict

        b. the mind

        c. free will

        d. none of the above

    8-2.   According to Skinner, much of our behavior is affected by reinforcement, punishment, or extinction—in other words, by the environmental _____ that follow our behavior. For example, if some individuals behave in a consistently aggressive manner (i.e., have aggressive personality traits), they do so because they have been _____ for behaving aggressively in the past.

    8-3.   Skinner recognized that there are differences between people and that people behave relatively consistent over time. This distinctiveness and consistency occur, however, not because of what's going on in an individual's *mind* but because of what has occurred previously in their _____.

8-4. Thus, for Skinner, personality is not mental, but environmental. People do not change their minds, their environment changes. Skinner makes a strong case for the point of view that our behavior is caused or _____ rather than free and that the determinants are largely _____ rather than genetic.

Answers: 8-1. d **8-2.** consequences (stimuli, events), reinforced **8-3.** environment **8-4.** determined, environmental.

9. Describe Bandura's contributions to personality theory.

9-1. In what respect is Bandura's point of view similar to Skinner's?

9-2. Bandura's major theoretical contribution is his concept of observational learning. What is observational learning?

9-3. According to Bandura whom do we imitate, and in what circumstances?

9-4. Explain Bandura's concept of self-efficacy.

Answers: 9-1. It is similar in that Bandura believes that personality is largely shaped through learning. **9-2.** Observational learning is the process through which we learn behaviors by observing someone else's (i.e., a model's) behavior. For example, we learn not only by being reinforced (Skinner) but by observing someone else being reinforced. **9-3.** We tend to imitate models whom we like, consider attractive or powerful, view as similar to ourselves, or see being reinforced. Children tend to imitate same-sex models. **9-4.** Self-efficacy is our belief in our ability to perform certain behaviors in order to obtain certain outcomes. Self-efficacy affects whether we undertake a task and how well we perform it.

10. Identify Mischel's major contribution to personality theory and indicate why his ideas have generated so much controversy.

10-1. Mischel's major contribution to personality theory is his contention that human behavior is determined to a much greater extent by the _____ than by _____.

10-2. Why is this such a controversial idea for personality theory?

Answers: 10-1. situation (situational factors), personality (personality traits) **10-2.** The notion is controversial because the very definition of personality involves the word *consistency*. Mischel's findings suggest that behavior is not as consistent as personality theorists may have thought, that it is strongly affected by an ever-changing situation.

11. **Summarize the strengths and weaknesses of the behavioral approach to personality.**

 11-1.   The major strengths of the behavioral approach have been its commitment to empirical
 _____, which keeps it open to new findings and ideas, and its identification of
 important _____ determinants of behavior.

 11-2.   The major weaknesses of the behavioral approach, according to its critics, have been its overdependence
 on research involving _____ subjects, its failure to integrate
 _____ factors into the theories, and its _____ view of personality.

 Answers: **11-1.** research, environmental (situational) **11-2.** animal, biological (genetic), fragmented.

HUMANISTIC PERSPECIVTES

12. **Explain how humanism was a reaction against both the behavioral and psychodynamic approaches and discuss the assumptions of the humanistic view.**

 12-1.   The humanistic movement reacted against (a) the behavioral approach, because of its mechanistic,
 fragmented view of personality and its emphasis on _____ research, and against (b) the
 psychoanalytic approach, because of its emphasis on _____ drives.

 12-2.   In addition, humanistic psychology objected to both movements because of their emphasis on
 _____, or absolute causation. The humanists also thought that the behaviorists and the
 Freudians failed to recognize the (<u>unique/common</u>) qualities of human behavior.

 12-3.   Humanistic psychology emphasizes the (<u>similarities/differences</u>) between human beings and the other
 animal species; believes we (<u>are controlled by/can rise above</u>) our biological heritage; asserts that we are
 largely (<u>rational/irrational</u>) creatures; and maintains that a person's (<u>subjective/objective</u>) view of the
 world is more important than _____ reality.

 Answers: **12-1.** animal, primitive (animalistic) **12-2.** determinism, unique **12-3.** differences, can rise above, rational, subjective, objective.

13. **Identify the single structural construct in Rogers's person-centered theory and summarize his view of personality development.**

 13-1.   Who are you? What are you like? What are your unique qualities? What is your typical behavior? Your
 answers to these questions are likely to reflect what Roger's called the _____.

 13-2.   Although Ralph is in fact a submissive and somewhat lazy person, he views himself as dynamic and
 hard-working.

 (a) What is Ralph's self-concept?

 (b) Is his self-concept congruent or incongruent?

(c) According to Rogers, what parental behavior may have led to this incongruence?

(d) According to Rogers, what parental behavior would have resulted in Ralph's achieving congruence rather than incongruence?

13-3. What is defensiveness for Rogers?

Answers: 13-1. self or self-concept **13-2.** (a) that he is hard-working, dynamic, and a leader (b) incongruent (c) conditional love, the condition being that the child must live up to another's expectations (d) unconditional love, full acceptance of the person that is not dependent on what he or she is or does **13-3.** As with Freud, people defend against anxiety by distorting or denying reality. For Rogers, people's defensiveness arises when people defend their self-concepts against inconsistent experiences. Thus, defensiveness is related to incongruence.

14. Explain Maslow's hierarchy of needs and his view of the healthy personality.

14-1. Maslow proposed that human needs are arranged in a hierarchy, usually depicted as a pyramid, with the most basic, physiological needs at the _____ and higher-level needs closer to the

_____.

14-2. The lower level needs include needs for food, water, and factors related to survival and security. Next in the hierarchy are needs for acceptance and love by others, followed by higher level needs, referred to as growth needs, for knowledge, order, and aesthetic beauty. Higher level needs would be activated (<u>just before/only after</u>) a lower level need is satisfied.

14-3. At the top of the pyramid is the need for _____, the need to express one's full potential.

14-4. Maslow proposed that people who are self-actualized have exceptionally healthy personalities. Which of the following, according to Maslow, are characteristic of self-actualized people? Place Y in the blank if the description applies, N if it does not.

_____ spontaneous

_____ has more profound emotional experiences than others

_____ uncomfortable being alone

_____ not dependent on others for approval

_____ thrive on their work

_____ extreme in personality (e.g., either conforming or rebellious)

Answers: 14-1. bottom, top **14-2.** only after **14-3.** self-actualization **14-4.** Y, Y, N, Y, Y, N.

15. **Summarize the strengths and weaknesses of the humanistic approach to personality.**

   15-1. To its credit, the humanistic movement called attention to the possibility that a person's _____ views may be more important than objective reality. The movement also emphasized the importance of the _____ or self-concept and stressed the study of the (normal/abnormal) personality.

   15-2. Critics have also identified several weaknesses of the humanistic formulations. Match the weaknesses listed below with the statements by placing the appropriate letters in the blanks.

   a. poor testability

   b. unrealistic view of human nature

   c. inadequate evidence

   _____ Humanistic psychologists tend to scorn research, so little experimental support for their views has emerged.

   _____ Even without research, some of the descriptions, such as of self-actualized personalities, have an idealized, perfectionistic ring.

   _____ Humanistic ideas are frequently difficult to define, so research on some concepts is difficult or impossible.

   Answers: **15-1.** subjective, self, normal **15-2.** c, b, a.

BIOLOGICAL PERSPECTIVES

16. **Describe Eysenck's biological theory of personality.**

   16-1. According to Eysenck, individual differences in personality can be understood in terms of a hierarchy of traits. At the top of the hierarchy are three fundamental higher-order traits from which all other traits derive: _____, _____, and _____.

   16-2. Eysenck asserted that a major factor in personality involves the ease with which people can be _____. Eysenck believed that differences in conditionability, like personality differences in general, are to a large extent (environmentally/genetically) determined.

   16-3. Conditionability, in turn, is related to extraversion-introversion. According to Eysenck (extraverts/introverts) have higher levels of physiological arousal, a characteristic that makes them (more/less) readily conditioned.

   16-4. Why would conditionability be related to introversion? Because easily conditioned people, according to Eysenck, are likely to be conditioned to fear (i.e., inhibited) social situations. Thus, in Eysenck's theory, people who are high in arousal are also highly conditionable and, therefore, likely to be _____.

   Answers: **16-1.** extraversion, neuroticism, psychoticism **16-2.** conditioned, genetically **16-3.** introverts, more **16-4.** introverts (introverted, inhibited).

17. **Summarize behavioral genetics research as it relates to the heritability of personality.**

    17-1. The most important and conclusive result from the various twin studies is the finding that the personalities of (identical/fraternal) twins reared (together/apart) were more similar than those of (identical/fraternal) twins reared (together/apart). This outcome has been found with several dependent measures, including the factors of the Big Five personality inventory as well as peer ratings.

    17-2. Approximately what percentage of the variance in personality is assumed to be caused by genetic factors?

        a. 10 to 20 percent

        b. 20 to 40 percent

        c. 40 to 60 percent

        d. 60 to 80 percent

    17-3. How important a determinant of personality is family environment, according to the results of these studies?

        a. of very little importance

        b. of about the same importance as heredity

        c. more important than heredity

Answers: 17-1. identical, apart, fraternal, together. This is the most important comparison because: even though the fraternal twins shared the same environment, their common environment did not make them nearly as similar as twins who did not have a common environment *but who shared the same heredity.* **17-2.** c **17-3.** a (Since many psychological theories have stressed the importance of the family environment for the development of personality, this has been a truly surprising finding.)

18. **Discuss evolutionary analyses of personality.**

    18-1. As group animals, we gain an advantage by being able to predict the behavior of other human beings. That is, the ability to recognize the "Big Five" characteristics in others has _____ value for our species.

    18-2. The big five traits are: neuroticism, extraversion, openness to experience, agreeableness, and conscientiousness. In terms of survival value, it is useful to know who in a group will fulfill their commitments, the trait of _____ ; who will fall apart under stress, the trait of _____ ; who will be a good problem solver, the trait of _____ , and so on.

    18-3. The fact that these traits appear as dimensions across a variety of cultures attests to their importance. For Buss, our ability to _____ these traits in others also has adaptive significance.

Answers: 18-1. adaptive (survival, evolutionary) **18-2.** conscientiousness, neuroticism, openness to experience **18-3.** recognize.

19. Summarize the strengths and weaknesses of the biological approach to personality.

19-1. Generally, parents are blamed for kids' personalities. I recently asked a friend of mine why she thought a mutual acquaintance of ours was so obnoxious. She said, "Well, raised with such crazy parents, what would you expect?" I said, "Is that an argument for environment or heredity?" That is one of the benefits of the twin studies: They put data in place of speculation. But what are some of the weaknesses of this research? One is that heritability ratios should be regarded only as _____ that will vary depending on sampling procedures. Another is that there is no comprehensive biological _____ of personality.

Answers: 19-1. estimates, theory.

CULTURE AND PERSONALITY

20. Summarize research on culture and personality.

20-1. For a decade or so after World War II, researchers using the Freudian model attempted to find a model personality type representative of each culture. This attempt was (successful/not successful).

20-2. With the current increased attention to cultural factors, interest in the relationship between personality and culture has again surfaced, and the new data have revealed both cross-cultural similarities and differences. With regard to similarity, precisely the same "_____" personality factors tend to emerge in different cultures.

20-3. With regard to differences, research by Markus and Kitayama clearly indicates that the individualistic orientation characteristic of the West is not universal across cultures. While Americans tend to value (independence/connectedness), Asians value (interdependence/uniqueness) among people. Similarly, while American parents encourage their children to (stand out/blend in), Asian parents emphasize taking pride in the accomplishments of (each individual/the group).

20-4. Even though the Big Five traits occur in widely different cultures, these traits do not necessarily mean the same things cross-culturally. For example, Eastern cultures emphasize (self-enhancement/self-criticism), which tends to be associated in the East, as is true in the West, with lower self-esteem. Somewhat surprisingly, however, self-esteem in Eastern cultures (is/is not) associated with subjective well-being.

Answers: 20-1. not successful 20-2. Big Five 20-3. independence, interdependence, stand out, the group 20-4. self-criticism, is not.

PUTTING IT IN PERSPECTIVE

21. Explain how this chapter highlighted three of the text's unifying themes.

21-1. We've just discussed one of the three themes emphasized in this chapter, that our behavior is influenced by our cultural heritage. Two other themes prominently demonstrated in the area of personality are that the field is theoretically _____ and that psychology evolves in a _____ context.

21-2. Freudian, behavioral, and biological perspectives of personality assume that behavior is determined; the _____ perspective does not. The biological perspective stresses genetic inheritance; the behavioral perspective stresses (heredity/the environment). As these examples illustrate, the study of personality has produced an enormous amount of theoretical _____.

21-3. Concerning sociohistorical context, it is clear that theories of personality have strongly affected our culture. For example, the surrealist art movement, begun in the 1920s, derives directly from _____ psychology, as do other movements in literature and the arts. And the current debate on the effects of media violence is to a large extent a product of research in social _____ theory.

21-4. In turn, culture has affected psychology. For example, it seems quite likely that the sexually repressive climate of Victorian Vienna caused Freud to emphasize the _____ aspects of human behavior; and it is clear, from Freud's own description, that World War I influenced his development of the second Freudian instinct, the _____ instinct. Thus, psychology evolves in a _____ context.

Answers: 21-1. diverse, sociohistorical **21-2.** humanistic, environment, diversity **21-3.** psychoanalytic (Freudian), learning **21-4.** sexual, aggression, sociohistorical.

APPLICATION • UNDERSTANDING PERSONALITY ASSESSMENT

22. **Describe self-report inventories and summarize their strengths and weaknesses.**

22-1. The MMPI, 16PF, and NEO personality inventories are (projective/self-report) tests. All three tests are also used to measure (single/multiple) traits.

22-2. Identify which tests (MMPI, 16PF, or NEO) are described by each of the following.

(a) _____ Originally designed to diagnose psychological disorders.

(b) _____, _____ Originally designed to assess the normal personality.

(c) _____ Contains 187 items.

(d) _____ Contains 567 items.

(e) _____ Measures the "big five" personality traits.

(f) _____ Includes four validity scales to help detect deception.

22-3. The major strength of self-report inventories, in comparison with simply asking a person what they are like, is that they provide a more precise and more (objective/personal) measure of personality.

22-4. The major weakness of self-report inventories is that they are subject to several sources of error, including the following: (1) Test-takers may intentionally fake responses, that is, may engage in deliberate _____. (2) While not realizing it, people may answer questions in ways to make themselves "look good," the _____ _____ bias. (3) In addition, some people tend either to agree or to disagree with nearly every statement on a test, a source of error involving _____ sets.

Answers: 22-1. self-report, multiple 22-2. (a) MMPI (b) 16PF, NEO (c) 16PF (d) MMPI (e) NEO (f) MMPI
22-3. objective 22-4. deception (lying), social desirability, response.

PERSONAL APPLICATION • UNDERSTANDING PERSONALITY ASSESSMENT

23. **Describe the projective tests and summarize their strengths and weaknesses.**

   23-1.   If you have ever looked at clouds and described the images you've seen, you've done something similar to taking a projective test. If you thought that the images you saw reflected something about your personality, then you also accepted the *projective hypothesis*. The projective hypothesis is the idea that people will tend to _____ their characteristics onto ambiguous stimuli, so that what they see reveals something about their personalities and problems.

   23-2.   Two major projective tests are the Rorschach, a series of _____, and the TAT, a series of simple _____.

   23-3.   The advantages of projective tests are that (1) since the way the tests are interpreted is not at all obvious, it is difficult for people to engage in intentional _____; and (2) projective tests may be sensitive to aspects of personality of which people are _____.

   23-4.   The major weaknesses of projective tests concerns inadequate evidence that they are _____ (consistent) or that they are _____ (measure what they are intended to measure). Nonetheless, the projective tests continue to be used and are valued by many clinicians.

Answers: 23-1. project 23-2. inkblots, pictures (scenes) 23-3. deception, unconscious (unaware) 23-4. reliable, valid.

CRITICAL THINKING APPLICATION • HINDSIGHT IN EVERYDAY ANALYSES OF PERSONALITY

24. **Discuss how hindsight bias affects everyday analyses of personality and scientific theorizing about personality.**

   24-1.   I am writing this sentence following a period of very substantial decline in the stock market. Somewhat surprising, to me at least, is the fact my colleagues say they saw it coming. If everyone saw it coming, why didn't everyone sell last year? Because we didn't see it coming. Rather, once exposed to information, we are inclined to believe that we already knew it, the cognitive tendency known as the _____.

   24-2.   Suppose you meet someone who is achievement motivated and fiercely independent. You learn that this person was brought up by adoptive parents who were somewhat distant and undemonstrative. Would you connect the events, thinking that the parent's child-rearing style accounted for their child's independence? Or, suppose that the person brought up by these parents is depressed and chronically unemployed. Would you connect the parenting and personality in this case, too? You might, because people tend to interpret _____ events in terms of _____, which is a definition of the hindsight bias.

24-3. What is the hindsight bias? Write a definition in the space below.

24-4. In what way might psychoanalytic interpretations involve the hindsight bias?

24-5. How might evolutionary theory's account of the emergence of the Big Five traits reflect the hindsight bias?

Answers: **24-1.** hindsight bias **24-2.** past (previous), present information (outcomes, current information) **24-3.** Once we know something, we tend to reinterpret past events in terms of that information. Or, once exposed to information, we tend to think we knew it all along. The hindsight bias is our tendency to mold our interpretation of the past to fit how events actually turned out. **24-4.** Once the analyst knows someone's personality traits, he or she can easily explain how their childhood experiences would account for these traits. **24-5.** Once exposed to the fact that the Big Five traits appear world-wide, an evolutionary theorist could easily explain the adaptive significance of this occurrence.

REVIEW OF KEY TERMS

Archetypes
Behaviorism
Collective unconscious
Compensation
Conscious
Defense mechanisms
Displacement
Ego
Extraverts
Fixation
Hierarchy of needs
Hindsight bias
Humanism
Id

Identification
Incongruence
Introverts
Model
Need for self-actualization
Observational learning
Oedipal complex
Personality
Personality trait
Pleasure principle
Preconscious
Projection
Projective tests
Psychodynamic theories

Psychosexual stages
Rationalization
Reaction formation
Reality principle
Regression
Repression
Self-actualizing persons
Self-concept
Self-efficacy
Self-report inventories
Striving for superiority
Superego
Unconscious

_____ 1. An individual's unique constellation of consistent behavioral traits.

_____ 2. A characteristic that represents a durable disposition to behave in a particular way in a variety of situations.

_____ 3. Instruments consisting of vague, ambiguous stimuli that people respond to in ways that may reveal people's needs, feelings, and personalities.

_____ 4. All the diverse theories, descended from the work of Sigmund Freud, that focus on unconscious mental forces.

_____ **5.** The primitive, instinctive component of personality that operates according to the pleasure principle.

_____ **6.** The id's demands for immediate gratification of its urges.

_____ **7.** The decision-making component of personality that operates according to the reality principle.

_____ **8.** The ego's delay of gratification of the id's urges until appropriate outlets and situations can be found.

_____ **9.** The moral component of personality that incorporates social standards about what represents right and wrong.

_____ **10.** Consists of whatever you are aware of at a particular point in time.

_____ **11.** Contains material just beneath the surface of awareness that can be easily retrieved.

_____ **12.** Contains thoughts, memories, and desires that are well below the surface of conscious awareness.

_____ **13.** The series of largely unconscious Freudian reactions that protect a person from unpleasant emotions such as anxiety or guilt.

_____ **14.** The defense mechanism that pushes distressing thoughts and feelings into the unconscious or keeps them from emerging into consciousness.

_____ **15.** Attributing your own thoughts, feelings, or motives to another.

_____ **16.** Creating false but plausible excuses to justify unacceptable behavior.

_____ **17.** Diverting emotional feelings (usually anger) from their original source to a substitute target.

_____ **18.** Behaving in a way that is exactly the opposite of one's true feelings.

_____ **19.** Reverting to immature patterns of behavior.

_____ **20.** Bolstering self-esteem by forming an imaginary or real alliance with some person or group.

_____ **21.** Developmental periods with a characteristic sexual focus that leave their mark on adult personality.

_____ **22.** A failure to move forward from one stage to another as expected.

_____ **23.** Characterized by erotically tinged desires for one's opposite-sex parent and hostility toward one's same-sex parent.

_____ **24.** A storehouse of latent memory traces inherited from our ancestral past.

_____ **25.** Emotionally charged images and thought forms that have universal meaning.

_____ **26.** People who tend to be preoccupied with the internal world of their own thoughts, feelings, and experiences.

_____ **27.** People who tend to be interested in the external world of people and things.

_____ **28.** A universal drive to adapt, to improve oneself, and to master life's challenges.

_____ **29.** Efforts to overcome imagined or real inferiorities by developing one's abilities.

_____ **30.** A theoretical orientation based on the premise that scientific psychology should study only observable behavior.

_____ **31.** Learning that occurs when an organism's responding is influenced by the observation of others.

_____ **32.** A person whose behavior is observed by another.

_____ **33.** Our belief about our ability to perform behaviors that should lead to expected outcomes.

_____ 34. A theoretical orientation that emphasizes the unique qualities of humans, especially their freedom and potential for personal growth.

_____ 35. A collection of beliefs about one's own nature, unique qualities, and typical behavior.

_____ 36. The degree of disparity between one's self-concept and one's actual experience.

_____ 37. The need to fulfill one's potential.

_____ 38. People with exceptionally healthy personalities, marked by continued personal growth.

_____ 39. The tendency to change our interpretations of previous events so that they fit what we know about the current situation.

_____ 40. Personality tests that ask people a series of questions about their characteristic behavior.

_____ 41. A systematic arrangement of needs, according to priority, in which basic, physiological needs must be met before social or growth needs are aroused.

Answers: 1. personality 2. personality trait 3. projective tests 4. psychodynamic theories 5. id 6. pleasure principle 7. ego 8. reality principle 9. superego 10. conscious 11. preconscious 12. unconscious 13. defense mechanisms 14. repression 15. projection 16. rationalization 17. displacement 18. reaction formation 19. regression 20. identification 21. psychosexual stages 22. fixation 23. Oedipal complex 24. collective unconscious 25. archetypes 26. introverts 27. extraverts 28. striving for superiority 29. compensation 30. behaviorism 31. observational learning 32. model 33. self-efficacy 34. humanism 35. self-concept 36. incongruence 37. need for self-actualization 38. self-actualizing persons 39. hindsight bias 40. self-report inventories 41. hierarchy of needs.

REVIEW OF KEY PEOPLE

Alfred Adler
Albert Bandura
Hans Eysenck

Sigmund Freud
Carl Jung
Abraham Maslow

Walter Mischel
Carl Rogers
B. F. Skinner

_____ 1. The founder of psychoanalysis.

_____ 2. Developed the theory called analytical psychology and anticipated the humanists' emphasis on personal growth and self-actualization.

_____ 3. Founder of an approach to personality named individual psychology.

_____ 4. Modern behaviorism's most prominent theorist, recognized for his theories on operant conditioning.

_____ 5. A contemporary behavioral theorist who elaborated the concept of observational learning.

_____ 6. His chief contribution to personality theory has been to focus attention on the extent to which situational factors govern behavior.

_____ 7. One of the fathers of the human potential movement, he called his approach a person-centered theory.

_____ 8. The humanist who developed a theory of self-actualization.

_____ 9. Proposed that conditionability and introversion-extraversion are largely genetically determined.

Answers: 1. Freud 2. Jung 3. Adler 4. Skinner 5. Bandura 6. Mischel 7. Rogers 8. Maslow 9. Eysenck.

SELF-QUIZ

1. Personality traits are characterized by:
   a. consistency and distinctiveness
   b. charm and wit
   c. change as a function of the situation
   d. lack of individual differences

2. Someone attributes his thoughts or feelings or conflicts to someone else. For example, although he chronically interrupts people, he thinks that other people interrupt him. What Freudian defense mechanism is illustrated?
   a. rationalization
   b. reaction formation
   c. regression
   d. projection

3. Which of the following is entirely unconscious, according to Freud?
   a. the id
   b. the ego
   c. the superego
   d. the archetype

4. Although Osmo at an unconscious level has great hatred for Cosmo, he believes that he likes Cosmo and, to the outside world, gives all the appearance of liking him. Which defense mechanism is Osmo using?
   a. regression
   b. reaction formation
   c. projection
   d. rationalization

5. The Oedipal complex occurs during the:
   a. oral stage
   b. anal stage
   c. phallic stage
   d. genital stage

6. Which of the following concepts did Carl Jung originate?
   a. id
   b. superego
   c. inferiority complex
   d. introversion-extraversion

7. Which of the following did Adler emphasize in his theory of personality?
   a. striving for superiority
   b. castration anxiety
   c. introversion-extraversion
   d. the collective unconscious

8. Much of the behavior that we call personality results from reinforcement and observational learning, according to:
   a. Jung
   b. Skinner
   c. Bandura
   d. Adler

9. Which of the following tends to emphasize freedom and personal growth in its view of human behavior?
   a. the psychoanalytic approach
   b. the biological approach
   c. the behavioral approach
   d. the humanistic approach

10. According to Rogers, what causes incongruence?
    a. an inherited sense of irony
    b. conditional acceptance or affection
    c. unconditional acceptance or affection
    d. unconditioned stimuli

11. Herb had the desire and potential to be a violinist but became, instead, a trader in hog futures. He decided never to touch the violin again. What is wrong with Herb, according to Maslow?
    a. He suffers from incongruence.
    b. He suffers from castration anxiety.
    c. He has not achieved self-actualization.
    d. He has an inferiority complex.

12. Which of the following views personality in terms of the adaptive significance to the Big Five traits?
    a. Abraham Maslow
    b. William James
    c. the behavioral approach
    d. the evolutionary approach

13. Your friend spends money like water. When you learn that he is from a poverty-stricken background, you attribute his spending patterns to his earlier deprivation. According to the critical thinking analysis, you are likely to do this because of:
    a. the hindsight bias
    b. a self-serving attribution
    c. the consistency and distinctiveness of personality
    d. circular reasoning

14. According to Mischel, what is the major factor that predicts human behavior?
    a. childhood experience
    b. specifics of the situation
    c. extraversion and introversion
    d. central and peripheral traits

15. You are asked to tell stories about a series of pictures. Which test is being administered to you?
    a. Rorschach
    b. MMPI
    c. TAT
    d. 16PF

Answers: 1. a 2. d 3. a 4. b 5. c 6. d 7. a 8. c 9. d 10. b 11. c 12. d 13. a 14. b 15. c.

INFOTRAC

Defense Mechanisms	Oedipal Complex	Personality Trait
Extraverts (see extraversion or introversion)	Puberty	Projective Tests

13 STRESS, COPING, AND HEALTH

REVIEW OF KEY IDEAS

THE NATURE OF STRESS

1. **Discuss the nature of stress.**

   1-1. The text defines stress as any circumstances that threaten or are perceived to threaten one's well-being. This definition would indicate that the perception of stress is a/an (<u>subjective</u>/<u>objective</u>) experience. Or to put it another way, stress lies in the mind of the _____.

   1-2. What is the source of most stress?

   Answers: 1-1. subjective. beholder **1-2.** everyday events.

2. **Describe the four principal types of stress discussed in the text.**

   2-1. The text lists four principal types of stress: *frustration, conflict, change,* and *pressure*. Identify these types of stress in the following situations.

   (a) You have three major exams coming up next week and you are also in charge of your sorority's fast-approaching homecoming celebration.

   (b) You leave your small home town and go off to a large city to enroll in a university.

   (c) You are late for an appointment and stuck in a traffic jam.

(d) You are forced to choose between two good movies on television.

2-2. There are two kinds of pressure. One is the pressure to get things accomplished, or the pressure to _____. The other is the pressure to abide by rules, or the pressure to _____.

Answers: **2-1.** (a) pressure (b) change (c) frustration (d) conflict **2-2.** perform, conform.

3. Identify the three basic types of conflict and discuss which types are most troublesome.

3-1. Many persons do not want to pay their income taxes, but on the other hand they don't want to go to jail either. These persons are faced with an _____-_____ conflict.

3-2. Getting married has both positive and negative aspects that make it an excellent example of an _____-_____ conflict.

3-3. Consider the problem of the student who has to choose between scholarships for two different universities. Since she can't accept both he is faced with an _____-_____ conflict.

3-4. Now that you have identified the three basic types of conflict, list them below in their order of troublesomeness, beginning with the least troublesome.

(a) _____

(b) _____

(c) _____

Answers: **3-1.** avoidance-avoidance **3-2.** approach-avoidance **3-3.** approach-approach **3-4.** (a) approach-approach (b) approach-avoidance (c) avoidance-avoidance.

4. Summarize evidence on life change as a form of stress.

4-1. The Social Readjustment Rating Scale (SRRS), measures the stress induced by _____ in daily living routines. The developers of this scale theorized that all kinds of life changes, both pleasant and unpleasant, would induce stress. Early research showed that high scores on the SRRS were correlated with psychological problems and a variety of _____ illnesses.

4-2. Later research began to indicate that the SRRS (does/does not) measure change exclusively. Moreover, high scores on an inventory measuring _____ are even more closely related to mental distress than high scores on the SRRS.

Answers: **4-1.** changes, physical **4-2.** does not, pressure.

RESPONDING TO STRESS

5. **Identify some common emotional responses to stress and discuss the effects of emotional arousal.**

   5-1.   The text describes three different dimensions of emotions that are particularly likely to be triggered by stress. Identify which of these dimensions is most likely to be present in the following situations.

   (a) The emotions in this dimension are likely to be found as a person begins to feel more and more helpless and unable to cope (e.g., you're failing in many of your classes and the semester is rapidly coming to an end).

   (b) The emotions in this dimension are likely to be found as a person begins to feel increasingly frustrated, put upon, and treated unfairly (you're being falsely accused of a deed you didn't commit).

   (c) The emotions in this dimension are likely to be found as a person faces increasing degrees of conflict, pressure, and uncertainty (you're driving on the highway and the fog is gradually becoming thicker).

   5-2.   According to optimal-arousal theories, what happens to the optimal arousal level as tasks become more complex?

   Answers: 5-1. (a) dejection, sadness, and grief (b) annoyance, anger, and rage (c) apprehension, anxiety, and fear
   5-2. The optimal arousal level decreases.

6. **Describe the three stages of the general adaptation syndrome.**

   6-1.   Indicate which of the three stages of the General Adaptation Syndrome is being described in each of the following.

   (a) This is the initial stage in which the body prepares for the fight-or-flight response.

   (b) This is the second stage in which the body stabilizes its physiological changes as it begins to effectively cope with the stress.

   (c) This is the third stage in which the body's coping resources are becoming depleted and the resistance to many diseases declines.

   Answers: 6-1. (a) stage of alarm (b) stage of resistance (c) stage of exhaustion.

7. **Discuss the two major pathways along which the brain sends signals to the endocrine system in response to stress.**

7-1.   Fill in the missing parts in the diagram below detailing the two major pathways along which the brain sends signals to the endocrine system.

CEREBRAL CORTEX

(a) _____

SYMPATHETIC NS   PITUITARY GLAND

                                                    ACTH

(b) _____ (GLAND)   (c) _____ (GLAND)

CATECHOLAMINES   CORTICOSTEROIDS
Increases heart rate &   Increases energy, inhibits
respiration, etc.   tissue inflammation, etc.

7-2.   Which one of these two categories of hormones (catecholamines or corticosteroids) is involved in the fight-or-flight response?

Answers: **7-1.** (a) hypothalamus (b) adrenal medulla (c) adrenal cortex **7-2.** catecholamines.

8. **Evaluate aggression and self-indulgence as behavioral responses to stress.**

8-1.   Answer the following questions regarding aggression and self-indulgence as responses to stress.

(a) Which of these responses is frequently, but not always, triggered by frustration?

(b) Which of these responses is illustrated by the saying, "When the going gets tough, the tough go shopping"?

Answers: **8-1.** (a) aggression (b) self-indulgence.

9. **Discuss defensive coping and constructive coping as mechanisms for dealing with stress.**

9-1.   Indicate whether each of the following situations illustrates defensive or constructive coping.

(a) This kind of coping is much more oriented to reality. _____

(b) This kind of coping is largely unconscious, although it can occur at conscious levels.

_____

(c) This kind of coping uses self-deception to distort reality. _____

(d) This kind of coping is much more task-relevant and action-oriented. _____

(e) This kind of coping avoids the problem and delays a possible solution. _____

9-2.   What might be a useful defensive coping technique when faced with a temporary period of frustration that you can do little about?

Answers: 9-1. (a) constructive (b) defensive (c) defensive (d) constructive (e) defensive 9-2. Engage in "positive illusions."

THE EFFECTS OF STRESS ON PHYSICAL HEALTH

10. **Summarize the evidence linking Type A behavior, emotional reactions, and depression to heart disease.**

10-1.   Tell whether the following characteristics are found in Type A or Type B persons.

_____ (a) easy going

_____ (b) competitive

_____ (c) impatient

_____ (d) amicable

_____ (e) hostile

10-2.   Which aspect of the Type A behavior seems to be most highly related to coronary heart disorder?

10-3.   What is the increased coronary risk for Type A's when compared to Type B's?

10-4.   Research has shown that negative emotions can trigger acute symptoms of heart disease. What other line of evidence, having to do with preventing a second heart attack, supports this relationship between emotions and heart disease?

10-5. Which of the following statements appears to best reflect the relationship between depression and heart disease?

(a) Heart disease can lead to depression.　　(b) Depression can lead to heart disease.

Answers: 10-1. (a) Type B (b) Type A (c) Type A (d) Type B (e) Type A **10-2.** hostility **10-3.** double (or twice as likely) **10-4.** Engaging in stress management training reduces the risk. **10-5.** b.

11. Discuss evidence linking stress to immunosuppression and a variety of physical illnesses.

11-1. Research has found stress to be related to numerous diseases and disorders. What effect on the lymphocytes (the specialized white blood cells that are important in initiating the immune response) appears to be the link between stress and so many disorders?

11-2. While many studies have shown a relationship between stress and numerous physical illness, we can still not state definitely that stress leads to physical illnesses. Why is this?

Answers: 11-1. Stress appears to suppress the proliferation of the lymphocytes (thus suppressing the immune system in general) **11-2.** Because almost all of the data are correlational (and you cannot infer cause and effect relationships from these kinds of data).

12. Discuss how social support, optimism, and conscientiousness moderate individual differences in stress tolerance.

12-1. What physical effect was found with students who had high social support during the stress of final exams?

12-2. What difference was found between optimists and pessimists with respect to physical health?

12-3. What trait was found to predict longevity in a long-term study that followed gifted children throughout most of their life span?

Answers: 12-1. They had improved immunal functioning (increases in an antibody that fights off respiratory infections). **12-2.** Optimists were more likely to enjoy good physical health **12-3.** conscientiousness.

13. Discuss the negative impact of smoking, poor nutrition, and lack of exercise on physical health.

13-1. Answer the following questions regarding the negative impact of smoking on physical health.

(a) How many fewer years can a 25-year-old smoker expect to live than a 25-year-old non-smoker?

(b) What are the two most frequent diseases that kill smokers?

(c) What does evidence suggest to smokers who have tried and failed to stop smoking?

13-2. Answer the following true-false questions regarding the effects of poor nutrition and lack of exercise.

_____ (a) Among Americans, health-impairing diets are the result of the inability to afford healthy foods.

_____ (b) Lack of regular physical exercise may increase chances of obesity.

_____ (c) Exercise is associated with reduced risk of coronary disease.

Answers: 13-1. (a) 8 years, or 8.3 years (b) lung cancer and heart disease (c) They should keep on trying to stop (readiness to stop smoking builds gradually as they try, fail, and continue to try). **13-2.** (a) false (b) true (c) true.

14. Discuss the relationship between behavioral factors and AIDS.

14-1. What two bodily fluids are most likely to transmit HIV from one person to another?

14-2. What are the two principal behaviors that may lead to HIV infection?

14-3. Why can you not be sure that someone who shows no symptoms of AIDS does not have HIV infection?

Answers: 14-1. blood and semen **14-2.** sexual contact and the sharing of needles **14-3.** The symptoms may take years to develop after the initial HIV infection.

REACTIONS TO ILLNESS

15. **Discuss individual differences in willingness to seek medical treatment.**

   15-1.   Indicate whether the following statements regarding individual differences in willingness to seek medical treatment are true or false.

   _____ (a) Delay in seeking treatment is perhaps the biggest problem here.

   _____ (b) The perception of pain and illness is highly subjective.

   Answers: **15-1.** (a) true (b) true.

16. **Discuss factors that influence communication with health providers and adherence to medical advice.**

   16-1.   The text lists three reasons for failure to comply with medical advice. One is that patients often fail to completely _____ treatment instructions. A second is that the treatment may prove to be quite _____. The third reason is not directly related to either instructions or treatment, but rather to the patient's attitude toward the _____. A negative attitude makes compliance (more/less) likely.

   16-2.   What appears to be of critical importance in increasing compliance with medical advice?

   Answers: **16-1.** understand, unpleasant (or aversive), physician or doctor, less **16-2.** Improving the communication process between doctor and patient.

PUTTING IT IN PERSPECTIVE

17. **Explain how this chapter highlighted two of the text's unifying themes (*multifactoral causation* and *the subjectivity of experience*).**

   17-1.   The fact that the amount of stress in any given situation primarily lies in the eyes of the beholder nicely illustrates the theme that experience is _____.

   17-2.   The fact that stress interacts with numerous other factors that affect health illustrates the theme of _____ _____.

   Answers: **17-1.** subjective **17-2.** multifactoral causation.

PERSONAL APPLICATION • IMPROVING COPING AND STRESS MANAGEMENT

18. **Summarize Albert Ellis's ideas about controlling one's emotions.**

   18-1.   The main idea behind Albert Ellis's rational-emotive therapy is that stress is largely caused by _____ thinking. Therefore, by changing one's catastrophic thinking and taking a more rational approach one can then reduce _____.

18-2. Ellis illustrates this theory by postulating an A-B-C series of events. Describe below what is going on during each of these events.

(A) activating event:

(B) belief:

(C) consequence:

18-3. Since the emotional turmoil in the A-B-C sequence is caused by the _____ sequence, effort must be directed towards changing irrational beliefs. Ellis proposes two techniques for doing this. One must first learn to _____ instances of irrational beliefs. Then one must learn to actively _____ these irrational beliefs.

Answers: 18-1. catastrophic, stress **18-2.** (A) The activating event that initiates the stress (B) The belief about the event (C) The emotional consequences that result from the belief **18-3.** B, detect or recognize, dispute.

19. Discuss the coping value of humor and releasing pent-up emotions.

19-1. Besides helping to release tension, what other role does humor play in easing stress in difficult situations?

19-2. Why might writing about a problem or talking with a sympathetic friend prove useful when experiencing stress?

Answers: 19-1. It allows for redefining the problem in a less threatening way. **19-2.** It may help to release pent-up tension.

20. Discuss the coping value of relaxation and exercise.

20-1. Complete the following statements regarding the coping value of relaxation and exercise.

(a) A quiet environment, a mental device, a passive attitude, and a comfortable position are conditions that facilitate _____.

(b) Along with humor, releasing pent-up emotions, and relaxation, a regular exercise program may help to minimize physical _____.

Answers: 20-1. (a) relaxation (b) vulnerability.

21. **Describe some important considerations in evaluating health statistics and making health decisions.**

· 21-1. Which kind of faulty statistical reasoning (*correlation is no assurance of causation, statistical significance is not equivalent to practical significance*, and *failure to consider base rates*) is illustrated by the following statements?

(a) Using cell phones may cause brain cancer.

(b) Since heart disease and depression are correlated, heart disease must cause depression.

(c) In a large sample population it was observed that the prevalence of hypertension was statistically significantly higher in higher sodium intake individuals. Therefore, everyone should reduce their sodium intake.

21-2. In addition to seeking information to reduce uncertainty, what other two basic principles of quantitative reasoning does the text suggest?

21-3. What should one do after reaching a decision and initiating action?

Answers: 21-1. (a) failure to consider base rates (and also forgetting that correlation is no assurance of causations) (b) correlation is no assurance of causation (c) statistical significance is not equivalent to practical significance **21-2.** Make risk-benefit assessments and list alternative courses of action **21-3.** Continue to reevaluate the decision (in light of treatment progress, new options, etc.).

REVIEW OF KEY TERMS

Acquired immune deficiency syndrome (AIDS)	Constructive coping	Life changes
Aggression	Coping	Optimism
Approach-approach conflict	Defense mechanisms	Pressure
Approach-avoidance conflict	Frustration	Rational-emotive therapy
Avoidance-avoidance conflict	General adaptation syndrome	Social support
Biopsychosocial model	Health psychology	Stress
Catastrophic thinking	Immune response	Type A personality
Conflict	Internet addiction	Type B personality

_____ 1. Holds that physical illness is caused by a complex interaction of biological, psychological, and sociocultural factors.

_____ 2. Concerned with how psychosocial forces relate to the promotion and maintenance of health, and the causation, prevention, and treatment of illness.

_____ 3. Any circumstances that threaten or are perceived to threaten our well-being and thereby tax our coping abilities.

_____ 4. Occurs in any situation in which the pursuit of some goal is thwarted.

_____ 5. Occurs when two or more incompatible motivations or behavioral impulses compete for expression.

_____ 6. Occurs when a choice must be made between two attractive goals.

_____ 7. Occurs when a choice must be made between two unattractive goals.

_____ 8. Occurs when a choice must be made whether to pursue a single goal that has both attractive and unattractive aspects.

_____ 9. Any noticeable alterations in one's living circumstances that require readjustment.

_____ 10. Expectations or demands that one behave in a certain way.

_____ 11. A model of the body's stress response consisting of three stages: alarm, resistance, and exhaustion.

_____ 12. An active effort to master, reduce, or tolerate the demands created by stress.

_____ 13. Involves any behavior that is intended to hurt someone, either physically or verbally.

_____ 14. Consists of spending an inordinate amount of time on the internet and inability to control online use.

_____ 15. Largely unconscious reactions that protect a person from unpleasant emotions such as anxiety and guilt.

_____ 16. Relatively healthy efforts to deal with stressful events.

_____ 17. A behavior pattern marked by competitive, aggressive, impatient, hostile behavior.

_____ 18. A behavior pattern marked by relaxed, patient, easy-going, amicable behavior.

_____ 19. The body's defensive reaction to invasion by bacteria, viral agents, or other foreign substances.

_____ 20. Various types of aid and succor provided by members of one's social network.

_____ 21. A general tendency to expect good outcomes.

_____ 22. An approach to therapy that focuses on altering clients' patterns of irrational thinking to reduce maladaptive emotions and behavior.

_____ 23. Unrealistic and pessimistic appraisal of stress that exaggerates the magnitude of a problem.

_____ 24. A disorder in which the immune system is gradually weakened and eventually disabled by the human immunodeficiency virus (HIV).

Answers: 1. biopsychosocial model **2.** health psychology **3.** stress **4.** frustration **5.** conflict **6.** approach-approach conflict **7.** avoidance-avoidance conflict **8.** approach-avoidance conflict **9.** life changes **10.** pressure **11.** general adaptation syndrome **12.** coping **13.** aggression **14.** internet addiction **15.** defense mechanisms **16.** constructive coping **17.** Type A personality **18.** Type B personality **19.** immune response **20.** social support **21.** optimism **22.** rational-emotive therapy **23.** catastrophic thinking **24.** acquired immune deficiency syndrome (AIDS).

REVIEW OF KEY PEOPLE

Robin DiMatteo   Thomas Holmes & Richard Rahe   Hans Selye
Albert Ellis   Richard Lazarus   Shelly Taylor
Meyer Friedman & Ray Rosenman

_____ 1. Observed that minor hassles were more closely related to mental health than were major stressful events.

_____ 2. These researchers developed the Social Readjustment Rating Scale.

_____ 3. Coined the word "stress" and described the General Adaptation Syndrome.

_____ 4. These researchers found a connection between coronary risk and what they called Type A behavior.

_____ 5. Showed several lines of evidence indicating that illusions may sometimes be adaptive for mental and physical health.

_____ 6. The developer of Rational-Emotive Therapy.

_____ 7. A leading expert on medical patient behavior.

Answers: 1. Lazarus **2.** Holmes & Rahe **3.** Selye **4.** Friedman & Rosenman **5.** Taylor **6.** Ellis **7.** DiMatteo.

SELF-QUIZ

1. Which of the following statements is correct?
   a. Stress is a subjective experience.
   b. Minor hassles can be as stressful as major ones.
   c. One should not seek to avoid all stress.
   d. All of the above are correct.

2. You've been invited to dinner at a nice restaurant on the final night of a TV mini series you've been watching and thus find yourself confronted with:
   a. pressure
   b. frustration
   c. an approach-avoidance conflict
   d. an approach-approach conflict

3. The week of final exams subjects most students to what kind of stress?
   a. pressure
   b. change
   c. frustration
   d. conflict

4. High scores on the Social Readjustment Rating Scale were found to be correlated with mental distress and:
   a. defensive coping
   b. physical illness
   c. pessimistic attitudes
   d. Type A personality

5. According to optimal-arousal theories, which of the following situations would be least affected by a high level of arousal?
   a. taking a psychology exam
   b. interviewing for a job
   c. buttoning a shirt
   d. typing a term paper

6. The General Adaptation Syndrome shows that the body:
   a. gradually adapts to a particular stress
   b. gradually adapts to all forms of stress
   c. may gradually weaken and become susceptible to many diseases
   d. can react rapidly to all forms of stress

7. Which of the following organs is involved in both of the body's two major stress pathways?
   a. the adrenal gland
   b. the sympathetic nervous system
   c. the pituitary gland
   d. the pineal gland

8. Aggression is frequently triggered by:
   a. helplessness
   b. frustration
   c. loneliness
   d. change

9. Which of the following characteristics is/are likely to be found with defensive coping?
   a. self-deception
   b. both conscious and unconscious awareness
   c. delay of a possible solution
   d. all of the above are likely to be found

10. One of the key links between stress and physical illness may be that the body's response to stress:
    a. increases the optimal-arousal level
    b. suppresses the immune system
    c. decreases the optimal-arousal level
    d. suppresses the adrenal gland

11. Smoking is to lung cancer as Type A behavior is to:
    a. coronary disease
    b. AIDS
    c. defensive coping
    d. mental disorders

12. Which of the following behavioral responses to stress may result in internet addiction?
    a. defensive coping
    b. self-indulgence
    c. positive illusions
    d. giving up

13. A major idea behind Rational-Emotive Therapy is that stress is caused by:
    a. conflict
    b. frustration
    c. catastrophic thinking
    d. pressure

14. Social support, optimism, and conscientiousness are related to:
    a. the Type B personality pattern
    b. a low level of stress
    c. defensive-coping strategies
    d. good physical health

15. The best way to deal with stress is to:
    a. avoid it as much as possible
    b. learn defensive coping strategies
    c. learn constructive coping strategies
    d. avoid it as much as possible and learn defensive coping strategies

16. Analyzing the possible gains and losses before undertaking a health-treatment program is an example of:
    a. seeking information to reduce uncertainty
    b. listing alternative courses of action
    c. making a risk-benefit analysis
    d. analyzing base rates

Answers: 1. d **2.** d **3.** a **4.** b **5.** c **6.** c **7.** a **8.** b **9.** d **10.** b **11.** a **12.** b **13.** c **14.** d **15.** c **16.** c.

INFOTRAC

Constructive Coping   Internet Addiction   Type B Personality
Health Psychology   Type A Personality

14 PSYCHOLOGICAL DISORDERS

REVIEW OF KEY IDEAS

ABNORMAL BEHAVIOR: MYTHS, REALITIES, AND CONTROVERSIES

1. Describe and evaluate the medical model of abnormal behavior.

1-1. A model is a metaphor or theory that is useful in describing some phenomenon. For example, the computer is frequently used as a model of thinking. The *medical model* uses physical illness as a model of psychological disorders. Under the medical model, maladaptive behavior is referred to as mental

_____.

1-2. The term "mental illness" is so familiar to all of us that we rarely think about the meaning of the concept and whether or not the analogy with disease is a good one. Among the model's critics, Thomas Szasz asserts that words such as *sickness*, *illness*, and *disease* are correctly used only in reference to the

_____, and that it is more appropriate to view abnormal behavior as a deviation from accepted social _____ than as an illness.

1-3. The text takes an intermediate position. The medical concepts of diagnosis, etiology, and prognosis have proven useful in treatment and study of psychological disorders, so while there are problems with the medical model, it may be of value as long as one understands that it is just a/an _____ and not a true explanation.

Answers: **1-1.** illness (disease, sickness) **1-2.** body, norms (behavior, standards) **1-3.** analogy (model).

2. **Explain the most commonly used criteria of abnormality and the evolutionary view of defining mental illness.**

    2-1. What does abnormal mean? The three criteria most frequently used are *deviance*, *maladaptive behavior*, and *personal distress*.

        (a) _____: Does not *conform* to cultural norms or standards.

        (b) _____: Behavior that *interferes with* the individual's social or occupational functioning.

        (c) _____: Intense *discomfort* produced by depression or anxiety.

    2-2. Following are three statements that describe a person with a particular type of disorder. Which criterion of abnormal behavior is illustrated by each statement? Place the letters from the list above in the appropriate blanks.

        ____ Ralph washes his hands several dozen times a day. His handwashing interferes with his work and prevents him from establishing normal friendships.

        ____ Even if Ralph's handwashing compulsion did not interfere with his work and social life, his behavior still would be considered strange. That is, most people do not do what he does.

        ____ It is also the case that Ralph's skin is very raw, and he becomes extremely anxious when he does not have immediate access to a sink.

    2-3. In some cultures, hearing voices or speaking with gods may be valued. In our culture, however, such behavior is likely to be considered abnormal. While the major categories of disorder may transcend culture, our assessments of abnormality are nonetheless value judgments that are strongly influenced by our _____. Thus, one of the problems involved in defining abnormality is that the criteria for psychological disorders are not entirely _____ -free.

    2-4. Evolutionary psychologists have recently proposed that abnormalities be considered simply as evolutionary _____, evolved mechanisms that are not functioning effectively. For example, as a mechanism for alerting the organism to danger, anxiety has _____ value; as a persistent emotion in the absence of danger, however, it interferes with functioning. While this approach is an attempt to make the criteria of mental illness less _____ -laden, critics question whether or not the viewpoint will in fact yield more objective criteria.

Answers: **2-1.** (a) deviance (b) maladaptive behavior (c) personal distress **2-2.** b, a, c **2-3.** culture (society), value (culture) **2-4.** dysfunctions, adaptive (survival, evolutionary), value.

3. **Describe the DSM-IV diagnostic system.**

    3-1. Below are descriptions of the five axes of the DSM-IV classification system. Label each with the correct axis number (I through V).

        ____ Listing of physical disorders

        ____ Diagnosis of long-running personality disorders or mental retardation

_____ Diagnosis of most of the disorders

_____ Estimates of the individual's current level of adaptive functioning (social and occupational)

_____ Notes concerning the severity of stress experienced by the individual in the past year

Answers: 3-1. III, II, I, V, IV.

ANXIETY DISORDERS

4. **List four types of anxiety disorders and describe the symptoms associated with each.**

   4-1.   List the names of the four anxiety syndromes in the space below. As hints, the initial letters of some key words are listed at the left.

   GAD: _____

   PhD: _____

   OCD: _____

   PDA: _____ and _____

   4-2.   Match the anxiety disorders with the symptoms that follow by placing the appropriate letters (from the previous question) in the blanks.

   (a) _____   Sudden, unexpected, and paralyzing attacks of anxiety

   (b) _____   Not tied to a specific object or event

   (c) _____   Senseless, repetitive rituals

   (d) _____   Brooding over decisions

   (e) _____   Fear of specific objects or situations

   (f) _____   Persistent intrusion of distressing and unwanted thoughts

   (g) _____   Free-floating anxiety

   (h) _____   Frequently includes fear of going out in public

Answers: 4-1. generalized anxiety disorder, phobic disorder, obsessive-compulsive disorder, panic disorder and agoraphobia 4-2. (a) PDA (in this example, panic attacks) (b) GAD (c) OCD (d) GAD (e) PhD (f) OCD (g) GAD (h) PDA (in this case, agoraphobia).

5. **Discuss the contribution of biological, cognitive, personality, conditioning, and stress factors to the etiology of anxiety disorders.**

   5-1.   Several types of studies suggest there are inherited differences between people in the extent to which they are predisposed to anxiety disorders. For example, twin studies find higher concordance rates for anxiety among _____ twins than _____ twins.

5-2. Other biological evidence implicates disturbances at synapses using GABA for some types of anxiety disorders and of serotonin for panic attacks and obsessive-compulsive disorder. Thus, the body chemicals known as _____ appear to play an important role in anxiety.

5-3. Conditioning or learning clearly plays a role as well. For example, if an individual is bitten by a dog, he or she may develop a fear of dogs through the process of _____ conditioning. The individual may then avoid dogs in the future, a response maintained by _____ conditioning.

5-4. People are more likely to be afraid of snakes than of hot irons. Using Seligman's notion of preparedness, explain why.

5-5. Two types of anecdotal evidence do not support the conditioning point of view. For example, people with phobias (always can/frequently cannot) recall a traumatic incident, and people who have experienced extreme traumas (always/frequently do not) develop phobias.

5-6. As discussed in Chapter 6, the conditioning models are being extended to include a larger role for cognitive factors. For example, children probably acquire fears by _____ the behavior of anxious parents.

5-7. In addition, cognitive theorists indicate that certain *thinking styles* contribute to anxiety. For example, as indicated in your text, the sentence "The doctor examined little Emma's Growth" could refer either to height or to a tumor. People who are high in anxiety will tend to perceive the (tumor/height) interpretation. People's readiness to perceive threat, in other words, appears to be related to their tendency to experience _____ .

5-8. Personality also plays a role. Not surprisingly, people who score high on the _____ trait of the "big five" personality factors have an elevated prevalence of anxiety disorders and a poorer prognosis for recovery.

5-9. Finally, *stress* is related to the anxiety disorders. Studies described in your text indicate that stress is related both to _____ disorder and to the development of social _____.

Answers: 5-1. identical, fraternal **5-2.** neurotransmitters **5-3.** classical, operant **5-4.** Preparedness is Seligman's notion that human beings have evolved to be more prepared or more ready to be conditioned to some stimuli than to others. We have evolved to be more afraid of snakes than of hot irons, the latter having appeared only relatively recently in our evolutionary history. (As a whole, research has provided only modest support for the idea of preparedness in acquisition of phobias.) **5-5.** frequently cannot, frequently do not **5-6.** observing **5-7.** tumor, anxiety **5-8.** neuroticism **5-9.** panic, phobia.

SOMATOFORM DISORDERS

6. **Compare and contrast the three somatoform disorders and discuss their etiology.**

    6-1. For each of the following symptoms, indicate which disorder is described by placing the appropriate letters in the blanks: S for somatization, C for conversion, and H for hypochondriasis.

_____ Serious disability that may include paralysis, loss of vision or hearing, loss of feeling, and so on

_____ Many different minor physical ailments accompanied by a long history of medical treatment

_____ Cannot believe the doctor's report that the person is not really ill

_____ Symptoms that appear to be organic in origin but don't match underlying anatomical organization

_____ Diverse complaints that implicate many different organ systems

_____ Usually does not involve disability so much as overinterpreting slight possible signs of illness

_____ "Glove anesthesia"; seizures without loss of bladder control

6-2. In the film *Hannah and Her Sisters,* Woody Allen is convinced that certain minor physical changes are a sign of cancer. When tests eventually find no evidence of cancer, he is sure the tests have been done incorrectly. Which of the somatoform disorders does this seem to represent? _____

6-3. The somatoform disorders are associated with certain personality types, with particular cognitive styles, and with learning. Among personality types, the self-centered, excitable, and overly dramatic _____ personalities are more at risk for developing these disorders.

6-4. With regard to cognitive factors, focusing excessive attention on internal _____ factors, or believing that good health should involve a complete lack of discomfort, may also contribute to somatoform disorders.

6-5. With regard to learning, the sick role may be positively reinforced through, for example, _____ from others or negatively reinforced by _____ certain of life's problems or unpleasant aspects.

Answers: 6-1. C, S, H, C, S, H, C **6-2.** hypochondriasis **6-3.** histrionic **6-4.** physiological **6-5.** attention (kindness, etc.), avoiding (escaping).

DISSOCIATIVE DISORDERS

7. Describe the dissociative disorders and discuss their etiology.

7-1. The three dissociative disorders involve memory and identity. Two of the disorders involve fairly massive amounts of forgetting, dissociative _____ and dissociative _____.

7-2. People who have been in serious accidents frequently can't remember the accident or events surrounding the accident. This type of memory loss, which involves specific traumatic events, is known as dissociative _____.

7-3. An even greater memory loss, in which people lose their memories for their entire lives along with their sense of identity, is termed dissociative _____.

7-4. You may have seen media characterizations of individuals who can't remember who they are—what their names are, where they live, who their family is, and so on. While popularly referred to as amnesia, this type of dissociative disorder is more correctly called dissociative _____.

7-5. A few years ago there was a spate of appearances on talk shows by guests who claimed to have more than one identity or personality. This disorder is still widely known as _____- _____ disorder (MPD), but the formal name in the DSM-IV is _____ _____ disorder. The disorder is also often (<u>appropriately/mistakenly</u>) called schizophrenia.

7-6. What causes dissociative disorders? Dissociative amnesia and dissociative fugue are related to excessive _____, but little else is known about why these extreme reactions occur in a tiny minority of people.

7-7. With regard to multiple-personality disorder, the diagnosis is controversial. Although many clinicians believe that the disorder is authentic, Spanos argues that it is the product of media attention and the misguided probings of a small minority of psychotherapists. In other words, Spanos believes that MPD (<u>is/is not</u>) a genuine disorder.

7-8. While the majority of people who show the characteristics of multiple-personality disorders report having been emotionally and sexually _____ in childhood, little is known about the causes of this controversial diagnosis.

Answers: **7-1.** amnesia, fugue **7-2.** amnesia **7-3.** fugue **7-4.** fugue **7-5.** multiple-personality, dissociative identity, mistakenly **7-6.** stress **7-7.** is not **7-8.** abused.

MOOD DISORDERS

8. Describe the two mood disorders.

8-1. While the terms *manic* and *depressive* describe mood, they refer to a number of other characteristics as well, listed below. With one or two words for each characteristic describe the manic and depressive episodes. (Before you make the lists, it may be a good idea to review Table 14.1 and the sections on depressive and bipolar mood disorders.)

	Manic	*Depressive*
mood:	_____	_____
sleep:	_____	_____
activity:	_____	_____
speech:	_____	_____
sex drive:	_____	_____

8-2. Be sure to note that mania and depression are not the names of the two affective disorders. What is the name of the disorder accompanied only by depression? _____ By both manic and depressive states? _____

Answers: **8-1.** mood: euphoric (elated, extremely happy, etc.) vs. depressed (blue, extremely sad); sleep: goes without or doesn't want to vs. can't (insomnia); activity: very active vs. sluggish, slow, inactive; speech: very fast vs. very slow; sex drive: increased vs. decreased **8-2.** unipolar disorder (major depressive disorder), bipolar disorder.

9. **Explain how genetic and neurochemical factors may be related to the development of mood disorders.**

9-1.   Twin studies implicate genetic factors in the development of mood disorders. In a sentence, summarize the results of these studies.

9-2.   While the exact mechanism is not known, correlations have been found between mood disorders and the activities of _____ such as norepinephrine and serotonin. Recent research suggests that of these two neurotransmitters _____ may be the more important factor in mood disorders.

Answers: 9-1. For mood disorders, the concordance rate for identical twins is much higher than that for fraternal twins (about 67% for the former compared to 15% for the latter). **9-2.** neurotransmitters (neurochemicals), serotonin.

10. **Explain how cognitive factors, interpersonal factors, and stress may be related to the development of mood disorders.**

10-1.   Martin Seligman's model of depression is referred to as the learned _____ model. While he originally based his theory of depression on an animal conditioning model involving exposure to unavoidable aversive stimuli, he has more recently emphasized (cognitive/behavioral) factors.

10-2.   According to the revised version of learned helplessness, people with a _____ explanatory style are particularly prone to depression. For example, people who attribute obstacles to (situational factors/personal flaws) are more likely to experience depression.

10-3.   Building on learned helplessness theory, _____ theory maintains that a pessimistic explanatory style is just one of several factors—stress and low self-esteem are others—that contribute to depression. For example, people who repetitively focus or _____ about their depression are more likely to remain depressed.

10-4.   With regard to interpersonal factors, depressed people tend to lack _____ skills. How does this characteristic affect the ability to obtain reinforcers?

10-5.   Why do we tend to reject depressed people?

10-6.   What is the relationship between stress and the onset of mood disorders?

Answers: **10-1.** helplessness, cognitive **10-2.** pessimistic (negative), personal flaws **10-3.** hopelessness, ruminate **10-4.** social (interpersonal). Lack of social skills makes it difficult to obtain certain reinforcers, such as good friends and desirable jobs. **10-5.** Because they are not pleasant to be around. Depressed people complain a lot, are irritable, and tend to pass their mood along to others. **10-6.** There is a moderately strong link between stress and the onset of mood disorders.

SCHIZOPHRENIC DISORDERS

11. **Describe the general characteristics (symptoms) of schizophrenia.**

    11-1.   Before we review the different types of schizophrenia, consider some general characteristics of the schizophrenic disorders, as follows.

        (a) Irrational thought: Disturbed thought processes may include the false beliefs referred to as _____ (e.g., the false belief that one is a world-famous political figure who is being pursued by terrorists).

        (b) Deterioration of adaptive behavior: The deterioration usually involves social relationships, work, and neglect of personal _____.

        (c) Distorted perception: This category may include hearing (or sometimes seeing) things that aren't really there. These sensory experiences are known as _____.

        (d) Disturbed emotion: Emotional responsiveness may be disturbed in a variety of ways. The person may have little or no responsiveness, referred to as _____ affect, or they may show _____ emotional responses, such as laughing at news of a tragic death.

Answers: **11-1.** (a) delusions (b) hygiene (cleanliness) (c) hallucinations (d) flat (flattened, blunted), inappropriate (erratic, bizarre).

12. **Describe two classification systems for schizophrenic subtypes.**

    12-1.   Write the names of the four recognized subcategories of schizophrenia next to the descriptions that follow.

        (a) _____ type: Particularly severe deterioration, incoherence, complete social withdrawal, aimless babbling and giggling, delusions centering on bodily functions.

        (b) _____ type: Muscular rigidity and stupor at one extreme, or random motor activity, hyperactivity, and incoherence at the other; now quite rare.

        (c) _____ type: Delusions of persecution and grandeur.

        (d) _____ type: Clearly schizophrenic, but doesn't fit other three categories.

    12-2.   Several critics have asserted that there are no meaningful differences among the categories listed above and have proposed an alternative classification system. Nancy Andreasen and others have described a classification system consisting of only two categories, one that consists of _____ symptoms and the other of _____ symptoms.

12-3. In Andreasen's system, "positive" and "negative" do not mean pleasant and unpleasant. Positive symptoms *add* something to "normal" behavior (like chaotic speech), and negative symptoms *subtract* something (like social withdrawal). Indicate which of the following are positive and which negative by placing a P or an N in the appropriate blanks.

_____ flattened emotions

_____ hallucinations

_____ bizarre behavior

_____ social withdrawal

_____ apathy

_____ non-stop babbling

_____ doesn't speak

12-4. Theorists hoped that classification of schizophrenia into positive and negative symptoms would provide more meaningful categories in terms of etiology and prognosis. Some differentiation between the two types of symptoms has been found; for example, *positive* symptoms seem to be associated with (better/ worse) adjustment prior to the onset of schizophrenia and a (better/worse) prognosis. All in all, however, this system (has/has not) produced a classification that can replace the traditional subtypes.

Answers: **12-1.** (a) disorganized (b) catatonic (c) paranoid (d) undifferentiated **12-2.** positive, negative **12-3.** N, P, P, N, N, P, N **12-4.** better, better, has not.

13. Explain how genetic vulnerability, neurochemical factors, and structural abnormalities in the brain may contribute to the etiology of schizophrenia.

13-1. As with mood disorders, twin studies implicate genetic factors in the development of schizophrenia. In a sentence, summarize the general results of these studies.

13-2. As with mood disorders, neurotransmitter substances in the brain are implicated in the etiology of schizophrenia. Although the evidence is somewhat clouded, what is the name of the neurotransmitter thought to be involved? _____

13-3. In addition to possible neurochemical factors, certain differences in brain structure may be associated with schizophrenia. One of these differences involves enlarged _____, hollow, fluid-filled cavities in the brain. Current thinking, however, is that this brain abnormality is an _____ rather than a cause of schizophrenia.

Answers: **13-1.** For schizophrenia, the concordance rate is higher for identical than for fraternal twins. (The actual concordance rates have been found to be about 48% for identical and 17% for fraternal twins. For comparison, the respective percentages found for mood disorders were about 67% and 15%.) **13-2.** dopamine (thought to be a factor because most drugs useful in treating schizophrenia decrease dopamine activity in the brain) **13-3.** ventricles, effect.

14. **Summarize evidence on how neurodevelopmental processes, family dynamics, and stress may be related to the development of schizophrenia.**

   14-1.   The _____ hypothesis of schizophrenia maintains that schizophrenia is caused in part by early neurological damage that occurs either prenatally or during the birth process.

   14-2.   Among the causes of neurological damage are _____ infections; _____ which may occur, for example, during famine; and complications that occur during _____.

   14-3.   Expressed emotion refers to the extent to which a patient's relatives are overly critical or protective or are in other ways overly emotionally involved with the patient. Patients returning to families that are high in expressed emotion have a relapse rate that is much (higher/lower) than that of families low in expressed emotion.

   14-4.   What role does stress play in the etiology of schizophrenia? Stress is a fact of life, and it is obvious that not everyone who experiences stress develops schizophrenia. Current thinking is that stress may be a precipitating factor for people who are biologically or for other reasons already _____ to schizophrenia.

   Answers: 14-1. neurodevelopmental **14-2.** viral (flu), malnutrition (starvation), delivery (birth, the birth process) **14-3.** higher **14-4.** vulnerable (predisposed).

PSYCHOLOGICAL DISORDERS AND THE LAW

15. **Distinguish between the legal concepts of insanity and involuntary commitment.**

   15-1.   While the words *insane* and *schizophrenic* may in some cases apply to the same person, the terms do not mean the same thing. The term _____ is a legal term, while _____ is a descriptive term used in psychological diagnosis. For example, an individual troubled by hallucinations and delusions probably fits the category of _____. An individual who is judged by a court not to be responsible for his or her actions would be classified (under the M'naghten rule) as _____.

   15-2.   With regard to the insanity defense, which of the following are true? (Mark T or F.)

   _____   The insanity defense is used in fewer than 1% of homicide cases.

   _____   Available evidence suggests that in by far the majority of cases in which is it used, the insanity defense is successful defense (i.e., wins the case).

   15-3.   More frequent than judgments of insanity are proceedings related to involuntary commitment to a psychiatric facility. Answer the following questions about involuntary commitment.

   (a)   What three criteria are used to determine whether an individual should be committed?

(b) What is required to temporarily commit an individual for one to three days?

(c) What is required for longer-term commitment?

Answers: 15-1. insane, schizophrenic, schizophrenic, insane **15-2.** T, F **15-3.** (a) In general, for people to be involuntarily committed, mental health and legal authorities must judge them to be (1) dangerous to themselves or (2) dangerous to others or (3) in extreme need of treatment. (b) Temporary commitment (usually 24 to 72 hours) may be done in emergencies by a psychologist or psychiatrist. (c) Longer-term commitments are issued by a court and require a formal hearing.

CULTURE AND PATHOLOGY

16. **Discuss the effects of culture on pathology.**

16-1. Your text divides viewpoints about culture and pathology into *relativists* and *panculturalists*. The _____ believe that there are basic standards of mental health that are *universal* across cultures. The _____ believe that psychological disorders *vary as a function of culture*.

16-2. Some data support the pancultural view. For example, most investigators agree that the three most serious categories of disorder, listed below, are universal:

_____

_____

_____

16-3. On the other hand, in some cultures hypochondria, somatization, generalized anxiety disorder, and some of the other (<u>milder/more severe</u>) disturbances are not considered full-fledged disorders in some cultures.

16-4. In addition, some disorders exist in some cultures and not others. For example, the obsessive fear about one's penis withdrawing into one's abdomen is found only among Chinese males in Malaya; and, until recently, _____ nervosa was found only in affluent Western societies.

16-5. In summary, are psychological disorders universal, or do they vary across cultures?

a. There are some universal standards of normality and abnormality.

b. There are some disorders that are specific to particular cultures.

c. Both of the above: some aspects of psychopathology are universal, some vary as a function of culture.

Answers: 16-1. panculturalists, relativists **16-2.** schizophrenia, depression, bipolar disorder **16-3.** milder **16-4.** anorexia **16-5.** c.

17. **Explain how this chapter highlighted four of the text's unifying themes.**

   17-1.   Below are examples of the highlighted themes. Indicate which theme fits each example by writing the appropriate abbreviations in the blanks: MC for multifactorial causation, HE for the interplay of heredity and environment, SH for sociohistorical context, and C for the influence of culture.

   (a) Mood and schizophrenic disorders will occur if one has a genetic vulnerability to the disorder *and* if one experiences a considerable amount of stress. ____

   (b) Psychological disorders are caused by neurochemical factors, brain abnormalities, styles of child rearing, life stress, and so on. ____

   (c) Anorexia nervosa occurs almost exclusively in affluent Western societies. ____

   (d) Decades ago homosexuality was classified as a disorder; in recent DSMs it is not. ____ and ____

   Answers: **17-1.** (a) HE (b) MC (c) C (d) SH, C.

PERSONAL APPLICATION • UNDERSTANDING EATING DISORDERS

18. **Describe the symptoms and medical complications of anorexia nervosa and bulimia nervosa.**

   18-1.   What are the names of the two major categories of eating disorder? _____ and

   _____

   18-2.   The most obvious feature of anorexia nervosa is the drastic weight loss that accompanies the disorder. Other characteristics include an intense _____ of gaining weight, a disturbed _____ (they think they are fat, no matter how emaciated they become), and (struggling/ refusal) to maintain normal weight.

   18-3.   The two major subtypes of anorexia have in common a dangerous weight loss. In one case this is accompanied by _____ (severely limiting food eaten) and in the other by bingeing and then _____ (vomiting, using laxatives and diuretics) as well as excessive exercise.

   18-4.   The weight loss that accompanies anorexia nervosa is substantial, typically 25-30% below normal weight. A critical diagnostic criterion for anorexia nervosa in women is amenorrhea, the loss of the _____ cycle.

   18-5.   There are other consequences as well, including serious gastrointestinal difficulties, heart and circulatory problems, and osteoporosis, all of which may lead to death in approximately ____% of cases. Anorexia nervosa patients (usually/rarely) seek treatment on their own.

   18-6.   Bulimia nervosa shares many of the characteristics of the binge-eating/purging type of anorexia. Its main differentiating feature is the fact that people with bulimia maintain a (relatively normal/drastically decreased) body weight. They are also somewhat more likely to recognize that there is a problem and to cooperate with treatment.

   Answers: **18-1.** anorexia nervosa, bulimia nervosa **18-2.** fear, body image, refusal **18-3.** restricting, purging **18-4.** menstrual **18-5.** 2-10%, rarely **18-6.** relatively normal.

19. **Discuss the history, prevalence, and gender distribution of eating disorders.**

19-1.   Anorexia nervosa was extremely (common/rare) and bulimia nervosa (omnipresent/nonexistent) prior to the middle of the 20th century. Obviously, culture has a great deal to do with this disorder; the combination of abundant food and the desire for thinness seem to have been a major impetus for the problem. Thus, eating disorders are in large part a product of (Western/developing) cultures.

19-2.   Probably as a result of the greater pressure on women to fit the current fashion of thinness, about ____% of individuals with eating disorders are female. Studies suggest that about 1-1.5% of young women develop _____ nervosa and about 2-3% _____ nervosa. The typical age of onset of the disorders is (before/after) age 21. Therapeutic interventions claim some success, but it is estimated that only about ____% of patients experience a full recovery.

Answers: **19-1.** rare, nonexistent, Western **19-2.** 90-95%, anorexia, bulimia, before, 40-50%.

20. **Discuss various etiological factors that may contribute to eating disorders.**

20-1.   Data from _____ studies and studies of relatives of individuals with eating disorders suggest that there is some degree of genetic predisposition for the disorders.

20-2.   There are also personality traits that may reflect an underlying vulnerability. For example, people who are impulsive, overly sensitive, and low in self-esteem are more likely to suffer from (bulimia/anorexia) nervosa. People characterized as neurotic, obsessive, and rigid are more likely to have (bulimia/anorexia) nervosa.

20-3.   As mentioned previously, cultural values are clearly implicated as well. Over the last half of the 20th century eating disorders (increased/decreased) in prevalence as the ideal body weight (increased/decreased). Although one cannot make causal conclusions it seems likely that the cultural milieu is a major factor in eating disorders.

20-4.   It is very difficult to sort out cause and effect in case and informal studies, but some theorists contend that parents who are (underinvolved/overly involved) in their children's lives unintentionally push their adolescent children to exert autonomy through pathological eating patterns. Other theorists contend that mothers pass along the thinness message by _____ unhealthy dieting practices.

20-5.   Disturbed thinking seems to accompany eating disorders, but whether it is a cause or a result of the disorders is hard to say. (For example, studies of food deprivation in volunteer subjects also find disturbed thinking processes.) In any case, the type of thinking may be characterized as _____ thinking (e.g., If I am not thin, I am nothing; if I eat, I am not in control of my life.)

Answers: **20-1.** twin **20-2.** bulimia, anorexia **20-3.** increased, decreased **20-4.** overly involved, modeling (endorsing, agreeing with, passing on) **20-5.** rigid (all or none, dichotomous).

21. **Discuss how mental heuristics can distort estimates of cumulative and conjunctive probabilities.**

21-1. Basing an estimate of probability on the similarity of an event to a prototype (or mental representation) is a distortion in thinking referred to as the _____ heuristic.

21-2. Over a lifetime, what is the probability that someone will be afflicted with mental illness? Higher than most people think, about one chance in three. People underestimate this probability in part because when they think of mental illness, they think of severe disturbances, such as schizophrenia. When a _____ such as this comes to mind, people tend to ignore information about _____. This bias in our thinking is called the _____.

21-3. In fact, the lifetime mental illness referred to could be schizophrenia, or obsessive-compulsive disorder, or phobia, or substance abuse disorder, or any of an enormous number of other disorders. Each "or" in this instance should involve (adding/subtracting) estimates of the appropriate probabilities, an example of (conjunctive/cumulative) probabilities. The representativeness heuristic, however, results in our estimating probabilities based on similarity to a _____.

21-4. Here is another probability question: Which of the following is more likely (a or b)?

a. having a phobia

b. having a phobia and being obsessive-compulsive

You don't have to know anything about these disorders or their actual probabilities to know that the answer is ____. In this example, you implicitly know that the likelihood of two events occurring together is less than that of either of these events occurring alone. This example illustrates "and" relationships or _____ probabilities.

21-5. Sometimes the answer is not so apparent. Consider this question: John was reported to have been brain damaged at birth. At age 14, John's IQ was measured as 70. Of the following which is most likely? ____

a. John wins a Nobel prize at age 40.

b. John is given an experimental treatment for retardation; John wins a Nobel prize at age 40.

c. John was mixed up with another baby; John's IQ test was scored incorrectly; John wins a Nobel prize at age 40.

21-6. The answer to the previous question is another example of _____ probabilities. If you, like most people that I have shown this problem, picked some answer other than "a," you made the error known as the _____ fallacy.

21-7. Why do we make the conjunction fallacy? In part the mistake results, again, from our tendency to be influenced by prototypes, the _____ heuristic. Even though we know that, logically, the likelihood of two events occurring together is less than the probability of either occurring alone, the additional "explanation" makes the combined result seem more reasonable. In fact, it is just another example of _____ probabilities.

21-8. When you first read about mood disorders, or obsessive-compulsive disorder, or generalized anxiety disorder, or hypochondriasis, did you tend to think that each description might fit you or one of your friends? If so, you were probably influenced by the _____ heuristic.

21-9. The availability heuristic involves the ease with which we can bring something to _____. The more readily we can think of some event, the more likely it is to influence our judgment about its frequency or _____.

21-10. Review. If one estimates probability based on a mental image or prototype, one is using the _____. If we think that it is more likely that two events will occur together than that either will occur alone, we have made the error known as the _____. If we base our estimate of probability on the ease with which something comes to mind, we are using the _____.

Answers: 21-1. representativeness **21-2.** prototype (mental representation), probability, representativeness heuristic **21-3.** adding, cumulative, prototype **21-4.** a, conjunctive **21-5.** a **21-6.** conjunctive, conjunction **21-7.** representativeness, conjunctive **21-8.** availability **21-9.** mind, probability **21-10.** representativeness heuristic, conjunction fallacy, availability heuristic.

REVIEW OF KEY TERMS

Agoraphobia
Anorexia nervosa
Antisocial personality disorder
Anxiety disorders
Availability heuristic
Bipolar disorders
Bulimia nervosa
Catatonic schizophrenia
Comorbidity
Concordance rate
Conjunction fallacy
Conversion disorder
Culture-bound disorders
Cyclothymic disorder
Delusions
Diagnosis
Disorganized schizophrenia

Dissociative amnesia
Dissociative disorders
Dissociative fugue
Dissociative identity disorder
Dysthymic disorder
Eating disorders
Epidemiology
Etiology
Generalized anxiety disorder
Representativeness heuristic
Hallucinations
Hypochondriasis
Insanity
Involuntary commitment
Major depressive disorder
Medical model

Mood disorders
Multiple-personality disorder
Negative symptoms
Obsessive-compulsive disorder (OCD)
Panic disorder
Paranoid schizophrenia
Personality disorders
Phobic disorder
Positive symptoms
Prevalence
Prognosis
Psychosomatic diseases
Schizophrenic disorders
Somatization disorder
Somatoform disorders
Undifferentiated schizophrenia

_____ **1.** Proposes that it is useful to think of abnormal behavior as a disease.

_____ **2.** Involves distinguishing one illness from another.

_____ **3.** Refers to the apparent causation and developmental history of an illness.

_____ **4.** A forecast about the possible course of an illness.

_____ **5.** An eating disorder characterized by fear of gaining weight, disturbed body image, refusal to maintain normal weight, and dangerous measures to lose weight.

_____ **6.** A class of disorders marked by feelings of excessive apprehension and anxiety.

_____ 7. Disorder marked by a chronic high level of anxiety that is not tied to any specific threat.

_____ 8. Disorder marked by a persistent and irrational fear of an object or situation that presents no realistic danger.

_____ 9. Disorder that involves recurrent attacks of overwhelming anxiety that usually occur suddenly and unexpectedly.

_____ 10. Disorder marked by persistent uncontrollable intrusions of unwanted thoughts and urges to engage in senseless rituals.

_____ 11. A fear of going out in public places.

_____ 12. Physical ailments with a genuine organic basis that are caused in part by psychological factors.

_____ 13. A class of disorders involving physical ailments that have no authentic organic basis and are due to psychological factors.

_____ 14. Disorder marked by a history of diverse physical complaints that appear to be psychological in origin.

_____ 15. Disorder that involves a significant loss of physical function (with no apparent organic basis), usually in a single-organ system.

_____ 16. Disorder that involves excessive preoccupation with health concerns and incessant worrying about developing physical illnesses.

_____ 17. A class of disorders in which people lose contact with portions of their consciousness or memory, resulting in disruptions in their sense of identity.

_____ 18. A sudden loss of memory for important personal information that is too extensive to be due to normal forgetting.

_____ 19. People's loss of memory for their entire lives along with their sense of personal identity.

_____ 20. Older term, still widely used, that describes the coexistence in one person of two or more personalities.

_____ 21. The new term that replaced multiple-personality disorder in the DSM-IV.

_____ 22. A class of disorders marked by depressed or elevated mood disturbances that may spill over to disrupt physical, perceptual, social, and thought processes.

_____ 23. Severe disturbances in eating behavior characterized by preoccupation with weight concerns and unhealthy efforts to control weight; includes the syndromes anorexia nervosa and bulimia nervosa.

_____ 24. A disorder marked by persistent feelings of sadness and despair and a loss of interest in previous sources of pleasure.

_____ 25. Disorders marked by the experience of both depressive and manic periods.

_____ 26. Statistic indicating the percentage of twin pairs or other pairs of relatives who exhibit the same disorder.

_____ 27. Estimating the probably of an event based on the ease with which relevant instances come to mind.

_____ 28. A class of disorders marked by disturbances in thought that spill over to affect perceptual, social, and emotional processes.

_____ 29. False beliefs that are maintained even though they clearly are out of touch with reality.

_____ 30. Sensory perceptions that occur in the absence of a real, external stimulus, or gross distortions of perceptual input.

_____ 31. Type of schizophrenia dominated by delusions of persecution, along with delusions of grandeur.

_____ 32. Type of schizophrenia marked by striking motor disturbances, ranging from muscular rigidity to random motor activity.

_____ 33. Type of schizophrenia marked by a particularly severe deterioration of adaptive behavior.

_____ 34. Type of schizophrenia marked by idiosyncratic mixtures of schizophrenic symptoms.

_____ 35. A legal status indicating that a person cannot be held responsible for his or her actions because of mental illness.

_____ 36. Legal situation in which people are hospitalized in psychiatric facilities against their will.

_____ 37. Abnormal syndromes found only in a few cultural groups.

_____ 38. Estimating the probability of an event based on how similar the event is to a prototype.

_____ 39. An error in thinking that involves estimating that the odds of two uncertain events happening together are greater than the odds of either event happening alone.

_____ 40. An eating disorder that involves binge eating followed by unhealthy compensatory efforts such as vomiting, fasting, abuse of laxatives and diuretics, and excessive exercise.

_____ 41. The coexistence of two or more disorders in the same individual.

Answers: 1. medical model **2.** diagnosis **3.** etiology **4.** prognosis **5.** anorexia nervosa **6.** anxiety disorders **7.** generalized anxiety disorder **8.** phobic disorder **9.** panic disorder **10.** obsessive-compulsive disorder **11.** agoraphobia **12.** psychosomatic diseases **13.** somatoform disorders **14.** somatization disorder **15.** conversion disorder **16.** hypochondriasis **17.** dissociative disorders **18.** dissociative amnesia **19.** dissociative fugue **20.** multiple-personality disorder **21.** dissociative identity disorder **22.** mood disorders **23.** eating disorders **24.** major depressive disorder **25.** bipolar disorders **26.** concordance rate **27.** availability heuristic **28.** schizophrenic disorders **29.** delusions **30.** hallucinations **31.** paranoid schizophrenia **32.** catatonic schizophrenia **33.** disorganized schizophrenia **34.** undifferentiated schizophrenia **35.** insanity **36.** involuntary commitment **37.** culture-bound disorders **38.** representativeness heuristic **39.** conjunction fallacy **40.** bulimia nervosa **41.** comorbidity.

REVIEW OF KEY PEOPLE

Nancy Andreasen   Martin Seligman   Thomas Szasz

_____ 1. Critic of the medical model; argues that abnormal behavior usually involves a deviation from social norms rather than an illness.

_____ 2. Proposes a classical conditioning view of phobias modified by the biological concept of "preparedness."

_____ 3. Proposed an alternative approach to subtyping that divides schizophrenic disorders into just two categories based on the presence of negative versus positive symptoms.

Answers: 1. Szasz **2.** Seligman **3.** Andreasen.

SELF-QUIZ

1. Which of the following concepts or people asserts that abnormal behavior is best thought of as an illness?
   a. the behavioral model
   b. the medical model
   c. Thomas Szasz
   d. Arthur Staats

2. The concordance rate for mood disorders has been found to be about 67% among identical twins and 17% among fraternal twins. These data suggest that the mood disorders:
   a. are caused primarily by stress
   b. have an onset at an early age
   c. are due primarily to family environment
   d. are caused in part by genetic factors

3. In Rosenhan's study involving admission of pseudopatients to psychiatric facilities, most of the "patients" were:
   a. diagnosed as seriously disturbed
   b. diagnosed as suffering from a mild neurosis
   c. dismissed within two days
   d. misdiagnosed by the ward attendants but correctly diagnosed by the professional staff

4. An individual gets sudden, paralyzing attacks of anxiety and also fears going out in public away from her house. Which anxiety disorder does this describe?
   a. generalized anxiety disorder
   b. phobic disorder
   c. obsessive-compulsive disorder
   d. panic attack and agoraphobia

5. Ralph cleans and scrubs the cupboards in his house seven times each day. Which anxiety disorder does this describe?
   a. generalized anxiety disorder
   b. phobic disorder
   c. obsessive-compulsive disorder
   d. panic disorder

6. Human beings may have evolved to be more easily conditioned to fear some stimuli than others. This is Seligman's notion of:
   a. preparedness
   b. anxiety differentiation
   c. somatization
   d. learned helplessness

7. Delusions and hallucinations are likely to characterize:
   a. major depressive disorder
   b. hypochondriasis
   c. phobias
   d. schizophrenia

8. Paralysis or loss of feeling that does not match underlying anatomical organization may be a symptom of:
   a. somatization disorder
   b. conversion disorder
   c. hypochondriasis
   d. malingering

9. A disorder that was extremely rare prior to the last half of the 20th century is the syndrome:
   a. manic-depressive disorder
   b. schizophrenia
   c. obsessive-compulsive disorder
   d. anorexia nervosa

10. The disorder marked by striking motor disturbances ranging from rigidity to random motor activity and incoherence is termed:
    a. catatonic schizophrenia
    b. multiple personality
    c. dissociative disorder
    d. paranoid schizophrenia

11. Which of the following are disorders that occur in all cultures?
    a. generalized anxiety disorder and panic disorder
    b. hypochondriasis, somatization, conversion disorder
    c. schizophrenia, bipolar mood disorder, depression
    d. bulimia and anorexia nervosa

12. A disorder characterized by amenorrhea (loss of the menstrual cycle) in women is the syndrome termed:
    a. generalized anxiety disorder
    b. bipolar mood disorder
    c. anorexia nervosa
    d. bulimia nervosa

13. An individual thinks he is Jesus Christ. He also believes that, because he is Christ, people are trying to kill him. Which of the following would be the most likely diagnosis? (Assume that he is not Christ and that people are not trying to kill him.)
    a. multiple personality
    b. paranoid schizophrenia
    c. obsessive-compulsive disorder
    d. catatonic schizophrenia

14. A court declares that, because of a mental illness, an individual is not responsible for his criminal actions (did not know right from wrong). The individual is:
    a. insane
    b. psychopathic
    c. psychotic
    d. schizophrenic

15. Being careful not to make the conjunction fallacy, indicate which of the following is more probable:
    a. Ralph is an alcoholic; Ralph wins a major world tennis tournament.
    b. Ralph is an alcoholic; Ralph enters a treatment program; Ralph wins a major world tennis tournament.
    c. Ralph is an alcoholic; Ralph enters a treatment program; Ralph has been sober for a year; Ralph wins a major world tennis tournament.
    d. Ralph is an alcoholic; Ralph enters a treatment program; Ralph has been sober for a year; Ralph practices tennis 50 hours a week; Ralph wins a major world tennis tournament.

   Answers: 1. b 2. d 3. a 4. d 5. c 6. a 7. d 8. b 9. d 10. a 11. c 12. c 13. b 14. a 15. a.

INFOTRAC

Agoraphobia	Hypochondriasis (see hypochondria)	Paranoid Schizophrenia
Anorexia Nervosa	Major Depressive Disorder	Somatoform Disorders
Availability Heuristic	Obsessive-compulsive Disorder	

15 PSYCHOTHERAPY

REVIEW OF KEY IDEAS

THE ELEMENTS OF THE TREATMENT PROCESS

1. Identify the three categories of therapy and discuss who seeks therapy.

   1-1. Even though she already owns more than a thousand pairs of shoes, Imelba cannot resist the urge to buy more. She checks the Yellow Pages and calls three different psychotherapists regarding possible treatment for her compulsion.

   (a) One therapist tells her that treatment will require her to talk with the therapist so as to develop a better understanding of her inner feelings. This therapist probably belongs to the _____ school of psychotherapy.

   (b) Another therapist suggests that some form of medication may help alleviate her compulsion. This therapist probably pursues the _____ approach to psychotherapy.

   (c) The third therapist is of the opinion that her urge to buy shoes results from learning, and correcting it requires that she unlearn this compulsion. This therapist probably pursues the _____ approach to psychotherapy.

   1-2. Indicate whether the following statements about people who seek and choose not to seek psychotherapy are true or false.

   _____ (a) The two most common presenting symptoms are excessive anxiety and depression.

   _____ (b) Persons seeking psychotherapy always have identifiable disorders.

   _____ (c) Only a minority of persons needing psychotherapy actually received treatment.

   _____ (d) Many people feel that seeking psychotherapy is an admission of personal weakness.

Answers: 1-1. (a) insight (b) biomedical (c) behavioral **1-2.** (a) true (b) false (c) true (d) true.

2. **Describe the various types of mental health professionals involved in the provision of psychotherapy.**

   2-1.   Identify the following kinds of mental health professionals:

   (a) Medically trained persons (physicians) who generally use biomedical and insight approaches to psychotherapy.

   (b) Persons with doctoral degrees who emphasize behavioral and insight approaches to psychotherapy in treating a full range of psychological problems (two types).

   (c) Nurses who usually work as part of the treatment team in a hospital setting.

   (d) Persons with a degree in social work who often work independently to provide a wide range of therapeutic services with both patients and their families.

   (e) Persons who usually specialize in particular types of problems, such as vocational, drug, or marital counseling.

   Answers: 2-1. (a) psychiatrists (b) clinical and counseling psychologists (c) psychiatric nurses (d) clinical social workers (e) counselors.

INSIGHT THERAPIES

3. **Explain the logic of psychoanalysis and describe the techniques by which analysts probe the unconscious.**

   3-1.   Freud believed that psychological disturbances originate from unresolved conflicts deep in the unconscious levels of the mind. His theory of personality, which he called _____, would be classified as an _____ approach to psychotherapy. The psychoanalyst plays the role of psychological detective, seeking out problems thought to originate from conflicts left over from early _____.

   3-2.   The psychoanalyst employs two techniques to probe the unconscious. One technique requires the patient to tell whatever comes to mind no matter how trivial. This technique is called _____ _____. The other technique requires the patient to learn to remember his or her dreams, which are then probed for their hidden meaning by the psychoanalyst. This technique is called _____ _____.

3-3. Freud believed most people (<u>do/do not</u>) want to know the true nature of their inner conflicts and will employ various strategies so as to offer _____ to the progress of therapy. As therapy progresses, the patient often begins to relate to the therapist as though he or she was actually one of the significant persons (mother, father, spouse, etc.) in the patient's life. This phenomenon is called _____.

Answers: **3-1.** psychoanalysis, insight, childhood **3-2.** free association, dream analysis. **3-3.** do not, resistance, transference.

4. Identify the elements of therapeutic climate and discuss the therapeutic process in Rogers's client-centered therapy.

4-1. Carl Rodgers felt that personal distress results from inconsistency, or _____, between a person's self-concept and _____.

4-2. Rogers holds that there are three important aspects necessary for a good therapeutic climate. These are genuineness, unconditional positive regard, and empathy. Match these terms with the correct definitions as given below.

(a) The ability to truly see the world from the client's point of view and communicate this understanding to the client.

(b) The therapist's openness and honesty with the client.

(c) The complete and nonjudgmental acceptance of the client as a person without necessarily agreeing with what the client has to say.

4-3. For client-centered therapy, the major emphasis is to provide feedback and _____ as the client expresses his or her thoughts and feelings. The idea here is that the client (<u>does/does not</u>) need direct advice. What is needed is help in sorting through personal confusion in order to gain greater _____ into true inner feelings.

Answers: **4-1.** incongruence, reality **4-2.** (a) empathy (b) genuineness (c) unconditional positive regard **4-3.** clarification, does not, insight or understanding.

5. Discuss the logic, goals, and techniques of cognitive therapy.

5-1. Answer the following questions regarding the logic, goals, and techniques of cognitive therapy.

(a) What is the basic logic behind cognitive therapy? Or to put it another way, what is the origin of many psychological problems according to cognitive therapy?

(b) What is the primary goal of cognitive therapy?

(c) How do cognitive therapists go about trying to change a client's negative illogical thinking?

Answers: 5-1. (a) negative illogical thinking (b) to change the client's negative illogical thinking (c) through argument and persuasion.

6. Describe how group therapy is generally conducted.

6-1. When conducting group therapy, the therapist generally plays a(an) (<u>active/subtle</u>) role, one that is primarily aimed at promoting _____ cohesiveness. Participants essentially function as _____ for each other, exposing problems and providing acceptance and emotional support.

Answers: 6-1. subtle, group, therapists.

7. Discuss evidence on the efficacy of insight therapies.

7-1. Answer the following questions about the efficacy (effectiveness) of insight therapies.

(a) What does the text conclude about the superiority of insight therapies over no treatment or placebo treatment?

(b) What did a majority of patients conclude about the efficacy of their own treatment?

Answers: 7-1. (a) They are superior. (b) They felt they had gained considerable benefit (from the therapy).

BEHAVIOR THERAPIES

8. Summarize the general principles underlying behavioral approaches to therapy.

8-1. In contrast to insight therapists who believe that pathological symptoms are signs of an underlying problem, behavior therapists believe that the _____ are the problem. Thus, behavior therapists focus on employing the principles of learning to directly change maladaptive _____. The two general principles underlying this approach are (1) one's behavior is a product of _____, and (2) what has been learned can be _____.

Answers: 8-1. symptoms, behavior, learning, unlearned.

9. **Describe the goals and procedures of systematic desensitization, aversion therapy, and social skills training.**

   9-1.   State whether the following situations would be most applicable to systematic desensitization or to aversion therapy.

   (a) The treatment goal is to lessen the attractiveness of particular stimuli and behaviors that are personally or socially harmful.

   (b) The treatment goal is to reduce irrational fears such as found in phobias and other anxiety disorders.

   (c) The three-step treatment involves pairing an imagined anxiety hierarchy with deep muscle relaxation.

   (d) Treatment involves presenting an unpleasant stimulus, such as electric shock, while a person is engaged in performing a self-destructive, but personally appealing, act.

   (e) This would be the treatment of choice for students who are unduly anxious about public speaking.

   9-2.   As the name implies, social skills training is a behavior therapy designed to improve a client's social or _____ skills. Three different behavioral techniques are employed. First, one is required to closely watch the behavior of socially skilled persons, a technique called _____. Next the client is expected to imitate and practice the behavior he or she has just witnessed, a technique called _____. Finally, the client is expected to perform in social situations requiring increasingly more difficult social skills, a technique called _____ ,

   Answers: 9-1. (a) aversion therapy (b) systematic desensitization (c) systematic desensitization (d) aversion therapy (e) systematic desensitization **9-2.** interpersonal, modeling, rehearsal, shaping.

10. **Discuss evidence on the effectiveness of behavior therapies.**

    10-1.   Compared to the evidence in support of insight therapies, the evidence in favor of behavior therapy is moderately (weaker/stronger) at least for some disorders. It is important to remember, however, that behavior therapies are best suited for treating (specific/general) psychological disorders and that all of the various behavioral techniques (are/are not) equally effective.

    Answers: 10-1. stronger, specific, are not.

BIOMEDICAL THERAPIES

11. **Discuss evidence on the effects and problems of drug treatments for psychological disorders.**

    11-1.   Valium and Xanax, popularly called tranquilizers, are used to treat psychological disorders in which anxiety is a major feature. Thus, they are collectively called _____ drugs.

11-2. Another class of drugs is used to treat severe psychotic symptoms, such as hallucinations and confusion. These drugs are collectively called _____ drugs.

11-3. Three classes of drugs–tricyclics, MAO inhibitors, and selective serotonin reuptake inhibitors–have been found to be useful in alleviating depression. These drugs are collectively called _____ drugs.

11-4. A rather unique drug can function as both an antidepressant and antimanic agent thus proving useful in the treatment of bipolar disorders. This drug is _____.

11-5. Drug therapies have proven useful in the treatment of many psychological disorders, some that are resistant to treatment by other forms of therapy. However, they remain controversial for at least three reasons. Use the hints below to describe these three reasons.

(a) resolve problems

(b) two areas having to do with excesses

(c) cure is worse than the disease

Answers: 11-1. antianxiety **11-2.** antipsychotic **11-3.** antidepressant **11-4.** lithium **11-5.** (a) They alleviate rather than cure psychological distress. (b) They are overprescribed and patients are over-medicated. (c) The side effects may be worse than the disease.

12. **Describe ECT and discuss its therapeutic effects and its risks.**

12-1. Answer the following questions about the nature, therapeutic effects, and risks of ECT.

(a) What is the physical effect of the electric shock on the patient?

(b) What general class of disorders warrant conservative use of ECT as a treatment technique?

(c) What does research evidence show regarding the effectiveness of ECT?

(d) What is the major risk of ECT?

Answers: 12-1. (a) It produces convulsive seizures. (b) severe mood disorders (especially depression) (c) There is enough favorable evidence to justify conservative use at this time. (d) It produces short-term intellectual impairment and may produce long-term intellectual impairment.

CURRENT TRENDS AND ISSUES IN TREATMENT

13. **Summarize the concerns that have been expressed about the impact of managed care on the treatment of psychological disorders.**

   13-1.   Why might the impact on mental health care be more negative with managed health care than for other treatment specialties in carrying out medically necessary treatment programs?

   13-2.   What are some cost-cutting strategies, in addition to denial of treatment and prescribing older rather than newer drugs, that are often employed by HMO's?

   Answers: 13-1. The question of what is medically necessary is more subjective (in the case of mental health treatment). **13-2.** under diagnosing conditions, failing to make needed referrals, limiting treatment times, rerouting patients to less highly trained professionals (in any order).

14. **Explain what is meant by empirically validated treatments.**

   14-1.   What two conditions must a treatment meet to become empirically validated?

   Answers: 14-1. It must be found to be superior to placebo or no treatment for a specific disorder and the studies must be conducted by two or more independent research teams.

15. **Discuss the merits of blending or combining different approaches to therapy.**

   15-1.   A significant trend in modern psychotherapy is to blend or combine many different treatment approaches. Psychologists who advocate and use this approach are said to be _____. Multiple approaches are most likely when a (therapist/treatment team) provides the therapy. Evidence suggests that there is (some/no) merit in combining approaches to treatment.

   Answers: 15-1. eclectic, treatment team, some.

16. **Discuss the barriers that lead to underutilization of mental health services by ethnic minorities and possible solutions to the problem.**

   16-1.   The text lists three general barriers (*cultural, language, and institutional*) to mental health services for ethnic minorities. Indicate which of these barriers is represented in the following statements.

   _____ (a)   Very few mental health facilities are equipped to provide culturally responsive services.

   _____ (b)   There is a limited number of bilingual therapists.

_____ (c) Psychotherapy was developed by whites in the Western world to treat whites in the Western world.

16-2. What would be an optimal, but perhaps impractical, solution to the problems of language and cultural differences between therapists and clients?

16-3. What kind of training was recommended for therapists dealing with ethnic minorities?

Answers. 16-1. (a) institutional (b) language (c) cultural **16-2.** Ethnically match therapists and clients. **16-3.** cultural sensitivity training.

INSTITUTIONAL TREATMENT IN TRANSITION

17. Explain why people grew disenchanted with mental hospitals.

17-1. After more than a century of reliance on state mental hospitals, the evidence began to grow that these institutions were hurting more than helping many patients. What condition unrelated to funding and staffing was partly responsible for this state of affairs?

Answer: 17-1. The removal of patients from their communities separated them from essential support groups.

18. Describe the deinstitutionalization trend and evaluate its effects.

18-1. The transferring of mental health care from large state mental hospitals to community-based facilities is what is meant by the term _____. As a result of deinstitutionalization, the number of patients in large mental hospitals has (increased/decreased) remarkably. The opening of community-based treatment facilities and the emergence of effective _____ therapies were the major factors that accounted for this remarkable decline.

18-2. While deinstitutionalization has resulted in a decrease in the number of patients, the number of admissions to psychiatric hospitals has actually _____. This is because of a large number of readmissions for short-term care, which the text calls "the _____ _____ problem." Another problem brought about by deinstitutionalization is that a large number of discharged patients who have meager job skills and no close support groups make up a sizeable portion of the nation's _____ persons.

Answers: 18-1. deinstitutionalization, decreased, drug **18-2.** increased, revolving door, homeless.

PUTTING IT IN PERSPECTIVE

19. Explain how this chapter highlighted two of the text's unifying themes.

19-1. What point does the text make about how theoretical diversity influenced the treatment techniques employed in psychotherapy?

19-2. The approaches to psychotherapy discussed in this chapter are not universally accepted or used, and some are actually counterproductive in many cultures. Why is this?

Answers: 19-1. It has resulted in better treatment techniques **19-2.** Cultural factors influence psychological processes.

PERSONAL APPLICATION • LOOKING FOR A THERAPIST

20. Discuss where to seek therapy and the potential importance of a therapist's sex, theoretical approach, and professional background.

20-1. Most therapists (are/are not) in private practice. In addition to talking to friends and acquaintances, the text lists many places (Table 15.2) where one might seek psychotherapy. The general idea here is to _____ _____ when looking for a therapist.

20-2. The text concludes that the kind of degree and theoretical approach held by the psychotherapist is (less/more) important than the therapist's personal skills, although a verifiable degree indicating some kind of professional training is important. The sex of the therapist should be chosen according to the feelings of the _____; it is unwise to engage a therapist whose sex makes the client feel uncomfortable.

Answers: 20-1. are not, look around **20-2.** less, client (patient).

21. Summarize what one should look for in a prospective therapist and what one should expect out of therapy.

21-1. The text lists three areas to evaluate when looking for a therapist. Complete the following statements describing these areas.

(a) Can you talk to the therapist _____?

(b) Does the therapist appear to have _____?

(c) Does the therapist appear to be _____?

21-2. What did the Ehrenbergs say about what to expect from psychotherapy?

Answers: 21-1. (a) openly (in a candid, nondefensive manner) (b) understanding (c) confident 21-2. It takes time, effort, and courage.

CRITICAL THINKING APPLICATION • FROM CRISIS TO WELLNESS–BUT WAS IT THE THERAPY?

22. **Explain how placebo effects and regression toward the mean can complicate the evaluation of therapy.**

   22-1.   In addition to therapy itself, what other two factors can influence the outcome of a treatment program?

   22-2.   Which of these two factors is least effected by having only a small sample?

   22-3.   Which of these factors leads us to predict that persons who score the healthiest on a mental health questionnaire will actually score lower on this questionnaire following a brief therapy intervention?

Answers: 22-1. placebo effects and regression toward the mean 22-2. placebo effects 22-3. regression toward the mean.

REVIEW OF KEY TERMS

Antianxiety drugs
Antidepressant drugs
Antipsychotic drugs
Aversion therapy
Behavior therapies
Biomedical therapies
Client-centered therapy
Clinical psychologists
Cognitive therapy
Counseling psychologists

Deinstitutionalization
Dream analysis
Electroconvulsive therapy (ECT)
Free association
Group therapy
Insight therapies
Interpretation
Lithium
Mental hospitals
Placebo effects

Psychiatrists
Psychoanalysis
Psychopharmacotherapy
Regression toward the mean
Resistance
Social skills training
Systematic desensitization
Tardive dyskinesia
Transference

_____   1.   Two groups of professionals with doctoral degrees in psychology that specialize in the diagnosis and treatment of psychological disorders and everyday behavioral problems.

_____   2.   Physicians who specialize in the treatment of psychological disorders.

_____   3.   Therapies that involve verbal interactions intended to enhance client's self-knowledge and thus produce healthful changes in personality and behavior.

_____   4.   An insight therapy that emphasizes the recovery of unconscious conflicts, motives and defenses through techniques such as free association and dream analysis.

_____   5.   A technique in which clients are urged to spontaneously express their thoughts and feelings with as little personal censorship as possible.

_____   6.   A technique for interpreting the symbolic meaning of dreams.

_____ 7. A therapist's attempts to explain the inner significance of a client's thoughts, feelings, memories, and behavior.

_____ 8. A client's largely unconscious defensive maneuvers intended to hinder the progress of therapy.

_____ 9. Process that occurs when clients start relating to their therapist in ways that mimic critical relationships in their lives.

_____ 10. An insight therapy that emphasizes providing a supportive emotional climate for clients who play a major role in determining the pace and direction of their therapy.

_____ 11. An insight therapy that emphasizes recognizing and changing negative thoughts and maladaptive beliefs.

_____ 12. The simultaneous treatment of several clients in a group.

_____ 13. Therapies that involve the application of learning principles to change a client's maladaptive behaviors.

_____ 14. A behavior therapy used to reduce clients' anxiety responses through counterconditioning.

_____ 15. A behavior therapy in which an aversive stimulus is paired with a stimulus that elicits an undesirable response.

_____ 16. A behavior therapy designed to improve interpersonal skills, that emphasizes shaping, modeling, and behavioral rehearsal.

_____ 17. Therapies that use physiological interventions intended to reduce symptoms associated with psychological disorders.

_____ 18. The treatment of mental disorders with drug therapy.

_____ 19. Drugs that relieve tension, apprehension, and nervousness.

_____ 20. Drugs that gradually reduce psychotic symptoms.

_____ 21. A neurological disorder marked by chronic tremors and involuntary spastic movements.

_____ 22. Drugs that gradually elevate mood and help bring people out of a depression.

_____ 23. A chemical used to control mood swings in patients with bipolar mood disorder.

_____ 24. A treatment in which electric shock is used to produce cortical seizure accompanied by convulsions.

_____ 25. A medical institution specializing in the provision of inpatient care for psychological disorders.

_____ 26. Transferring the treatment of mental illness from inpatient institutions to community-based facilities that emphasize outpatient care.

_____ 27. Occurs when people's expectations lead them to experience some change even though they receive a fake treatment.

_____ 28. Occurs when people who score extremely high or low on some trait are measured a second time and their new scores fall closer to the mean.

Answers: 1. clinical and counseling psychologists **2.** psychiatrists **3.** insight therapies **4.** psychoanalysis **5.** free association **6.** dream analysis **7.** interpretation **8.** resistance **9.** transference **10.** client-centered therapy **11.** cognitive therapy **12.** group therapy **13.** behavior therapies **14.** systematic desensitization **15.** aversion therapy **16.** social skills training **17.** biomedical therapies **18.** psychopharmacotherapy **19.** antianxiety drugs **20.** antipsychotic drugs **21.** tardive dyskinesa **22.** antidepressant drugs **23.** lithium **24.** electroconvulsive therapy (ECT) **25.** mental hospitals **26.** deinstitutionalization **27.** placebo effects **28.** regression toward the mean.

REVIEW OF KEY PEOPLE

Aaron Beck   Carl Rogers   Joseph Wolpe
Sigmund Freud

_____   1.   Developed a systematic treatment procedure that he called psychoanalysis.
_____   2.   The developer of client-centered therapy.
_____   3.   Noted for his work in the development of cognitive therapy.
_____   4.   The developer of systematic desensitization.

Answers: 1. Freud **2.** Rogers **3.** Beck **4.** Wolpe.

SELF-QUIZ

1. Which approach to psychotherapy is most likely to use medication as part of the treatment package?
    a. insight
    b. biomedical
    c. behavioral
    d. group

2. Which of the following is not a true statement?
    a. Only a minority of persons who need psychotherapy actually receive it.
    b. The two most common problems that lead to psychotherapy are sexual problems and depression.
    c. Persons seeking psychotherapy don't always have identifiable problems.
    d. All psychotherapists are not equally effective.

3. Which of the following mental health professional is most likely to employ both biomedical and insight approaches to psychotherapy?
    a. psychiatrists
    b. clinical psychologists
    c. psychiatric nurses
    d. counselors

4. Psychoanalysis is an example of what kind of approach to psychotherapy?
    a. insight
    b. learning
    c. biomedical
    d. a combination of learning and biomedical

5. A client who begins to relate to her psychoanalyst as she would her mother would be said to be exhibiting:
    a. transference
    b. free association
    c. catharsis
    d. restructuring

6. The major emphasis in client-centered therapy is to provide the client with:
    a. interpretation of unconscious thinking
    b. cognitive restructuring
    c. feedback and clarification
    d. good advice

7. Which of the following is likely to be commonly found in behavior therapy?
   a. free association
   b. emphasis on non-verbal cues
   c. transference
   d. social skills training

8. Which of the following is not likely to be found in cognitive therapy?
   a. a search for automatic negative thoughts
   b. reality testing
   c. an emphasis on rational thinking
   d. dream interpretation

9. Which kind of therapists are likely to play the least active (most subtle) role in conducting therapy?
   a. behavior therapists
   b. cognitive therapists
   c. group therapists
   d. psychoanalytic therapists

10. Which of the following therapies is most likely to see the symptom as the problem?
    a. psychoanalysis
    b. Gestalt
    c. behavior
    d. cognitive

11. Which of the following behavior therapy techniques would most likely be used to treat a fear of flying?
    a. systematic desensitization
    b. aversive conditioning
    c. modeling
    d. rehearsal

12. Electroconvulsive therapy (ECT) is now primarily used to treat patients suffering from:
    a. anxiety
    b. phobia
    c. severe mood disorders
    d. psychosis

13. Which of the following trends in psychotherapy have been facilitated by the impact of managed health care?
    a. the development of eclectic approaches
    b. an increasing emphasis on group rather than individual therapy
    c. an increasing emphasis on biomedical approaches
    d. the development of empirically validated treatment techniques

14. The trend toward deinstitutionalization largely came about because large mental institutions:
    a. were becoming too expensive
    b. were actually worsening the condition of many patients
    c. could not be properly staffed
    d. relied too much on drugs

15. Which of the following factors can affect the outcome of a treatment program?
    a. the efficacy of the treatment itself
    b. regression toward the mean
    c. placebo effects
    d. all of the above

Answers: 1. b 2. b 3. a 4. a 5. a 6. c 7. d 8. d 9. c 10. c 11. a 12. c 13. d 14. b 15. d.

INFOTRAC

Aversion Therapy
Deinstitutionalization

Electroconvulsive Therapy

Placebo Effects

16 SOCIAL BEHAVIOR

REVIEW OF KEY IDEAS

PERSON PERCEPTION: FORMING IMPRESSIONS OF OTHERS

1. **Describe how various aspects of physical appearance may influence our impressions of others.**

   1-1. In general, we attribute _____ characteristics to good-looking people. In judging personality, we see attractive people as warmer, friendlier, better-adjusted, and more poised. In assessing competence, although differences are not as great for personality, we tend to view attractive people as (less/more) intelligent and successful than less attractive people.

   1-2. While good looks in general have relatively little impact on judgments of honesty, people do tend to view baby-faced individuals (large eyes, rounded chin) as more _____, helpless, and submissive than others. What about the notorious criminal, Baby-faced Nelson? Well, recent data indicates that our perceptions of baby-faced people (is/is not) a good match for their actual traits.

   Answers: **1-1.** positive (desirable, favorable) characteristics, more **1-2.** honest, is not.

2. **Explain how schemas and stereotypes contribute to subjectivity in person perception.**

   2-1. Briefly define the following:

   (a) schemas:

   (b) stereotypes:

2-2. Men are competitive, women are sensitive: these are stereotypes. Stereotypes are broad generalizations that tend to ignore the _____ within a group. People who hold stereotypes do not necessarily assume that all members of a particular group have the same characteristics but merely that there is an increased _____ that they do.

2-3. Whether probabilistic or absolute, schemas in general and stereotypes in particular direct our perception, so that we tend to see the things we expect to see. Such selective perception results in an overestimation of the degree to which our expectations match actual events, a phenomenon referred to as _____ correlation.

2-4. In one study discussed in the text participants watched a videotape of a woman engaged in various activities (including drinking beer and listening to classical music). For one set of subjects she was described as a librarian and for another as a waitress. What effect did the occupational labels have on subjects' recall of the woman's *activities*? Which of the following is(are) true?

  a. Subjects in the "librarian" condition tended to recall her listening to classical music.

  b. Subjects in the "waitress" condition tended to recall her drinking beer.

  c. Both of the above.

2-5. The study just described illustrates subjectivity in person perception. Our schemas, in this case the _____ that we have about categories of people, affect how we perceive and what we remember.

Answers: **2-1.** (a) clusters of ideas about people and events (b) a type of schema; widely held beliefs about people based on group membership **2-2.** diversity (variability), probability (likelihood) **2-3.** illusory **2-4.** c **2-5.** stereotypes.

3. **Explain the evolutionary perspective on bias in person perception.**

3-1. How does one explain bias or prejudice in terms of evolution? To explain anything in terms of evolution one has to assume that a trait had _____ value in our evolutionary past. For example, the bias in favor of physical attractiveness might have signaled health and _____ potential in women and the ability to acquire _____ in men. The attribution of submissiveness and honesty to _____ individuals could simply be fallout from our adaptive reaction to infants.

3-2. Evolutionary theorists also assert that we needed a quick way to categorize people as friend or enemy or, in more technical terms, as members of our _____ or members of the _____.

3-3. The question still remains: how could prejudice and bias be adaptive? It must be clear that what was adaptive in our evolutionary past (is also/may not be) adaptive now. Nonetheless, from the point of view of evolutionary theory, cognitive mechanisms involving bias have been shaped by natural _____.

Answers: **3-1.** adaptive (survival), reproductive, resources, baby-faced **3-2.** ingroup, outgroup **3-3.** may not be, selection.

4. **Describe the distinction between internal and external attributions and summarize Weiner's theories of attribution.**

4-1. Why are you reading this book? The search for causes of events, and of our own and others' behavior, is termed _____. For example, you might _____ your behavior to an upcoming test (or to personal interest, quest for knowledge, etc.)

4-2. Attributions are inferences that people make about the _____ of events and about their own and others' behavior.

4-3. We may attribute to *internal* causes (personality traits or dispositions) or to *external* causes (the situation or environment). Which of the following involve internal and which external attributions? Label each sentence with an I or an E.

_____ He flunked because he's lazy.

_____ Our team lost because the officials were biased against us.

_____ The accident was caused by poor road conditions.

_____ He achieved by the sweat of his brow.

_____ Criminal behavior is caused by poverty.

_____ His success is directly derived from his parents' wealth and influence.

4-4. Weiner proposed that attributions are made not only in terms of an internal-external dimension but also in terms of a stable-unstable dimension. Suppose that Sally makes a high score on an exam. She could attribute her score to her ability, an (internal/external) factor that is also (stable/unstable). If she attributed her success to her good mood, the attribution would be (internal/external) and (stable/unstable).

4-5. Or, Sally may think she did well because these types of test are easy, an (internal/external) and (stable/unstable) attribution. If she attributes her score to luck, the attribution would be (internal/external) and (stable/unstable).

Answers: 4-1. attribution, attribute **4-2.** causes **4-3.** I, E, E, I, E, E **4-4.** internal, stable, internal, unstable **4-5.** external, stable, external, unstable.

5. **Describe several types of attributional bias and cultural differences in attributional tendencies.**

5-1. Define or describe the following:

(a) fundamental attribution error:

(b) actor-observer bias:

(c) defensive attribution:

(d) self-serving bias:

5-2. Recent research has indicated that the attributional biases described above may not apply to all cultures. Since collectivist societies emphasize accomplishing the goals of the group over individual achievement, collectivist cultures are (less/more) likely to attribute other's behavior to *personal traits*. In other words, people from collectivist cultures tend to be (less/more) prone to the *fundamental attribution error.*

5-3. Some evidence also indicates that people from collectivist societies are more likely to attribute their *successes* to (the ease of a task/unusual ability). Similarly, they are more likely to attribute their *failures* to (bad luck/lack of effort). Thus, in contrast with people from individualistic societies, people from collectivist cultures appear to be (less/more) prone to the *self-serving bias.*

Answers: 5-1. (a) the tendency for observers to attribute an individual's behavior to *internal* rather than *external* factors (b) the tendency for observers to attribute an actor's behavior to internal rather than external factors *and the tendency for actors to attribute their own behavior to external causes* (Yes, there is overlap between these two concepts. The fundamental attribution error is part of the actor-observer bias.) (c) the tendency to attribute other people's misfortunes to internal causes, that is, the tendency to blame the victim (d) the tendency to attribute our *successes* to internal factors and our *failures* to situational factors **5-2.** less, less **5-3.** the ease of a task, lack of effort, less.

INTERPERSONAL ATTRACTION • LIKING AND LOVING

6. **Summarize evidence on how physical attractiveness, similarity, and reciprocity influence attraction.**

   6-1. What factors influence liking, friendship, and love? The key determinant of romantic attraction for (males/females/both sexes) is physical _____.

   6-2. While everyone might prefer to have a relationship with the most attractive person, people take their own attractiveness into account. What is the matching hypothesis?

   6-3. Do opposites attract, or do birds of a feather flock together? An overwhelming amount of research supports the idea that we are attracted to others who are (similar to/different from) us in attitudes, personality, social background, etc.

   6-4. We also tend to like others who like us, the principle of _____. In many cases we are particularly fond of those who exaggerate our good characteristics and overlook our bad. For married or dating couples, for example, the happiest couples seem to be those who hold a reciprocated and (accurate/idealized) view of their partners.

Answers: **6-1.** both sexes, attractiveness **6-2.** The matching hypothesis asserts that people tend to date and marry others of the opposite sex who are *approximately equal* to themselves in physical attractiveness. **6-3.** similar to **6-4.** reciprocity, idealized.

7. Describe efforts to analyze love into types and components.

7-1. Hatfield and Berscheid divide love into two types, the intense emotional and sexual feelings of _____ love and the warm and tolerant affection of _____ love.

7-2. Sternberg further divides companionate love into _____, characterized by closeness and sharing, and _____, an intention to maintain a relationship in the face of difficulties.

7-3. Thus, Sternberg lists three factors or types of love. Of these _____ love appears to peak early and drop off rapidly, while _____ and _____ gradually increase over time.

7-4. Commitment seems to be a particularly important factor in determining the durability of a relationship. For example, in a study of dating couples, _____ was more predictive of whether or not the relationship would continue than was overall love.

Answers: **7-1.** passionate, companionate **7-2.** intimacy, commitment **7-3.** passion, intimacy, commitment **7-4.** commitment.

8. Discuss cross-cultural research on romantic relationships and evolutionary analyses of mating patterns.

8-1. While there is considerable cross-cultural overlap in what the two sexes want in mates (e.g., kindness, intelligence, dependability), David Buss has found nearly universal differences as well. Buss's data indicate that _____ want mates who can acquire resources that can be invested in children, while _____ want mates who are beautiful, youthful, and in good health. These gender differences in mate preference appear to occur (<u>in virtually all/only in Western</u>) societies.

8-2. There are also differences among cultures in their views on the relationship between romantic love and marriage. The idea that one should be in love in order to marry is in large part an 18th-century invention of (<u>Eastern/Western</u>) culture. Arranged marriages, in which romantic love is less important, tend to be characteristic of (<u>collectivist/individualist</u>) societies.

8-3. If men emphasize physical attractiveness and women resources, how does this affect *tactics* that the sexes use in pursuing the opposite sex? In support of the evolutionary perspective, Buss has found that men tend to use tactics that emphasize their (<u>looks/resources</u>) and women tactics that emphasize their (<u>looks/resources</u>). For example, _____ might talk about their jobs or display what they own while _____ would try to enhance their makeup or clothing.

8-4. A recent study by Schmitt and Buss further specifies that the tactic used by the two sexes may depend in part on the type of romance they are looking for. Signals of sexual availability (e.g., dressing seductively) were rated as most effective for women seeking a _____-term relationship. Signals of sexual exclusivity (e.g., rejecting overtures from other men) were considered most effective for women seeking a _____ -term relationship. For men an immediate display of resources was rated the most effective tactic for a _____ -term relationship and an emphasis on potential for acquiring resources as most effective for a _____ -term relationship.

8-5. With regard to the use of tactics involving deception, (<u>males/females</u>) anticipate more deception from prospective dates and underestimate men's potential commitment, perhaps as an _____ strategy for protection against consenting to sex and being abandoned. Men tend to overestimate women's _____ interest, perhaps as an evolved tactic of not overlooking sexual opportunities.

Answers: 8-1. women, men, in virtually all **8-2.** Western, collectivist **8-3.** resources, looks, men, women **8-4.** short, long, short, long **8-5.** females, evolved (adaptive, survival), sexual.

9. Discuss evidence on the hypothesized relationship between love and attachment.

9-1. In Chapter 11 we discussed types of *attachment patterns* that occur between infants and their caregivers. According to Hazen and Shaver, type of infant-caregiver attachment is predictive of adult love relationships. Write the names of the three infant attachment styles next to the appropriate letters below.

S: _____

A-A: _____

A: _____

9-2. Using the letters from the previous question, identify the types of romantic relations predicted by the infant attachment styles.

_____ As adults these individuals tend to use casual sex as a way of getting physically close without the vulnerability of genuine intimacy and commitment.

_____ These people experience more emotional highs and lows in their relationships, find conflict stressful, have more negative feelings after dealing with conflict.

_____ These individuals easily develop close, committed, well-adjusted, long-lasting relationships.

Answers: 9-1. secure, anxious-ambivalent, avoidant **9-2.** A, A-A, S.

ATTITUDES • MAKING SOCIAL JUDGMENTS

10. Describe the components and dimensions of attitudes.

10-1. Attitudes are positive or negative _____ of objects of thought. Objects of thought may include *issues* (e.g., gun control), *groups* (e.g., Irish people), or _____ (e.g., your best friend).

10-2. Attitudes may include three components: cognition (thought), affect (emotion), and behavioral predispositions. People may have attitudes toward any object of thought—political views, art, other people, cottage cheese. Take cottage cheese. List the three possible components of attitudes next to the examples below.

_____ He hates cottage cheese.

_____ If cottage cheese touches his plate he scrapes it into the garbage.

_____ He thinks: "Cottage cheese seems kind of lumpy."

10-3. Attitudes also vary along various dimensions, as follows:

_____ The importance, vested interest, or knowledge about the attitude object.

_____ How easily the attitude comes to mind.

_____ The degree to which the attitude includes both positive and negative aspects.

10-4. Attitude strength is a function of several factors, including how _____ the attitude is to the person, the extent to which the attitude involves a _____ interest that directly affects them, and the degree of _____ that they have about the attitude object.

Answers: 10-1. evaluations, individuals **10-2.** affect, behavior, cognition. (Note that the components may be remembered as the ABCs of attitude.) **10-3.** strength, accessibility, ambivalence **10-4.** important, vested, information.

11. Summarize evidence on how source, message, and receiver factors influence persuasion.

11-1. If you are the *source* of a communication (i.e., the message giver):

(a) What factors mentioned in your text would you use to make yourself more *credible*?
_____ and _____

(b) What else would you hope to emphasize about yourself? _____

11-2. With regard to *message* factors:

(a) Which is generally more effective, a one-sided message or a two-sided message?

_____

(b) In presenting your argument, should you use every argument that you can think of or emphasize just the stronger arguments? _____

(c) Is simple repetition a good strategy, or should you say something just once? _____

(d) What is the *validity effect?* _____

(e) Do fear appeals tend to work? _____ When? _____

11-3. With regard to *receiver* factors in persuasive communications:

(a) If you know that someone is going to attempt to persuade you on a particular topic you will be (harder/easier) to persuade. This is the factor referred to as _____.

(b) Resistance to persuasion is greater when an audience holds an attitude incompatible with the one being presented. In this case the receiver will tend to view the arguments with greater (credulity/ skepticism) and scrutinize them for a longer period of time.

(c) In addition, in part because they may be anchored in networks of other beliefs that may also require change, _____ attitudes are more resistant to change.

Answers: 11-1. (a) expertise, trustworthiness (b) likability (for example, by increasing your physical attractiveness or emphasizing your similarity with the message receiver) **11-2.** (a) In general, two-sided (That's the kind of speech Mark Antony gave over the body of Caesar in Shakespeare's *Julius Caesar*.) (b) stronger only (c) repetition (causes people to believe it's true, whether it is or isn't) (d) the finding that simply repeating a statement, whether it's true or not, makes it more believable (e) yes, *if* they arouse fear (and especially if the audience thinks the consequences are very unpleasant, likely to occur, and avoidable) **11-3.** (a) easier, forewarning (b) skepticism (c) stronger.

12. **Explain how cognitive dissonance can account for the effects of counterattitudinal behavior and effort justification.**

12-1.   (Dissonance is a truly complicated theory, but the following exercise should help. First read over the text, then see how you do on these questions. Here's a hint: Both problems that follow are contrary to common-sense ideas of reward and punishment; dissonance theory prides itself on making predictions contrary to these common-sense ideas. Item 17-1 indicates that we like behaviors accompanied by less, not more, reward; item 17-2 indicates that we like behaviors accompanied by more, not less, discomfort.)

Ralph bought a used car. However, the car uses a lot of gas, which he doesn't like because he strongly supports conserving energy. He rapidly concludes that conserving fuel isn't so important after all.

(a) Ralph has engaged in counterattitudinal behavior. What were the two contradictory cognitions? (One is a thought about his *behavior*. The other is a thought about an important *attitude*.)

(b) Suppose the car was a real beauty, a rare antique worth much more than the price paid. Alternatively, suppose that the car was only marginally worth what was paid for it. In which case would dissonance be stronger? In which case would the attitude about gas guzzling be more likely to change?

12-2.   Suppose Bruce decides to join a particular club. (1) One possible scenario is that he must travel a great distance to attend, the club is very expensive, and he must give up much of his free time to become a member. (2) Alternatively, suppose that the traveling time is short, the club is inexpensive, and he need not give up any free time. In which case (1 or 2) will he tend to value his membership more, according to dissonance theory? Briefly, why?

Answers: 12-1. (a) I know I bought the car. I'm against the purchase of cars that waste gas. (b) The additional reward in the first situation produces less dissonance and will tend to leave Ralph's original attitude about gas consumption intact. Ralph's attitude about gas consumption will change more when there is less justification (in terms of the value of the car) for his action. As described in your text, we tend to have greater dissonance, and greater attitude change, when *less reward* accompanies our counterattitudinal behavior. **12-2.** According to dissonance theory, he will value the membership more under alternative 1, even if the benefits of membership are slight, because people attempt to *justify the effort* expended in terms of the benefits received. (While dissonance is a true phenomenon with many of the characteristics that Festinger described in 1957, several other variables are operating, so it is difficult to predict when dissonance will occur.)

13. **Relate learning theory and the elaboration likelihood model to attitude change.**

13-1.   Following are examples that relate learning theory to attitude change. Indicate which type of learning—classical conditioning (CC), operant conditioning (OC), or observational learning (OL)—is being illustrated.

_____ Ralph hears a speaker express a particular political attitude that is followed by thunderous applause. Thereafter, Ralph tends to express the same attitude.

_____ Advertisers pair soft drinks (and just about any other product) with attractive models. The audience likes the models and develops a stronger liking for the product.

_____ If you express an attitude that I like, I will agree with you, nod, say "mm-hmm," and so on. This will tend to strengthen your expression of that attitude.

13-2.   To illustrate the elaboration likelihood model: Suppose that you are to travel in Europe and must decide between two options, renting a car or traveling by train (on a Eurailpass). In the blanks below indicate which persuasive route, central (C) or peripheral (P), is referred to in these examples.

____ On the basis of train brochures showing apparently wealthy and dignified travelers dining in luxury on the train while viewing the Alps, you opt for the train.

____ Your travel agent is an expert who has advised many of your friends, and she strongly recommends that you take the train. You decide on the train.

____ A friend urges you to consider details you hadn't previously considered: traffic, waiting in line, additional cab fare, and so on. After weighing the relative expenses and conveniences for four traveling together you decide to rent a car.

13-3.   In the elaboration likelihood model, the route that is easier, that involves the least amount of thinking, is the _____ route. The route in which relevant information is sought out and carefully pondered is the _____ route. Elaboration, which involves thinking about the various complexities of the situation, is more likely to occur when the _____ route is used.

13-4.   Elaboration leads to (more enduring/transient) changes in attitudes. In addition, elaboration (i.e., the more central route) is (more/less) likely to predict behavior.

Answers: 13-1. OL, CC, OC 13-2. P, P, C 13-3. peripheral, central, central 13-4. more enduring, more.

CONFORMITY AND OBEDIENC • YIELDING TO OTHERS

14. Describe Asch's work on conformity.

14-1.   Briefly summarize the general procedure and results of the Asch line-judging studies.

14-2.   Conformity increased as number of accomplices increased, up to a point. Conformity seemed to level off, so that increasing the number of accomplices beyond _____ has relatively little effect.

14-3.   Suppose there are five accomplices, one real subject, and another accomplice who dissents from the majority. What effect will this "dissenter" have on conformity by the real subject?

Answers: 14-1. Subjects were asked to judge which of three lines matched a standard line, a judgment that was actually quite easy to make. Only one of the subjects was a real subject, however; the others were accomplices of the experimenter, who gave wrong answers on key trials. The result was that a majority of the real subjects tended to conform to the wrong judgments of the majority on at least some trials. **14-2.** 4 **14-3.** Conformity will be dramatically reduced, to about one-fourth the frequency without a dissenter.

15. Describe Milgram's study on obedience to authority and the ensuing controversy.

15-1. Two individuals at a time participated in Milgram's initial study, but only one was a real subject. The other "subject" was an accomplice of the experimenter, an actor. By a rigged drawing of slips of paper the real subject became the _____ and the accomplice became the _____. There were a total of _____ subjects, or "teachers," in the initial study.

15-2. The experimenter strapped the learner into a chair and stationed the teacher at an apparatus from which he could, supposedly, deliver electric shocks to the learner. The teacher was to start at 15 volts, and each time the learner made a mistake the teacher was supposed to _____ the level of shock by 15 volts—up to a level of 450 volts.

15-3. What percentage of the subjects continued to obey instructions, increasing the shock all the way to 450 volts? _____

15-4. What is the major conclusion to be drawn from this study? Why are the results of interest?

15-5. As you might imagine, Milgram's studies on obedience were controversial, producing both detractors and defenders. Following are illustrations of the *generality* and *ethical* objections raised against the Milgram studies. Beneath each are possible counter-arguments asserted by either Milgram or his supporters. Complete the counter-arguments by selecting the appropriate alternatives.

(a) "Subjects in an experiment expect to obey an experimenter, so the results don't generalize to the real world."

Counter-argument: The flaw in this argument, according to Milgram's defenders, is that in many aspects of the real world, including the military and business worlds, obedience (is not/is also) considered appropriate. So, Milgram's results (do/do not) generalize to the real world.

(b) "Milgram's procedure, by which subjects were allowed to think that they had caved in to commands to harm an innocent victim, was potentially emotionally damaging to the subjects. Milgram's experiment was unethical."

Counter-argument: Milgram's defenders assert that the brief distress experienced by the subjects was relatively (slight/great) in comparison with the important insights that emerged.

Answers: 15-1. teacher, learner, 40 **15-2.** increase **15-3.** 5, none **15-4.** The major conclusion is that ordinary people will tend to obey an authority even when their obedience could result in considerable harm (and perhaps even death) to others. The result is of interest because it suggests that such obedience as occurs in war atrocities (e.g., in World War II, at Mai Lai in Viet Nam, and throughout history) may not be due so much to the evil *character* of the participants as to pressures in the *situation*. (Milgram's results are also of interest because most people would not expect them: even psychiatric experts predicted that fewer than 1% of the subjects would go all the way to 450 volts.) **15-5.** (a) is also, do (b) slight. (Many psychologists today share the critics' concerns, however, and the study has not been replicated in the United States since the 1970s.)

16. **Discuss cultural variations in conformity and obedience.**

16-1. As with other cross-cultural comparisons, replications in other countries yield some similarities and some differences. Indicate true (T) or false (F) for the following statements.

_____ The obedience effect found by Milgram seems to be a uniquely American phenomenon.

_____ In replications of the Milgram studies in several European countries, obedience levels were even higher than those in the United States.

_____ Replications of the Asch line-judging studies suggest that cultures that emphasize collectivism are somewhat more conforming than are those that emphasize individualism.

Answers: 16-1. F, T, T.

BEHAVIOR IN GROUPS • JOINING WITH OTHERS

17. **Discuss the nature of groups and the bystander effect.**

17-1. The word *group* doesn't have the same meaning for social psychologists that it does for everyone else. As I look out across my social psychology class on a Tuesday morning, I might say to myself, "Hm, quite a large group we have here today." Actually, my class is *not* a group in social psychological terms because it lacks one, and perhaps two, of the essential characteristics of a group. A group consists of two or more individuals who (a) _____ and (b) are _____.

17-2. Which of the following are groups, as defined by social psychologists?

_____ A husband and wife.

_____ The board of directors of a corporation.

_____ A sports team.

_____ Spectators at an athletic event.

_____ Shoppers at a mall.

17-3. What is the bystander effect?

17-4. Why does the bystander effect occur? In part because the presence of onlookers not doing anything produces an _____ situation (no one seems to be upset, so maybe it's not an emergency). In addition, the presence of others causes a _____ of responsibility (we're all responsible, or else someone else will do it.)

Answers: 17-1. (a) interact (b) interdependent 17-2. The first three are groups and the last two are not. 17-3. When people are in groups (or at least in the presence of others), they are less likely to help than when they are alone. Or, the greater the number of onlookers in an emergency, the less likely any one of them is to assist the person in need. 17-4. ambiguous, diffusion.

18. **Summarize evidence on group productivity and group decision making.**

18-1. Individual productivity is frequently less in large than in small groups. Two factors contribute to this decreased productivity: a loss of _____ among workers in larger groups (e.g., efforts of one person interfere with those of another) and decreased _____ resulting from *social loafing*.

18-2. Social loafing is the reduction in _____ expended by individuals working in groups as compared to people working alone. People in groups frequently don't work as hard as they would if they were working alone. Social loafing and the bystander effect seem to share a common cause: diffusion of _____.

18-3. Cultures that place a high priority on meeting group goals tend to show less social loafing, according to some studies. That is, social loafing tends to be less common in (collectivist/individualistic) societies.

18-4. This problem should help you understand the concept of group polarization. Suppose that a group of five corporate executives meet to decide whether to *raise or lower* the cost of their product, and by how much. Before they meet as a group, the decisions of the five executives (expressed as a percentage) are as follows: +32%, +17%, +13%, +11%, and +2%. After they meet as a group, which of the following is most likely to be the result? Assume that group polarization occurs.

a. +30%, +10%, +3%, +3%, and +2%

b. +32%, +19%, +19%, +15%, and +13%

c. -3%, -1%, 0%, +9%, and +11%

d. –10%, –7%, –3%, 0%, and +2%

18-5. What is group polarization?

18-6. Have you ever been in a group when you thought to yourself, "This is a stupid idea, but my best friends seem to be going along with it, so I won't say anything." If so, you may have been in a group afflicted with groupthink. Groupthink is characterized by, among other things, an intense pressure to _____ to group opinions accompanied by very low tolerance for dissent.

18-7. According to Janis, the major cause of groupthink is high group _____, the degree of attraction group members have for the group. Other factors that may contribute to groupthink include (directive/nondirective) leadership, stress accompanying making a major decision, and relative isolation.

18-8. While the groupthink theory has intuitive appeal, research support for Janis' conclusions has been (strongly supportive/mixed).

Answers: 18-1. efficiency (coordination), effort **18-2.** effort, responsibility **18-3.** collectivist **18-4.** b **18-5.** Group polarization is the tendency for a group's decision to shift toward a *more extreme position* in the direction that individual members are *already leaning*. **18-6.** conform **18-7.** cohesiveness, directive **18-8.** mixed.

PUTTING IT IN PERSPECTIVE

19. Explain how the chapter highlighted three of the text's unifying themes.

19-1. This chapter again illustrates psychology's commitment to empirical research. When people hear the results of psychological studies they frequently conclude that the research just confirms common sense. Dispute this view by listing and describing *at least one study* with results that are not predictable from common sense assumptions.

19-2. Cross-cultural differences and similarities also reflect one of the unifying themes. People conform, obey, attribute, and love throughout the world, but the manner and extent to which they do so are affected by cultural factors. Important among these factors is the degree to which a culture has an _____ or _____ orientation.

19-3. Finally, the chapter provides several illustrations of the way in which our view of the world is highly subjective. For example, we tend to make ability and personality judgments based on people's physical _____; see what we expect to see as a result of the cognitive structures termed social _____; distort judgments of physical lines based on pressures to _____ ; and make foolish decisions when we become enmeshed in the group phenomenon known as _____ .

Answers: 19-1. This chapter has described at least three studies that defy the predictions of common sense or of experts. (1) Concerning *Milgram's studies*, psychiatrists incorrectly predicted that fewer than 1% of the subjects would go to 450 volts. (2) Results from *cognitive dissonance* studies are frequently the opposite of common sense. For example, common sense would suggest that the more people are paid, the more they would like the tasks for which they receive payment; dissonance researchers found that the opposite is true; people paid *more* liked the tasks *less*. (3) Common sense might predict that the larger the number of people who see someone in need of help, the more likely any one is to offer help. Research on the *bystander effect* consistently finds the opposite result. **19-2.** individualistic, collectivistic **19-3.** attractiveness (appearance), schemas, conform, groupthink.

PERSONAL APPLICATION • UNDERSTANDING PREJUDICE

20. Relate person perception and attributional bias to prejudice.

20-1. Prejudice is a negative _____ toward others based on group membership. Like other attitudes, prejudice may include affective, _____, and behavioral components

20-2. The cognitive component of prejudice may be comprised of schemas about groups. This type of schema is frequently referred to as a _____

20-3. Stereotypes are part of the *subjectivity* of person perception. People tend to see what they expect to see, and when stereotypes are activated people see and remember information that (is/is not) congruent with their stereotype.

20-4. Stereotypes are highly accessible and frequently activated automatically, so that even though people reject prejudiced ideas, stereotypes (can not/may still) influence behavior.

20-5. Our *attributional biases* are also likely to maintain or augment prejudice. For example, observers tend to attribute success in men to (ability/luck) but success in women to (ability/luck).

20-6. People may also attribute other people's behavior to internal traits, the bias referred to as the _____ attribution error.

20-7. When people experience adversity such as prejudice, we are also likely to attribute their misfortune to character flaws, a predisposition referred to as defensive attribution or _____.

Answers: **20-1.** attitude, cognitive **20-2.** stereotype **20-3.** is **20-4.** may still **20-5.** ability, luck **20-6.** fundamental **20-7.** victim blaming.

21. Relate principles of attitude formation and group processes to prejudice.

21-1. Attitudes are to a large extent learned. For example, if someone makes a disparaging remark about an ethnic group that is followed by approval, the approval is likely to function as a _____ that increases that person's tendency to make similar remarks in the future. This is the learning process known as _____ . Or, if someone simply *observes* another person making such a remark, the observer may acquire the tendency to make similar remarks through the process known as

_____.

21-2. Ingroup members view themselves as different from the outgroup in several ways. First, they tend to see themselves as superior to outgroups, a tendency known as _____ . In addition, they seem themselves as relatively heterogeneous and outgroup members as relatively

_____.

21-3. In other words, ingroup members see outgroupers as highly (dissimilar/similar) to one another in appearance as well as behavior. In fact, studies have found that (blacks/whites/both) have difficulty distinguishing the faces of the other group. This important difference in the perception of outgroups by ingroups is termed the illusion of outgroup _____.

Answers: **21-1.** reinforcer, operant conditioning, observational learning (modeling) **21-2.** ethnocentrism, homogeneous **21-3.** similar, both, homogeneity.

CRITICAL THINKING APPLICATION• ANALYZING CREDIBILITY AND SOCIAL INFLUENCE TACTICS

22. Discuss some useful criteria for evaluating credibility and some standard social influence strategies.

22-1. We are constantly bombarded with information designed to persuade. Sometimes we are persuaded and happy about it and sometimes we regret the outcome. How can we resist attempts at manipulation? Two tactics are discussed in this section: evaluating the _____ of the source, and learning about several widely-used social _____ strategies.

22-2. To assess credibility, consider these questions: Do they have a _____ interest? If so, information they provide may not be objective. What are the source's _____? Although degrees do not certify competence, they may indicate relevant training.

22-3. Is the information inconsistent with _____ views on the issue? If not, one should ponder why others haven't arrived at the same conclusion. Finally, what was the _____ of analysis used? One should be particularly skeptical if the source relies on anecdotes or focuses on small inconsistencies in accepted beliefs.

22-4. In addition, learn to recognize social influence strategies. Following are several scenarios. Identify each with one of the four strategies discussed: *foot-in-the-door*, *reciprocity*, *lowball*, and *scarcity*.

_____ Scenario 1: Mail solicitation for a magazine subscription. "Enclosed is a packet of seeds, free of charge, just for you. We hope you enjoy the beautiful flowers they produce! Also, you will benefit from subscribing to Outdoor Beauty magazine. We've enclosed a free copy."

_____ Scenario 2: Newspaper ad. "This weekend only—mammoth blowout car deals!! These beauties will go fast!!!! Don't miss this once-in-a-lifetime opportunity!!"

_____ Scenario 3: A college development office calling alumni. First week: "We don't care about the amount, perhaps $5, just so that we can ensure full participation." You commit to $5. Next week: "Would you become one of our member donors with a contribution of $100?"

_____ Scenario 4. On the phone with a wholesale camera salesman. "Yes, we do have the XXY Camera at $499.00 plus tax. We'll ship that this afternoon. Now, did you want the new lens or the old lens with that? The new lens would be an additional $99. Did you want the carrying case also?" (Your assumption was that the so-called extras were included in the original price.)

_____ Scenario 5: Mail solicitation. First week: "Would you answer this brief survey for us? There are only 12 questions." Next week: "Thanks for responding to our survey! We desperately need money for this worthwhile (candidate, school, charity, etc.)."

_____ Scenario 6: At the car dealer. "We've got a deal, $22,900 plus tax! You'll be very happy with this car! Let me check with my manager to see if that price includes the radio and CD player." (Fifteen minutes pass while the salesman supposedly checks.) "Well, I tried, but the manager won't budge. Fortunately it's not much additional!"

Answers: 22-1. credibility, influence **22-2.** vested, credentials **22-3.** conventional, method **22-4.** reciprocity, scarcity, foot-in-the-door, lowball, foot-in-the-door, lowball.

REVIEW OF KEY TERMS

Attitudes
Attributions
Bystander effect
Channel
Cognitive dissonance
Collectivism
Commitment
Companionate love
Conformity
Defensive attribution
Discrimination
Ethnocentrism
External attributions
Foot-in-the-door technique
Fundamental attribution error

Group
Group cohesiveness
Group polarization
Groupthink
Illusory correlation
Individualism
Ingratiation
Ingroup
Internal attributions
Interpersonal attraction
Intimacy
Latitude of acceptance
Lowball technique
Matching hypothesis
Message

Obedience
Outgroup
Passionate love
Person perception
Prejudice
Receiver
Reciprocity
Reciprocity norm
Self-serving bias
Social loafing
Social psychology
Social schemas
Source
Stereotypes

_____ 1. The branch of psychology concerned with the way individuals' thoughts, feelings, and behaviors are influenced by others.

_____ 2. The process of forming impressions of others.

_____ 3. Clusters of ideas about categories of social events and people that we use to organize the world around us.

_____ 4. Widely held beliefs that people have certain characteristics because of their membership in a particular group.

_____ 5. Error that occurs when we estimate that we have encountered more confirmations of an association between social traits than we have actually seen.

_____ 6. Inferences that people draw about the causes of events, others' behavior, and their own behavior.

_____ 7. Attributing the causes of behavior to personal dispositions, traits, abilities, and feelings.

_____ 8. Attributing the causes of behavior to situational demands and environmental constraints.

_____ 9. The tendency of an observer to favor internal attributions in explaining the behavior of an actor.

_____ 10. The rule that we should pay back when we receive something from others; may be used in an influence strategy.

_____ 11. The tendency to attribute our positive outcomes to personal factors and our negative outcomes to situational factors.

_____ 12. Liking or positive feelings toward another.

_____ 13. Getting people to agree to a small request to increase the chances that they will agree to a larger request later.

_____ 14. The observation that males and females of approximately equal physical attractiveness are likely to select each other as partners.

_____ 15. Liking those who show that they like us.

_____ 16. Behaving differently, usually unfairly, toward the members of a group.

_____ 17. A complete absorption in another person that includes tender sexual feelings and the agony and ecstasy of intense emotion.

_____ 18. A warm, trusting, tolerant affection for another whose life is deeply intertwined with one's own.

_____ 19. A negative attitude held toward members of a group.

_____ 20. The strength of the liking relationships linking group members to each other and to the group itself.

_____ 21. Positive or negative evaluation of objects of thought; may include cognitive, behavioral, and emotional components.

_____ 22. The person who sends a communication.

_____ 23. The person to whom the message is sent.

_____ 24. The information transmitted by the source.

_____ 25. The medium through which the message is sent.

_____ 26. The group one belongs to and identifies with.

_____ 27. People who are not a part of the ingroup.

_____ 28. Situation that exists when related cognitions are inconsistent.

_____ 29. Yielding to real or imagined social pressure.

_____ 30. Involves getting someone to commit to an attractive deal before its hidden costs are revealed.

_____ 31. A form of compliance that occurs when people follow direct commands, usually from someone in a position of authority.

_____ 32. Involves putting group goals ahead of personal goals and defining one's identity in terms of the group one belongs to.

_____ 33. Involves putting personal goals ahead of group goals and defining one's identity in terms of personal attributes rather than group memberships.

_____ 34. Two or more individuals who interact and are interdependent.

_____ 35. The apparent paradox that people are less likely to provide needed help when they are in groups than when they are alone.

_____ 36. A reduction in effort by individuals when they work together as compared to when they work by themselves.

_____ 37. Situation that occurs when group discussion strengthens a group's dominant point of view and produces a shift toward a more extreme decision in that direction.

_____ 38. Phenomenon that occurs when members of a cohesive group emphasize concurrence at the expense of critical thinking in arriving at a decision.

_____ 39. The finding that the mere repetition of a message, whether it is true or not, causes it to be perceived as more valid.

Answers: 1. social psychology **2.** person perception **3.** social schemas **4.** stereotypes **5.** illusory correlation **6.** attributions **7.** internal attribution **8.** external attribution **9.** fundamental attribution error **10.** reciprocity norm **11.** self-serving bias **12.** interpersonal attraction **13.** foot-in-the-door technique **14.** matching hypothesis **15.** reciprocity **16.** discrimination **17.** passionate love **18.** companionate love **19.** prejudice **20.** group cohesiveness **21.** attitudes **22.** source **23.** receiver **24.** message **25.** channel **26.** ingroup **27.** outgroup **28.** cognitive dissonance **29.** conformity **30.** lowball technique **31.** obedience **32.** collectivism **33.** individualism **34.** group **35.** bystander effect **36.** social loafing **37.** group polarization **38.** groupthink **39.** validity effect.

REVIEW OF KEY PEOPLE

Solomon Asch   Elaine Hatfield   Irving Janis
Ellen Berscheid   Fritz Heider   Stanley Milgram
Leon Festinger

_____   1.   Was the first to describe how people make attributions in terms of internal or
                              external factors.

_____   2.   With Hatfield did research describing two types of romantic love: passionate
                              and companionate.

_____   3.   Originator of the theory of cognitive dissonance.

_____   4.   Devised the "line-judging" procedure in pioneering investigations of
                              conformity.

_____   5.   In a series of "fake shock" experiments studied the tendency to obey authority
                              figures.

_____   6.   Developed the concept of groupthink.

_____   7.   Under the name of Walster did early study on dating and physical
                              attractiveness; with Berscheid, described types of romantic love.

Answers: 1. Heider **2.** Berscheid **3.** Festinger **4.** Asch **5.** Milgram **6.** Janis **7.** Hatfield.

SELF-QUIZ

1. Which of the following characteristics do we tend to attribute to physically attractive people?
    a. low intelligence
    b. friendliness
    c. unpleasantness
    d. coldness

2. Cognitive structures that guide our perceptions of people and events are termed:
    a. attributions
    b. stigmata
    c. schemas
    d. denkmals

3. Inferences that we make about the causes of our own and others' behavior are termed:
    a. attributions
    b. stigmata
    c. schemas
    d. denkmals

4. Bruce performed very well on the examination, which he attributed to native ability and hard work. Which
    attributional bias does this illustrate?
    a. the fundamental attribution error
    b. the actor-observer bias
    c. the self-serving bias
    d. illusory correlation

5. According to this viewpoint, men emphasize physical attractiveness in mate selection while women emphasize the ability to acquire resources. Which theory does this describe?
   a. evolutionary theory
   b. cognitive dissonance
   c. sexual propensity theory
   d. attribution theory

6. Which of the following could be an example of the fundamental attribution error?
   a. Ralph described himself as a failure.
   b. Ralph thought that the reason he failed was that he was sick that day.
   c. Jayne said Ralph failed because the test was unfair.
   d. Sue explained Ralph's failure in terms of his incompetence and laziness.

7. Which influence technique involves asking for a small request in order to increase the likelihood of the target complying with a larger request later?
   a. foot-in-the-door
   b. feigned scarcity
   c. reciprocity norm
   d. lowball

8. Which of the following is, in general, likely to reduce the persuasiveness of a message?
   a. The receiver's viewpoint is already fairly close to that of the message.
   b. The receiver has been forewarned about the message.
   c. A two-sided appeal is used.
   d. The source is physically attractive.

9. Subjects in Group A are paid $1 for engaging in a dull task. Subjects in Group B are paid $20 for the same task. Which theory would predict that Group A subjects would enjoy the task more?
   a. balance
   b. cognitive dissonance
   c. reinforcement theory
   d. observational learning

10. In making a decision you rely on the opinion of experts and the behavior of your best friends. According to the elaboration likelihood model, which route to persuasion have you used?
    a. central
    b. peripheral
    c. attributional
    d. 66

11. Which of the following is the best statement of conclusion concerning Milgram's classic study involving the learner, teacher, and ostensible shock?
    a. Under certain circumstances, people seem to enjoy the opportunity to be cruel to others.
    b. People have a strong tendency to obey an authority even if their actions may harm others.
    c. The more people there are who observe someone in need of help, the less likely any one is to help.
    d. Aggression seems to be a more potent force in human nature than had previously been suspected.

12. Which of the following is most likely to function as a group?
    a. shoppers at a mall
    b. the audience in a theater
    c. the board of trustees of a college
    d. passengers in an airplane

13. Someone witnesses a car accident. In which of the following cases is that individual most likely to stop and render assistance?
    a. Only she saw the accident.
    b. She and one other individual saw the accident.
    c. She and 18 others saw the accident.
    d. The other observers are pedestrians.

14. Suppose the original decisions of members of a group are represented by the following numbers in a group polarization study: 3, 3, 4, 4, 6. The range of numbers possible in the study is from 0 to 9. Which of the following possible shifts in decisions would demonstrate polarization?
    a. 2, 3, 3, 4, 5
    b. 4, 4, 5, 5, 7
    c. 4, 5, 6, 6, 7
    d. 9, 9, 7, 7, 5

15. According to Janis, what is the major cause of groupthink?
    a. cognitive dissonance
    b. diffusion of responsibility
    c. the tendency of group members to grandstand
    d. strong group cohesion

Answers: 1. b 2. c 3. a 4. c 5. a 6. d 7. a 8. b 9. b 10. b 11. b 12. c 13. a 14. a 15. d.

INFOTRAC

Attitudes	Discrimination	Self-serving Bias
Attributions	Groupthink	Stereotype
Cognitive Dissonance		

APPENDIX B STATISTICAL METHODS

REVIEW OF KEY IDEAS

1. Describe several ways to use frequency distributions and graphs to organize numerical data.

1-1. Identify the following methods that are commonly used to present numerical data.

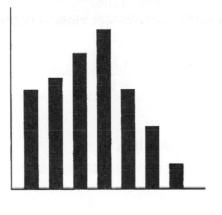 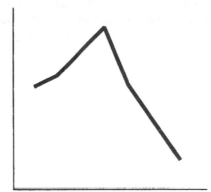

(a) _____   (b) _____

1-2. What data are usually plotted along the:

(a) horizontal axis?

(b) vertical axis?

Answers: 1-1. (a) histogram (b) frequency polygram **1-2.** (a) the possible scores (b) the frequency of each score

2. **Describe the measures of central tendency and variability discussed in the text.**

    2-1.   State which measure of central tendency, the mean, median, or mode, would be most useful in the following situations.

        (a) Which measure would be best for analyzing the salaries of all workers in a small, low-paying printshop that includes two high-salaried managers? Explain your answer.

        (b) Which measure would be best for selecting a single ice cream flavor for an upcoming party?

        (c) Which measure would be best for pairing players at a bowling match, using their individual past scores, so that equals play against equals?

        (d) Where do most of the scores pile up in a positively skewed distribution?

Answers: 2-1. (a) The median, because the high salaries of the two management persons would distort the mean (b) the mode (c) the mean (d) at the bottom end of the distribution.

3. **Describe the normal distribution and its use in psychological testing.**

    3-1.   Answer the following questions regarding the normal distribution.

        (a) What is the general shape of the normal distribution?

        (b) Where are most of the scores located in a normal distribution?

        (c) What is the unit of measurement in a normal distribution?

        (d) What percentage of scores falls above 2 standard deviations in a normal distribution (see Fig. B-6 in the text)?

(e) If your percentile ranking on the SAT was 84, what would your SAT score be (see Fig. B.7 in the text)?

Answers: 3-1. (a) It is a bell-shaped curve (b) near the center (c) the standard deviation (d) 2.14% (e) 600 (approximately).

4. Explain how the magnitude and direction of a correlation is reflected in scatter diagrams and how correlation is related to predictive power.

4-1.   Answer the following questions about the magnitude and direction of a correlation as reflected in scattergrams.

   (a) Where do the data points fall in a scattergram that shows a perfect correlation?

   (b) What happens to the data points in a scattergram when the magnitude of correlation decreases?

   (c) What does a high negative correlation indicate about the scores on variable Y if the scores on variable X are high?

4-2.   Answer the following questions regarding the predictive power of correlations.

   (a) How does one compute the coefficient of determination?

   (b) What does the coefficient of determination tell us?

   (c) What could we say if the sample study used in the text showed a correlation of -.50 between SAT scores and time watching television?

Answers: 4-1. (a) In a straight line (b) They scatter away from a straight line (c) Scores on variable Y would be low **4-2.** (a) By squaring the correlation coefficient (b) It incidates the percentage of variation in one variable that can be predicted based on the other variable (c) Knowledge of TV viewing habits allows one to predict 25% of the variation on SAT scores (.50 X .50 = .25).

5. **Explain how the null hypothesis is used in hypothesis testing and relate it to statistical significance.**

    5-1.   Answer the following questions regarding the null hypothesis and statistical significance.

        (a) In the sample study correlating SAT scores and television viewing, the findings supported the null hypothesis. What does this mean?

        (b) What level of significance do most researchers demand as a minimum before rejecting the null hypothesis?

        (c) What is the probability of making an error when a researcher rejects the null hypothesis at the .01 level of significance?

Answers: 5-1. (a) We cannot conclude that there is a significant negative correlation between SAT scores and television viewing (b) the .05 level (c) 1 in 100.

REVIEW OF KEY TERMS

Coefficient of determination	Mean	Positively skewed distribution
Correlation coefficient	Median	Scatter diagram
Descriptive statistics	Mode	Standard deviation
Frequency distribution	Negatively skewed distribution	Statistics
Frequency ploygon	Normal distribution	Statistical significance
Histogram	Null hypothesis	Variability
Inferential statistics	Percentile score	

    _____   **1.** The use of mathematics to organize, summarize, and interpret numerical data.

    _____   **2.** An orderly arrangement of scores indicating the frequency of each score or group of scores.

    _____   **3.** A bar graph that presents data from a frequency distribution.

    _____   **4.** A line figure used to present data from a frequency distribution.

    _____   **5.** Type of statistics used to organize and summarize data.

    _____   **6.** The arithmetic average of a group of scores.

    _____   **7.** The score that falls in the center of a group of scores.

    _____   **8.** The score that occurs most frequently in a group of scores.

    _____   **9.** A distribution in which most scores pile up at the high end of the scale.

    _____   **10.** A distribution in which most scores pile up at the low end of the scale.

_____ 11. The extent to which the scores in a distribution tend to vary or depart from the mean.

_____ 12. An index of the amount of variability in a set of data.

_____ 13. A bell-shaped curve that represents the pattern in which many human characteristics are dispersed in the population.

_____ 14. Figure representing the percentage of persons who score below (or above) any particular score.

_____ 15. A numerical index of the degree of relationship between two variables.

_____ 16. A graph in which paired X and Y scores for each subject are plotted as single points.

_____ 17. The percentage of variation in one variable that can be predicted based on another variable.

_____ 18. Statistics employed to interpret data and draw conclusions.

_____ 19. The hypothesis that there is no relationship between two variables.

_____ 20. Said to exist when the probability is very low that observed findings can be attributed to chance.

Answers: 1. statistics **2.** frequency distribution **3.** histogram **4.** frequency polygon **5.** descriptive statistics **6.** mean **7.** median **8.** mode **9.** negatively skewed distribution **10.** positively skewed distribution **11.** variability **12.** standard deviation **13.** normal distribution **14.** percentile score **15.** correlation coefficient **16.** scatter diagram **17.** coefficient of determination **18.** inferential statistics **19.** null hypothesis **20.** statistical significance.